China

China

Pamela Youde

B. T. Batsford Ltd, London

ISBN 0 7134 3795 2

Printed in Great Britain by
Butler & Tanner Ltd
Frome, Somerset,
for the Publishers
B.T. Batsford Ltd
4 Fitzhardinge Street
London W1H 0AH

Contents

List of Illustrations

Black and White

(Between pages 48 and 49)

6

Colour

MAPS

Acknowledgment

I should like to thank all my friends who have been so generous with their advice and encouragement while I have been writing this book, and to acknowledge my debt to the authors of the numerous books and periodicals of local history produced in China.

I also remember with pleasure and gratitude my travelling companions, Chinese friends, guides and China Travel Service officials who have been untiring in sharing with me their knowledge of the history and background of the many parts of China I have been fortunate enough to visit.

The author and publishers would like to thank the following for permission to reproduce their photographs:

G. and P. Corrigan for 1, 8, 14-17, 21, 22 and 25, and The Society for Anglo-Chinese Understanding for 19, 20, 23, 24, 27, 32-3 and 36-9.

The others are from the author's own collection.

The maps are by Patrick Leeson.

Introduction

A holiday in China is an adventure, a unique experience in a country unlike any other. A quarter of the world's population lives within its borders. Its climate varies from the humid tropical heat of the south to the bitter Siberian winters of the north. From the Pacific it stretches through areas of fertile wheat and ricefields westwards to the deserts of Central Asia and Tibet, the Roof of the World. Its scenery includes snowcapped mountains, awesome gorges along one of the world's largest rivers, and the greatest fortification ever built by man, the Great Wall.

Within a Communist state the magnificent palaces and tombs of an imperial age, together with hundreds of temples and monasteries, are still preserved. Its museums contain superb bronzes, porcelain and pictures. New archaeological finds constantly throw fresh light on Chinese history and culture; the unique terracotta army which guards the still unexcavated tomb of the builder of the Great Wall dates from the third century B.C., and was discovered only in 1974.

To help in the difficult choice of where to go in China, I have described in some detail those places which have most to offer the visitor, and given less attention to cities where, although they have an eventful history, there is little left to see. As so many temples are now open an outline of the main features of typical Buddhist, Daoist and Confucian foundations is included in the section on Religion, Monasteries and Temples (p.21). Description of individual temples is confined to points of particular interest.

In almost every case there is more than one version of the story and background to the sights of China, some firmly rooted in history, some entirely fanciful and based on folk stories. Where possible I have given the historical explanation, but have also drawn on myths and legends since they were such a powerful force in the old Chinese society, indeed the whole atmosphere of many places would be lost without them. The Chinese love to give romantic and evocative names to both places and buildings. To bring out the flavour of these names I have in many cases given (or attempted) an English equivalent, and, to help locate them on Chinese tourists maps, have added the Chinese names using the standard 'pin-yin' form of spelling (see p.160). Pin-yin is also used for the names of towns and cities, but where the older romanisation is more familiar in the west, it is given in brackets in the text; since it is so well known I have used 'Peking' instead of 'Beijing'.

1. Background

Geography and History

It is 2500 miles from Shanghai on China's eastern seaboard to Kashgar on its far western frontier, and about the same distance from the tropical island of Hainan to the northernmost point on the Amur River which forms China's frontier with Soviet Siberia. Only about 12 per cent of this vast land can be cultivated and most of that is in the east adjacent to the seaboard where 95 per cent of China's nearly one billion people now live. The western half is divided between the remote Tibetan highlands and the deserts and steppes of Xinjiang and Inner Mongolia.

China's civilisation began in the valley of the Yellow River, the northernmost of her three great eastward flowing rivers. The Yangtze River, which meets the sea near Shanghai, divides south China from the North China Plain. In the mountainous south the West River draws on many tributaries in its path to the sea near Guangzhou (Canton). In the north the main crops are millet, maize and wheat. The great rice growing and silk producing areas lie in the Yangtze Valley and the south, whose mountain slopes also produce the teas for which China is famous.

Over most of China a standard form of Chinese derived from Northern Mandarin is now spoken. In the southern provinces the people also maintain their own distinctive dialects, such as Cantonese, with a pronunciation so different and a tonal pattern so complex that they are unintelligible to their compatriots in the north. The southwestern provinces are the home of numerous minority peoples, including the Zhuang, the Dai, the Miao and the Yi. In Xinjiang the Kazaks and Uighurs still speak their own languages, as do the Mongols and the Tibetans, and all maintain their own distinctive ways of life.

Remains of early man in China going back to 700,000 B.C. have been found at Lantian near Xi'an, and the site at Zhoukoudian, southwest of Peking, where Peking Man was discovered, was occupied from about 500,000 B.C. Early Chinese civilisation grew up along the fertile Yellow and Wei River valleys in northwest China, and by 4000 B.C. communities there were living in neolithic villages similar to the one preserved in the museum at Banpo just outside Xi'an. Here they farmed and hunted and painted their pottery with geometric designs. To the east another group of peoples grew rice and made fine black pottery on the wheel.

For their earliest beginnings the Chinese look back to mythical rulers credited with the discovery of fire, agriculture, sericulture and the calendar, of whom the last three were called Yao, Shun and the Great Yu. Yu is said to have controlled the Great Flood and to have founded the first recorded dynasty, the Xia, believed to have existed during the early Bronze Age from about the twenty-first to the sixteenth century B.C. An often repeated pattern then began of strong dynasties becoming corrupt and weak enough to be overthrown by new and vigorous men. The Xia were conquered by the warlike Shang, whose kings governed from their palaces in walled capitals at Zhengzhou and later at Anyang. They used cowrie shell currency, worked jade and wrought superb bronze vessels unequalled anywhere in the world.

In about 1027 B.C. their vassals in the west, the Zhou, swept over north China and set up a new regime with a capital at Xi'an and another at Luoyang. They ruled through semi-independent vassal lords, and were the first to call themselves Sons of Heaven and to make the ceremonial sacrifices to heaven and to earth. Agriculture and irrigation improved, and philosophy flourished in China as it did in Greece, the Middle East and India. The Great Schools were founded and philosophers travelled round the capitals of states as advisors to local rulers. Confucius was one of these, and his teaching dominated and moulded Chinese life until recent times. Born in 551 B.C. in Qufu in Shandong, his home and the palace of his heirs are preserved near the sacred Mount Taishan. After the increasing power of their vassals had forced the Zhou rulers east to their capital at Luoyang, China collapsed into a group of Warring States. From the turmoil the leader of the totalitarian State of Qin, the builder of the Great Wall, emerged victorious to unite the whole of China for the first time.

The empire disintegrated in 206 B.C., soon after the first Emperor's death. It was reunited under Liu Bang, the founder of the Han empire which lasted four hundred years and became even larger than the almost contemporary Roman empire, reaching from the Pamirs to Korea and from Mongolia to Vietnam. The Chinese today still call themselves Men of Han. To the prosperous and cosmopolitan capital at Changan (modern Xi'an) came traders across the Silk Road, bringing about the exchange of ideas as well as merchandise between China and the west. Dissatisfaction with the ruinous cost of military expeditions led to the brief seizure of power by a rebel minister in 9 A.D., but in 25 A.D. Han rule was re-established with the capital at Luoyang. Two centuries later the now corrupt and failing empire was carved into Three Kingdoms, whose battles, romanticised by Chinese story-tellers, are still a favourite subject for the Peking Opera.

For the next three hundred years north China was occupied by northern invaders, and only the southern states were governed by Chinese rulers. Buddhism was encouraged by the unifiers of north China, the Northern Wei, who constructed great cave temples near their northern capital at Datong in north Shanxi province, and at their southern capital, Luoyang.

In 589 a general of mixed northern and southern blood united the country once again under the shortlived Sui dynasty. To furnish his capital with food and supply his troops, waterways and rivers were linked up to make a canal route south as far as Hangzhou, and north to Peking. But costly wars again brought collapse, and it fell to another general of mixed blood to found, in 618, the Tang empire, one of the most brilliant and extensive in Chinese history. Chinese from the south still call themselves People of Tang. Once more a magnificent capital at Changan became a centre of culture and sophistication where poetry, painting and all the arts flourished, and learning was the key to advancement. Towards the end of the seventh century Empress Wu Zetian, the only woman to seize power and rule China as Emperor, added superb figures to the Buddhist cave temples at Longmen near Luoyang.

The empire continued to prosper but its vast frontiers demanded professional armies, including 'barbarian' mercenaries, to garrison them. In the eighth century one of the border commanders, a disaffected general named An Lushan, attacked the capital, precipitating the flight to Sichuan province of the Emperor Xuan Zong and the death of his beautiful consort, Yang Guifei, on the way. Although restored to power, the Tang were in decline and fell early in the tenth century. Another period of disunity ended only in 960, when the Song rulers gained the upper hand and made their capital further east at Kaifeng.

Unable to regain the vast territories of the Tang, the Song were forced to pay annual tribute of silver and silk to buy off the northern tribes who established themselves in their southern capital, Peking, taking the reign title of Liao. Kaifeng was a cultured and wealthy city with a government in the hands of officials selected in reasonably fair competitive examinations. The production of porcelain reached new heights of excellence at this time. Military and political miscalculations by the Song brought another northern tribe, who had taken the title of the 'Jin', pouring down to capture Kaifeng together with the Emperor and his entourage in 1126. One of the Emperor's sons escaped to the rich and fertile south where he set up a new capital in the lakeside city of Hangzhou, soon to become even more splendid than Kaifeng. Unfortunately for the women, the sophisticated life of the city led to an increase in the seclusion of women, concubinage and the introduction of footbinding.

Little more than a century later the Mongol cavalry in its turn thundered across north China to force the Jin conquerors out of Peking and Kaifeng. It took them another fifty years to complete the defeat of the Southern Song. China was now united under a Mongol ruler for the first time. Kublai Khan, the grandson of Genghis, established the Yuan dynasty in 1271 and ruled as Son of Heaven from Khanbalik, or Cambulac, in present day Peking. With their empire extending from the Black Sea to the Pacific and south to Southeast Asia, the Mongols maintained an excellent communications system of roads, canals and couriers; the Grand Canal was completed by Kublai. But oppressive taxation and agricultural disasters again resulted in rebellion, and after less than a century the Mongols were driven back to their homelands.

They were defeated by a popular uprising led by a monk from the beautiful Lushan Mountains in north Jiangxi province, who founded the

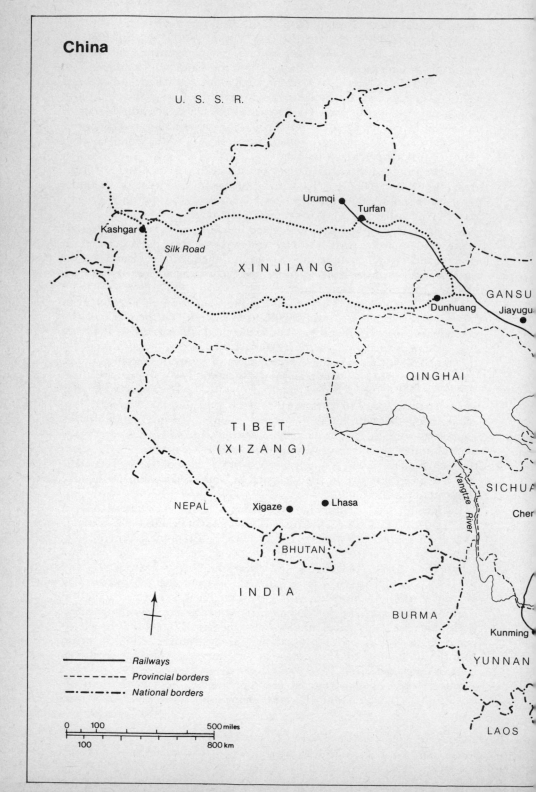

China

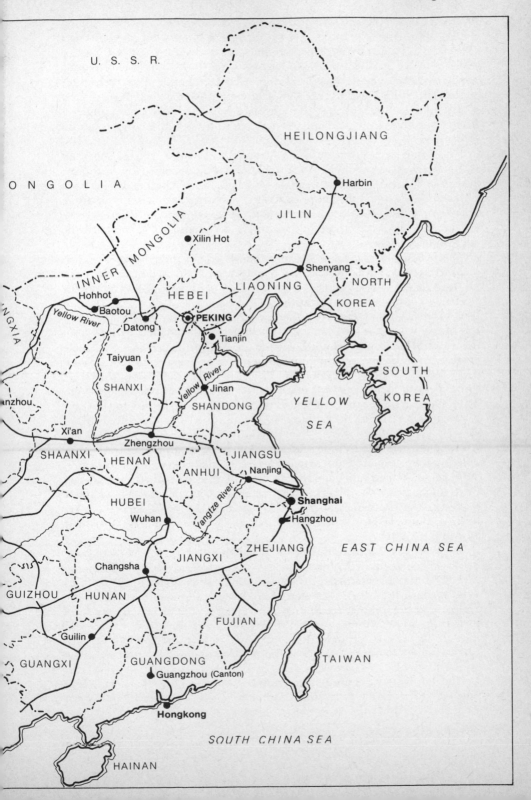

Background

Ming dynasty in Nanjing (Nanking) in 1368 and gave the country a long period of peace and stability. He began the custom of adopting one reign title for his whole reign, so from this time on Chinese Emperors are usually referred to not by their names but by those titles. In 1421 his son moved the capital to his own powerbase at Peking where he rebuilt the city on a larger scale. The Mings were great builders of military fortifications; ever on guard against the Mongols, they restored the Great Wall maintaining a huge army to man it, and erected massive walls around many provincial cities.

By the sixteenth century, despite all efforts to discourage them, European traders gained a foothold in Macao and later in Guangzhou. The first of the Jesuits, Matteo Ricci, was residing in Peking in 1601, and the Father's descriptions of life at the Imperial Court created an enthusiasm in Europe for all things Chinese. Jesuits and priests of other orders continued to serve the Chinese court as artists, astronomers and mathematicians until the early nineteenth century.

In due course weak rulers became dominated by eunuchs, whose extravagance at court and appropriation of public funds put an impossible strain on the economy. Costly wars and famine in the country triggered numerous uprisings culminating in the capture of Peking in 1644 by a peasant leader, Li Zicheng. At the Great Wall the imperial commander sought help from the Manchus, whose kingdom lay immediately to the north. He threw open the gates to his supposed allies who swept through to conquer the whole empire. For the second time an Emperor from beyond the Great Wall ascended the Dragon Throne. The Manchus called themselves the Great Qing dynasty. They were the last imperial dynasty and ruled China until 1911. Once in power they continued to govern through the existing bureaucracy, using many of the Chinese who had served them loyally in Manchuria. Government posts were generally duplicated, a Manchu and Chinese serving side by side with the Manchu in command of the troops. The Manchus repaired and extended the Forbidden City and Peking itself. They retained their language (which can still be seen beside the Chinese on the nameboards of buildings in the Forbidden City), their dress and their customs. They forbade Manchu mothers to bind the feet of their daughters in the Chinese fashion, and decreed that all Chinese men must wear their hair in the Manchu pigtail.

The two great Manchu Emperors, Kang Xi (1662-1723) and Qian Long (1736-96) consolidated Manchu power through Central Asia, Tibet and Mongolia and maintained a magnificent and cultured court in Peking. In 1793 the first British Ambassador, Lord Macartney, was received by the Emperor at his summer resort at Jehol (Chengde) but he was unsuccessful in his attempt to obtain improved facilities for foreign trade. The mid nineteenth century brought disaster. The Taiping and many other uprisings in the provinces threatened the empire just at the moment when the young Empress Dowager was seizing power. In a regime fatally weakened by the old evils of corruption and popular unrest, the Empress Dowager and her conservative court were unable to resist pressures from western countries and Japan for trading rights and special privileges. China's defeat in the Opium War led to the opening of a number of ports to foreign trade, the cession of Hong Kong to the British, and a free-for-all among the European nations and Japan vying for spheres of influence. In 1900 the court sought to capitalize on the anti-foreign Boxer Uprising to expel foreign influence from China, encouraging the Boxer forces to lay siege to the Legations in Peking. They were forced to flee the capital when the allied armies took Peking.

This final humiliation of the Manchu regime served to increase the appetite of the European powers and Japan for 'spheres of influence' in China, and the competition for control of the resources of Manchuria led to a war conducted on Chinese soil between Russia and Japan in 1904. The inevitable end soon came with the revolution inspired by Dr Sun Yat-sen and establishment of the republic in 1911, but the boy-emperor remained in the Forbidden City until 1924, loyally attended during the last five years by his British tutor, Reginald Johnston, a former member of the Colonial Civil Service.

For the next ten or more years the warlords divided and dominated China. It was not until the mid 1920s that Nationalist forces led by Chiang Kai-shek were able to strike north from Guangzhou and establish a new government and capital at Nanjing in 1927. In the same year Chiang turned on his erstwhile Communist allies, and mounted a coup against them in Shanghai in which many of them were hunted down and killed. During the next decade he set himself the objectives of consolidating his own power, of breaking the power of the warlords, and of driving the Communists first from their base in the wild hills of Jiangxi province south of the Yangtze, and later from the provinces of the northwest to which the Communist forces, now under the leadership of Mao Zedong, had moved after the Long March in 1934.

In the meantime the Japanese incursions into Manchuria in 1931, and the establishment of a puppet state there under the former Manchu boy Emperor Pu Yi added a new dimension to the scene. In 1937 Japanese troops clashed with Chinese forces at the Marco Polo Bridge just outside Peking, and the Sino-Japanese war began. Following the Japanese defeat in 1945 civil war broke out between the Nationalists and the Communists. Four years later the establishment of the People's Republic of China was declared by Mao Zedong from the Tianan Men Gate in Peking, on 1 October 1949.

With the coming of the Communist regime, political, social and economic change was rapid. Land reform campaigns eliminated the landlords, distributing their land amongst the peasants, and then led on to the establishment of co-operative farms and finally the system of communes which exists throughout China today. A massive industrialisation programme was begun with Soviet help, and although interrupted by the Sino-Soviet split in 1960, has continued to the point where China has in absolute, if not in per capita terms, a substantial industrial base.

But the process was not a smooth one. The Great Leap Forward at the end of the 1950s, an attempt at accelerated economic growth relying largely on indigenous resources, was a failure. In 1966-7 there occurred the Cultural Revolution, a political, social and economic upheaval on an enormous scale, in which large numbers of Communist leaders were ousted, officials, scholars and professional men humiliated, and economic advance largely halted. Relations with foreign countries deteriorated and in a dispute which arose out of disturbances in Hong Kong the British Mission in Peking was burned to the ground. In 1976, the year which saw the death both of Premier Zhou Enlai and Chairman Mao Zedong, the pendulum swung back. Four members of the Politbureau, known as the Gang of Four, were arrested and later condemned for their part in the Cultural Revolution. With the fall of the Gang, political institutions were restored, many of those disgraced were reinstated, and the programme of rapid modernisation and industrialisation resumed.

Chinese Life

Although the life of most Chinese has changed dramatically during this century, the observant visitor can even now learn much of how life was lived in old China. In the main museums carved or painted tiles from the tombs of the Han dynasty (206 B.C. - 220 A.D.) depict the methods of farming, spinning and weaving, the construction of buildings and the life of the privileged classes. Frescoes and figurines from the tombs of the imperial family of the Tang dynasty (618-907) in Xi'an illustrate vividly the dress, ceremony and leisure pursuits of the court at that time. In the Palace Museum in Peking the famous hand-scroll painting of 'Life along the River on the Eve of the Qingming Festival' attributed to Zhang Zedan illustrates life in the riverside streets of the Song capital of Kaifeng in the early twelfth century. Toiling porters unload the grain barges, crowds of people press through the city gates, the official rides in his sedan chair, and the merchants lead their pack horses; the water-carriers, itinerant craftsmen and cloth sellers use the ubiquitous bamboo carrying-pole. The Historical Museum in Peking has a Ming dynasty (1368-1644) painting showing 'Scenes from the Southern Capital' (Nanjing). Outside the cities life in country towns and villages was harder and prone to disaster from flood, drought and famine. With few exceptions the village was dependent on its own produce. A little of the luxury of the city might filter into the house of the local magistrate, landlord or merchant, but not more.

In old China the family system was strong. It required absolute respect for the elders. From the day he was born the Chinese child had his exactly defined place in the hierarchy. It was expected of all members that they should do all they could to advance the family interests. The family as a whole could be held responsible by officialdom for the conduct of its members.

A girl's life was largely confined first to her own family, and after marriage to that of her husband. She had no say in her own destiny and few girls received much education. The marriage of both sons and daughters was arranged by the parents. Elaborately dressed and veiled in red, the bride was carried in procession in a sedan chair to the home of her new husband for the wedding celebrations. If she did not soon produce a son to carry on the family line, her husband might take a second wife or concubine. Only with sons or advancing years did her status improve.

Throughout the year the monotony of domestic routine was broken by festivals. By far the most important was at the lunar New Year when homes were swept, debts settled, new clothes purchased and relatives and friends were visited during a three day celebration. The Lantern Festival followed quickly after the New Year. At the Festival of Pure Brightness (Qingming) in the second lunar month, the ancestral tombs were swept with willow branches and paper money burnt for the use of the dead. Dragon Boats raced at the Festival in the middle of the fifth month. The Mid Autumn Festival in the eighth month in honour of the Goddess of the Moon was the time for eating mooncakes filled with sweet beans, dates or savouries.

After the fall of the Manchu Qing dynasty in 1911 the youth of China revolted against the Confucian disciplines which their families sought to impose on them, and also against foreign domination of China. Students educated abroad brought with them a vision of society which contrasted sharply with the traditional Chinese form, and translations of western works had a tremendous impact on the new generation. With the establishment of the Communist regime in 1949 came a new and fundamental change in Chinese political, economic and social life.

Eighty per cent of the population of China still live in the countryside in communes, administrative units with a membership of anything from ten to sixty thousand or more people. The commune is divided into brigades and teams. The team is usually based on an old village, and thus a visit to a commune can provide an opportunity to see something of Chinese village life. The team is responsible for the cultivation of the land allocated to it, and its members draw their main income from it according to the work they perform. A fixed amount of the crop they produce must be sold to the state through the commune at a set price. The rest they may consume or, if there is a surplus, can be sold at a higher price. Villagers have modest private plots on which to grow vegetables or rear pigs, some of which they can sell at the market. They can build and own their own houses and many do. At the brigade level there will be food processing plants, repair workshops for maintaining the tractors and other agricultural equipment, and schools and clinics to support the 'barefoot doctors', the Chinese village equivalent of the western health visitor. At the commune level there may well be quite substantial local industries to contribute to the general income of the members and pay for the central services. The commune, often in co-operation with other communes nearby, organises major capital works such as reservoir construction, the digging of irrigation canals, land reclamation and the building of local roads. A committee structure provides for administration at all levels.

In the city the life of every Chinese is bound up in the organisation in which he or she works. Government departments and the larger factories provide housing, recreation and medical facilities, and sometimes pensions schemes for their employees. Private ownership of houses in cities is rare. Many people work in street co-operatives too small to provide their own facilities, and have to rely on municipal services. Although there is a limited toleration of exchanges of jobs, in the main it is the state system which decides where Chinese work and when they may move.

Education at primary level is almost universal, and secondary schools are widespread in the communes and cities. Although China now has many universities and technical colleges, the competition for higher education is intense. It is a matter of pride in China for a son or daughter to be accepted into the People's Liberation Army which, in addition to providing the country's defences, is a great school for technical training. The politically ambitious join the Communist Party which controls the political destiny of the state at all levels.

The great events of family life, births, marriages and deaths, are still marked as they always have been but with greater simplicity. No longer is the Chinese girl carried to her wedding in a sedan chair. She walks with her chosen companion to the local registry office where they declare their willingness to be joined in marriage and receive a pink wedding certificate. To ensure that no family pressure has been brought on them the registrar will wish to satisfy himself that the girl is marrying of her own free will. After the wedding they will probably splash out on a celebration at a local restaurant. The pressure of population in China is such that the young are strongly discouraged from marriage until they are in their mid-twenties, and from having more than one or two children.

City dwellers enjoy themselves in the parks on Sundays, in cinemas and theatres, at the sports stadiums, and increasingly in front of the television set in the local recreation hall, or at home if the family income stretches that far. In the countryside the radio and cinema provide the main diversion after the long working day. The important holidays are now New Year, the Spring Festival (the old Chinese New Year), May Day and the national holiday at the beginning of October — the Spring Festival still has a special place as a time for family reunions.

Theatre

The popular collections of stories from history and legend such as the *Three Kingdoms, Monkey* and *The Water Margin* provide many of the plots for Chinese operas which visitors see today. The classical Chinese opera, a combination of drama, singing and dance is quite different from its western counterpart. The techniques and the methods of voice production are highly stylised. Actors specialise in one of four types of role: the males, including military men; the female; the 'painted faces'; and the clowns. The 'painted faces' portray the larger-than-life personalities either good or bad. It can take the actor an hour to paint on his mask, whose colour and pattern symbolise his character. As a rough guide, red can indicate courage and loyalty; blue, ferocity; black, honesty; and white with black or grey pattern, treachery;

gold and silver indicate mythical figures. The clowns, easily recognisable by the white patch over the eyes and nose, play simple characters, either kind or malicious including mothers-in-law and go-betweens, somewhat in the Widow Twankey tradition.

The costly silk embroidered costumes worn on stage are loosely based on the dress of the Ming dynasty. But historical accuracy often bows to theatrical effect, and a lady wearing a wide Manchu headdress may well appear among characters dressed in Ming style in a play about the Tang dynasty, six centuries earlier. Yellow is worn only by the emperor and his family. Barbarian emperors and generals swagger in white foxtails.

Traditionally the Peking Opera uses no scenery, and in consequence mime and props are essential elements in the unfolding of the story. The waving of a tasselled stick indicates that the actor is riding a horse; boarding a boat is shown by jumping on board and rocking back and forth as if to balance the motion of the water; flags with a wheel pattern held at waist level symbolise a carriage. Among the most common mimes is the un-bolting and pushing open of doors and stepping over the high doorsill to indicate that the actor is entering or leaving a room. Emotions such as anger and embarrassment are expressed by graceful manipulation of long flowing sleeves, a difficult art which takes years to master. Martial characters toss, stroke or flick the long pheasant feathers in their headdress for the same purpose. Battle scenes are occasions for a dazzling display of sword play and acrobatics. Acquiring such skills demands a long apprenticeship often beginning in childhood. Even so, until the beginning of this century the social status of actors was low. Their descendants to the third generation were excluded from the official examinations. Actresses, who were some-times courtesans, were banned from the theatre in the eighteenth century and admitted again only after 1911, with the curious result that today they play female roles in a style largely developed by female impersonators in all-male companies, and sing the parts of young women in falsetto.

Chinese traditional music based on a five-note scale is not easily appre-ciated by westerners, although folk songs, including the music of the National Minorities, have an immediate appeal. The music with which an on-stage orchestra of traditional string, wind and percussion instruments accompany Chinese opera may sound strident to our ears, but to the Chinese it plays an essential part in creating the mood and heightening the atmosphere of the performance.

During the Cultural Revolution both the Peking Opera and modern drama were banned, and replaced by a limited repertoire of revolutionary opera and plays. But in recent years both have been reinstated, and western ballet, orchestral concerts, opera and drama in translation have also re-appeared on the Chinese stage.

Religion, Monasteries and Temples

Buddhism and Daoism (Taoism) were the religions with the most ad-herents in China. Buddhism spread from India to China in the early centuries of our era and although it drew heavily on its Indian origins it developed many distinctively Chinese characteristics and schools of thought. The Chinese adopted the Mahayana doctrine which admits the existence of more than one Buddha in the same era. The popularity of the cults of different Buddhas has changed both over time and regionally. This is reflected in the wide variety of Buddhist figures which appear in cave temples and monasteries in various parts of the country.

The historical Buddha, the last of the Buddhas to appear on earth, was born in India in the sixth century B.C. His name was Prince Siddhartha, his family was called Gautama, and they belonged to the Sakya clan. He is usually referred to in China as Sakyamuni (the Holy One of Sakya) Buddha.

Several episodes in his life are favourite subjects for paintings and sculpture in Chinese temples. They include: his conception – his mother Maya is depicted asleep while a child on an elephant comes from heaven towards her; his birth – he springs from his mother's side as she stands under a tree; his first steps: lotus flowers spring up as he walks; four occasions on which he leaves his palace and sees the misery of the world; renunciation – he leaves his wife and child asleep and rides away on his horse with a servant; he sends his horse home; temptation – the evil Mara tempts him under a Bodhi tree; enlightenment – beneath the Bodhi tree he attains enlightenment and becomes a Buddha; the Deer Park – Buddha preaches the Law in the Deer Park at Benares; Nirvana – Buddha's death, where he is shown lying down, with mourners, animals and flowers.

In temples a Buddha is easily recognised by his bare head with a cranial bump, or topknot of hair, his undergarment usually tied at the waist, with a cloak over one or both shoulders, and lack of jewellery. He may be standing or sitting, often with legs crossed and his hands in his lap in the position for meditation. Other common hand positions are the gesture of reassurance with the hand held up and palm out; of 'earth touching' with the tips of the fingers almost touching the earth, calling it to witness that he had achieved enlightenment; and 'discussion' with one or both hands up, with the thumb touching a finger. He, in common with other figures, has a round spot between the eyes, and the long earlobes now associated with holiness but which are believed to have their origin in ears weighed down with heavy princely jewellery.

Apart from Sakyamuni, among other Buddhas who frequently appear is Maitreya (Milo Fo) the Buddha of the Future. In the fifth and sixth centuries people believed that an era was about to come to an end and that Maitreya might appear on earth. His popularity was such that statues of him were large and impressive, for example in the caves at Yungang and Longmen and in the cliff at Leshan where his statue is 220 ft high. In the tenth century a mendicant monk is said to have died reciting a verse which led to the belief that he was the reincarnation of Maitreya, and since that date Maitreya has been depicted as a fat monk, the popular Laughing Buddha found in the first hall of temples. Another Buddha is Amitabha (Amito Fo), the Buddha of the Pure Land or Western Paradise, a being unknown in early Indian Buddhism who is often shown in the cave temples at Dunhuang sitting beneath jewelled trees, surrounded by new souls being born from lotus flowers, musicians, dancers and celestial beings. The cult of Amitabha which succeeded that of Maitreya, also rivalled that of Sakyamuni among ordinary people, as they had only to call devoutly on his name to be admitted to the Western Paradise. Another Buddha who appears in a common scene of 'Sakyamuni Buddha expounding the Lotus Sutra', is Prabhaturatna (Duo Bao), the Buddha Long in Nirvana, who is shown seated in a stupa with Sakyamuni and surrounded by a myriad Buddhas who have been summoned by the light shining from Sakyamuni's brow; these are the 'Thousand Buddhas' or 'Ten Thousand Buddhas' often found as tiny statues or painted on temple walls.

It is difficult to identify individual Buddhas correctly where there is no inscription or accompanying illustration because sculptors sometimes massproduced statues that were then named as they wished by the donors or the monks in the temple. This also applies to the Bodhisattvas, the 'saints' who turned back on the very threshold of Buddahood out of compassion for the suffering world. Bodhisattvas often wear high diadems and are covered in elaborate jewellery. Probably the most popular is Avalokitesvara, the Lord who Looks Down, sometimes depicted with many heads and 'a thousand' arms and eyes to see and save all souls. Avalokitesvara also appears as Guan Yin the Goddess of Mercy, who hears the cries of the world. Originally male, this deity has been shown in female form since the Tang dynasty, in Chinese dress, carrying a lotus or willow branch and a flask. The Bodhisattva Samantabhadra (Puxian), the Protector of all who Preach the Law, rides a white elephant and carries a lotus; he is patron saint of Mount Emei in Sichuan. The Bodhisattva of Wisdom, Manjusri (Wenshu) is patron saint of Mount Wutai in Shanxi and rides a lion, holding a sword in his right hand and a book on a lotus in his left. Manjusri is often shown holding the wand of discussion and debating with an old man, Vimalakirti, who sits on his bed fanning himself. In the crowd listening to them are a princess and a monk. As the monk vehemently affirms that women cannot quickly achieve enlightenment, the princess turns into a male Bodhisattva before his eyes.

Through the centuries the original Buddhist faith acquired many of the trappings of other religions including concepts of heavens and hells, an enormous canon of scriptures (sutra), contending schools of thought and a pantheon of deities. Among them, apart from the various manifestations of Buddha and Bodhisattvas, there appear lohan (or arhats), monks who have liberated themselves from the cycle of reincarnation, and a host of guardians of the faith.

In layout, no two Buddhist temples were exactly alike, and cave temples were usually simple with just a Main Hall and outer or inner room, but the layout of most, other than cave temples, will show some or all of the following features.

The gate will be protected from 'evil influences' by a Spirit Wall, so located that the gate can not be approached in a direct line. Inside the gate buildings, on each side, the gigantic guardians Heng and Ha tower over the passers-by. They represent the two brothers Shu Yu and Yu Lu who, in Chinese folklore, have power over disembodied spirits. The next hall will be dedicated to the Four Heavenly Kings, the Guardians of the East, West, South and North. In Buddhist tradition they defend the slopes of Mount Meru, the abode of the gods. Each is identified by his symbol of power, a guitar, a sword, a pearl and snake, or an umbrella. In the centre of the hall may sit the Laughing Buddha, Maitreya. Back to back with him, Wei Tuo the Guardian of Buddha, the Law and the Community, always faces the Great Hall.

The Great Hall (Daxiong Baodian) is the fulcrum of the temple. In it the Sakyamuni Buddha will often occupy the central lotus seat accompanied by two other Buddhas, such as Amithaba, Boundless Light, and Vaidurya (Yaoshi Fo) the Healing Buddha; or he may be flanked by his favourite disciples, the youthful Ananda and the elderly Kasyapa the keeper of Buddhist tradition; they in turn flanked by Buddhas, Bodhisattvas and sometimes by guardians. There are many different arrangements depending on the location of the temple and the wishes of the donors. Back to back with the Buddhas may be a large relief featuring Guan Yin the Goddess of Mercy or some other deity.

Along the walls of the Hall there are usually statues, sometimes paintings, of lohan, and in some monasteries the Five Hundred Lohan occupy a separate hall. Like ten thousand or a thousand, five hundred is a popular number meaning 'many'. There were said to be five hundred lohan at a famous synod in India four hundred years after Sakyamuni entered Nirvana. Statues numbered 108 in the Hall in the Hualin Temple in Guangzhou and in the Temple of the Azure Cloud (Biyun Si) in Peking are fancifully pointed out to visitors as Marco Polo.

Next in line on the central axis may be the Meditation Hall or Hall of the Law where the monks performed their devotions, in which statues of a variety of Buddhas may appear, and above it the library housing the sutras with, if the monastery produced its own editions of these, the blocks from which they were printed. The monks' quarters, abbot's rooms, guest rooms and kitchens are usually in the side buildings. Few monasteries lack a bell tower and drum tower just inside the gate, and a pagoda erected to protect some sacred relic and as a sign of piety. The larger monasteries had ordination platforms for the ceremonies admitting new monks. Not far away a crematorium may be hidden among the trees with a 'forest of stupas', pagoda-like structures raised over the remains of distinguished monks.

(I will describe Lamaistic Buddhism in the section on Tibet.)

The Daoist philosophy is well known in the west from the writings of Laotze, the supposed author of the *Daode Jing (Tao te ching)*. But more relevant for the visitor is religious Daoism which grew up in China in the early centuries of our era and which generated a vast pantheon of gods, superstitious practices, and secret societies far removed from the original philosophy. Religious Daoism is much concerned with the nourishment of vital forces by abstinence, respiratory exercises, and the interplay of the sexual forces of 'ying and yang', and with the attainment of immortal life through a search for elixirs and a constant attempt to maintain a relationship with numerous gods and with the immortals who inhabit the Daoist paradise. Key figures were the Jade Emperor (Yu Huang) who was raised to eminence only in the tenth century; Daojun, the controller of Yin and Yang; Laotze himself; and the Eight Immortals who are portrayed everywhere, sometimes individually and sometimes together on the slopes of paradise or in a boat on the way there.

In layout Daoist monasteries differ from Buddhist establishments. A good example was the White Cloud Monastery (Baiyun Guan) in Peking, once one of the most important monasteries of the Complete Perfection persuasion. On its main axis stood a series of shrine halls including one dedicated to the Jade Emperor. Other halls dedicated to the Immortals, Daoist patriarchs, Confucians and the God of War were dotted around the grounds. One of the central buildings was dedicated to the Patriarch Qiu, the founder of the Long Men sect whose tomb lies within the monastery.

Novices received instruction at smaller temples before seeking ordination at foundations like Baiyun Guan. Unlike his Buddhist counterpart whose shaven head was marked with round incense scars, the Daoist allowed his hair to grow long. When ready for ordination, his hair was tied into a knot on the top of his head in the Ceremony of the Crown and the Cloth, and secured by a pin and a flat cloth cap. Blue robes, white stockings and blue 'cloud' shoes with turned up toes were worn.

The Chinese were eclectic in their beliefs and did not find it necessary to confine a temple to one cult. In addition they have from the beginning canonised their folk heroes and dedicated temples to them. The famous Jin Ci in Taiyuan was originally dedicated to a prince of the eleventh century B.C., Prince Shu Yu of Tang, and later to his mother. In the Ancestral Temple (Zu Miao) in Foshan, near Guangzhou, the cult centres on the God of the North (Bei Di — the Pak Tai of Hong Kong temples). A strong cult among sailors and fishermen revered the Queen of Heaven (Tian Hou), the incarnation of a legendary fishergirl who saved her parents from a storm. She became the Daoist equivalent of the Buddhist Goddess of Mercy.

Guan Di, the God of War, was Guan Yu, a popular general of the period of the Three Kingdoms who became the patron deity of the Manchu dynasty. Temples were dedicated to him all over China and he also appears in Buddhist and Daoist temples. Another military hero to be canonised was Zhu Geliang, a statesman-general of the same period whose story is told in connection with the Warlord Temple dedicated to him in Chengdu.

Each city had its guardian god, honoured in the Temple of the Wall and Moat (Chenghuang Miao) who kept an account of the virtues and failings of the city dwellers, and who could in turn be commended for his own achievements on behalf of the city. As one of his first official acts a new magistrate was required to call or stay at the temple and read a sacrificial address, pledging himself not to engage in corruption or perpetrate injustice.

Background

For over a thousand years knowledge of the Confucian Classics was the key to success in the official examinations, and the teachings of Confucius had formed the basis for the state cult long before that. As over the centuries it grew in importance so did the attention lavished on his birthplace, Qufu (see page 94), and in time each city had its Confucian temples where officials and scholars paid homage to him. The layout was simple. The memorial tablet of Confucius was displayed on the central altar in the Great Hall north of the second courtyard. On each side were altars bearing the tablets of the four main disciples, including Mencius. On lesser altars in the same hall and in side halls were the tablets of other illustrious Confucianists, and in a separate hall at the back, five generations of his ancestors were honoured. As if to accentuate the link between the cult and the official examinations no gate could be opened in the south wall until a scholar from the district had headed the list in the Palace Examinations in Peking.

Nestorians brought Christianity to the Tang capital at Changan in the seventh century, and in the thirteenth the Catholic Father John de Montecorvino set up a lonely church in Peking. Neither church survived. Only after the Portuguese had established themselves in Macao did the Christian missionary effort in China begin in earnest. In 1601 Matteo Ricci, having spent a decade studying Chinese, obtained permission from the Ming Emperor Wan Li to reside in Peking, and was quick to recognise that initially Jesuits would be tolerated in the imperial capital only as scholars and scientists. His success and the success of those who followed him in maintaining a Christian presence at the Chinese court for over two centuries, in spite of many persecutions, was largely due to the scientific and artistic skills of the Jesuits and other priests who served there. Their missionary effort had limited success, partly because of their own intersectarian disputes. They argued interminably among themselves about the correct translation of the concept of 'God' in Chinese, and disputed for more than a hundred years about the acceptability or otherwise of the Chinese tradition of paying homage to their ancestors. By the early nineteenth century there were no Catholic missionaries left in Peking.

A new era of western missionary effort in China began after the treaty of 1842 when Europeans and Americans established themselves in treaty ports along the China coast. These became bases from which the missionary societies spread their activities all over China. With the Sino-Japanese war and the coming of the Communists to power, the role of the western missionaries came to an end and the churches became the responsibility of Chinese Christians. Both Protestant and Catholic churches were required to sever their relations with the west, and during the Cultural Revolution public religious observances were completely suppressed. In recent years churches have reopened and Chinese Christians are now permitted to resume limited contact with their co-religionists in the outside world. There are also numerous Chinese Moslems in the north and north-west, and mosques in major cities.

Sculpture

The sculpture to be seen in China falls into two broad categories: stone tomb sculpture, and Buddhist and other sculpture, mainly in clay, stone, bronze and wood, in caves and temples.

From very early times the Chinese placed guardian figures and animals at the approach to tombs to serve the dead and protect their resting place from evil spirits. Such figures and processions may still be seen at the imperial tombs at Xi'an, Nanjing, Gongxian and Peking.

With the spread of Buddhism from India came the Indian style cave temples described in the chapters on Dunhuang, Datong and Luoyang. Two other cave complexes of interest, both in Gansu province, are more difficult of access. At Maijishan, south of Tianshui, wooden galleries cling-ing to its cliff faces lead to nearly two hundred cave temples filled with painted clay sculptures dating from the sixth century. The remoteness of these caves has meant that some are still untouched and almost perfectly preserved in their original state. Of the same period the Bingling Si caves, carved from red sandstone cliffs in spectacular riverside scenery near Yongjing, were a popular place of pilgrimage and have suffered from constant restoration as well as from erosion. A hundred miles northwest of Chongqing in Sichuan province, the rock temples at Dazu date from the ninth to thirteenth century. At the two main sites, Beishan has exquisite late Tang and Song figures, and Baoding Shan has a monumental Sleeping Buddha, and a Great Buddha Crescent with a wealth of twelfth and thirteenth century carvings.

The cave temples provide a rich source of material for the study not only of Buddhist art but of Chinese architecture, social history and costume. As some knowledge of the rudiments of Buddhist iconography may add to the pleasure of visiting Buddhist monuments, a simplified guide to this notoriously difficult subject is given on pages 22-4.

Although many monasteries contain statues of no artistic interest, it is always worth making enquiries locally. Every few months buildings are reopened to the public, and some temples contain outstanding sculpture, for example, the Lower Huayan Monastery in Datong, the Jin Ci in Taiyuan, and the Bamboo Temple in Kunming. A number of local museums also exhibit good sculpture rescued from ruined temples and regional excavations.

Painting and Calligraphy

To the Chinese artist the brush, ink, inkstone, and paper or silk are the Four Treasures of painting and calligraphy. The brush is a tuft of finely pointed animal hairs glued into a hollow bamboo tube. The earliest brush found so far, dating back to 400 B.C., was made in the same way as a modern brush. The ink for painting is made of pine-soot mixed with glue and moulded into a stick decorated with characters or pictures. The inkstone, on which the inkstick is rubbed with water to make the ink, is of non-porous slate and may be exquisitely carved and of great value. Prepared silk was being used for painting and writing by the third century B.C. and is still used for intricate styles of work. Paper, first made in about 105 A.D., comes in many types and qualities for different styles. Chinese artists place their paper, or silk, flat on the table and stand while painting.

One of the earliest known paintings on silk, of the second century B.C., comes from a tomb in Changsha. Murals from tombs of the Han dynasty are exhibited in a number of museums throughout the country, and Tang painting (618-907 A.D.) can be seen in the Tang tombs at Xi'an as well as in the Buddhist cave temples at Dunhuang. The main museum collections, particularly at the Palace Museum in Peking and the Shanghai Museum include masterpieces from the Tang to Qing period.

In this century a number of artists began to explore western techniques, some of whom went to study in Japan and the west. And in recent years, after a period of stereotyped Socialist Realism, painters are again able to experiment both in traditional Chinese media and in oils.

Modern original paintings at reasonable prices can be found in art shops in most cities. In Peking the Rongbao Zhai studios in Liulichang produce excellent reproductions of old and new paintings by hand printing from woodblocks on paper and silk. Their copies of old Chinese masterpieces are made mainly for museums in China and abroad, but they also print inexpensive copies of the work of modern artists such as Qi Baishi (Ch'i Pai-shih: 1863-1957) known for his flowers, fish and shrimps; Xu Beihong (Hsu Pei-hung: 1895-1953) who studied with Matisse in Paris and is world famous for his horses; Wu Zuoren and Wang Xuetao known respectively for inkpaintings of camels and pandas and colourful cocks and flowers. This has been a favourite shop for artists in Peking to buy their materials for many years, and Chinese brushes, decorated inksticks, inkstones, porcelain palettes and waterpots, and boxes of decorated art paper make attractive presents for friends who paint.

Chinese paintings are usually finished with a poem or inscription written by the artist and signed with a seal bearing his name, style or personal insignia. The design and carving of seals is an art in its own right and their history goes back two thousand years. Already popular in the Han dynasty (206 B.C. − 220 A.D.), they have been used ever since for authenticating official documents, personal papers and paintings. Early seals were made of metal or jade, the softer stones being introduced later. High ranking mandarins are said to have entrusted their silver official seals to their wives for safekeeping as there were dire penalties for their loss. Large finely carved imperial seals can be seen in the Jiaotai Hall of the Palace Museum in Peking.

Collectors of paintings often added inscriptions and their own seals to paintings which they wished to authenticate or praise. Sometimes this was done on a separate slip of paper beside the painting, but some connoisseurs, of whom the Qian Long Emperor is one famous example, allowed their comments and seals to overcrowd and, to the western eye, deface the painting itself. Conversely, a colophon by a great calligrapher could enhance the value of a mediocre work. A personal seal, which can be cut in a seal shop and in some hotels within a day, makes an attractive memento of a visit to China.

Chinese schoolchildren still learn to write with a brush as well as with a pen, and must know about three to four thousand characters to read well. The simplest characters illustrate the meaning of words. One, two or three horizontal lines are easily recognised as the first three numerals. A rectangle disected vertically with a single line denotes 'middle'. Two symbols used together suggest an idea; the sun and moon are combined to mean 'bright'; a woman and child together mean 'good'. By far the greatest number of characters are produced by combining one of just over two hundred symbols denoting basic ideas (e.g. heart, to indicate feelings; water, to indicate liquids: a hand, to indicate action), with another character which acts as a rudimentary phoenetic. To assist the process of learning, simplified forms of characters have been introduced. The written language is common to all parts of the country no matter how widely divergent the local dialects.

The varied forms of Chinese characters allowed calligraphy to develop into an art closely allied to painting. It has been compared by the contemporary Chinese scholar Chiang Yee to 'an adventure in movement very similar to good dancing' with its beauty springing from its spontaneity, rhythm and strength. The visitor will see it everywhere and will soon enjoy recognising contrast between the stiff archaic pattern-like Seal Characters, the elegant formal Regular Script, the flow of the Running Script, and the artistic scribble of the Grass Script. Good and inexpensive prints and rubbings of calligraphy can be found in art shops all over the country.

Good rubbings of famous carvings, and particularly of calligraphy, are treasured by the Chinese and treated as works of art.

One method of taking a rubbing, popular in the Tang dynasty, is to dampen a piece of special paper and press it carefully into place over the stone. When the paper is dry, ink is applied with a pad to reproduce the design or inscription. The paper is removed when the ink is dry.

Rubbings and reproductions of rubbings may be found in art shops in many large cities. There are good stocks in shops at the Temple of Heaven in Peking.

Ritual Bronzes and Mirrors

In 1929 the existence of the Shang dynasty (sixteenth to eleventh century B.C.) which some had believed to be legendary, was proved conclusively by the discovery of hundreds of superbly cast bronze ritual vessels in Shang royal tombs at Anyang in Honan. The sudden appearance of such highly skilled workmanship was a puzzle to scholars until excavations at Zhengzhou, the old Shang capital, produced earlier and cruder bronzes. Vessels were cast in multipart moulds, many of which have been unearthed at both Anyang and Zhengzhou. The 'lost wax' process of casting was also being used by about the fifth century B.C.

Background

Many different types of ritual bronzes were made for ceremonies honouring the ancestors of the Emperor and the nobility. Some were for preparing and holding food, some for mixing, warming and drinking wine, and others for pouring water for ritual ablutions.

Bronze mirrors, usually round with polished front and decorated back, appeared about the fifth century B.C., and from about 200 B.C. they were placed over the heart of the deceased to ward off evil spirits. On some mirrors the imprint of the grave cloths can still be seen.

Jade

There are two different extremely hard stones called jade — nephrite and jadeite. Jadeite, the shining stone that polishes to an emerald-like brilliance, is found in all shades of green, as well as lilac, blue and black, and was introduced into China from Burma only in the eighteenth century. Nephrite is the stone so highly valued by the Chinese through the centuries. In its purest state it is white, but it is also found in colours ranging from palest to darkest green, brown, yellow, and grey to black. Its fibrous toughness makes it extremely difficult to work, but burial and burning can make it less hard, and opaque. The rich soft gleam of old jade is due to the less harsh abrasives used to work it before the thirteenth century. It was prized for its translucency, beautiful colours and musical tone when struck, as well as for its medicinal virtues (powdered jade was thought to prolong life) and its presumed power to preserve the body, which led to the creation of jade burial suits of small squares of jade stitched together with gold wire.

It can be difficult even for experts to identify real jade without scientific tests. The well known 'scratch test' with a penknife blade will detect soft soapstone but is of little use with hard quartz and serpentine. A modern stainless steel blade will mark these hard stones as well as true jade. If you wish to buy good jade it is best to go to a reliable shop with your guide.

Lacquer

Lacquer is made from the sap of the lac tree (rhus vernicifera). Completely waterproof, it can be painted, carved or inlaid, and pieces inlaid with silver, gold and tortoiseshell fetched fabulous sums in the prosperous Han cities. The base for lacquer could be wood, cloth glued to wood, or, for luxury articles a base of hempcloth alone, and after the fourteenth century a soft metal was also used. After an application of primer, several coats of lacquer were put on, each being allowed to dry in a humid atmosphere at a temperature of 70 to 80°F. By the Ming and Qing periods from thirty to two hundred coats were used for high quality work, some of which required the application of layers of differently coloured lacquer that would be revealed when the carving was done.

Peking and Suzhou are known for carved lacquer, and Guangzhou and Fuzhou for painted lacquer. The production process can be seen in Arts and Crafts Factories in a number of cities.

Ceramics

The form of Chinese art most universally appreciated in the western world is ceramics, and many excellent books have been written on the subject; a few are mentioned in the reading list at the end of this book for those who wish to learn more about it.

It was in the seventeenth century that Chinese porcelain first appeared in quantity in western Europe, and was so different from European earthenware that it seemed beyond belief that it was made from clay. When Mary II succeeded to the English throne towards the end of the century she brought 'China-mania' over from Holland with her. There was an enormous demand during the eighteenth century first for 'blue and white' and later for enamel painted china from the famous kilns at Jingdezhen which had produced classic wares for the Chinese court since the twelfth century. Also popular were the blue-green 'celadons' (named for a shepherd in a French seventeenth century play who wore green of a similar hue), and the white 'blanc de chine' Buddhist figurines and groups of figures in seventeenth century dress.

Much Chinese export porcelain was made to order from models and patterns sent from Europe and the USA to agents in Guangzhou, the only port open to western traders before the mid-nineteenth century. The agents dealt with Chinese merchants who travelled to or were represented in Jingdezhen and other potteries. As much as three years might elapse between ordering and delivery. The porcelain had to travel six hundred miles by land and river between Jingdezhen and Guangzhou, and the great sailing ships, the East Indiamen, were dependent on the trade winds to bring them back to Europe. To the astonishment, not to say exasperation of purchasers, designs were copied so exactly that the finished product sometimes included the instructions written on the patterns, or even the smudged colours that resulted from the pattern having become wet. Some orders were completed at the potteries, others were sent to be decorated in Guangzhou under the supervision of the foreign agent. In 1709 Bottger succeeded in producing porcelain at Dresden, but it was some time before European porcelain could compete with Chinese export ware.

Today much research is being done in China on the production of high quality modern porcelain and on reproducing the great wares of the past. Potteries, a number of which are manufacturing for export, may be visited in many centres such as Foshan near Guangzhou, Jingdezhen, Gongxian near Luoyang, Peking and Hangzhou.

The main national collections, constantly being enriched by new finds, are at the Palace Museum in Peking and the Shanghai Museum. Provincial museums such as those at Xi'an, Jinan, Hangzhou, Kunming, Nanjing, Changsha, Chongqing, Dehua and Guangzhou have good regional collections.

Background

Reign Marks

During the fifteenth century it became a regular practice to place a reign mark, usually of four or six characters, on Chinese ceramics. With a mark of six characters the first two denoted the name of the dynasty: e.g. the Great Qing. The second two gave the reign title of the emperor: e.g. Qian Long. The next character meant 'year', and the last character meant either 'made by imperial order' or just 'made'. With a mark of four characters the name of the dynasty may be omitted. The first two characters of this mark denoted the reign title of the Emperor, and the last two as above.

The mark does not necessarily give the date of manufacture. A potter copying an antique piece also copied the mark, and a piece in a certain style was often made with the mark appropriate to that period. There are of course also frauds.

The characters in marks were written either in the normal style for writing or in a special antique style of characters used for seals. They may be found on any part of the vessel, but are most often on the base in underglaze blue.

Silk and Embroidery

The discovery by the Chinese of the techniques of silk production is lost in history. For many centuries silk was so important economically that the production process was kept a closely guarded secret, the death penalty being imposed on anyone attempting to take silkworm cocoons out of the country. Right up to the end of the last century the empress or her representative presented offerings at the altar to sericulture in the Beihai Park in Peking.

The art of embroidery is probably as old as that of silk weaving. The earliest silk found dates from the third century B.C. and the earliest embroidery (now in the Changsha Museum) from the second. Since that time there have been many skilful embroiderers such as Lu Mei, who in the ninth century stitched a complete Buddhist scripture on one foot of silk in minute characters, and the Gu family of the Fragrant Dew Garden who lived in Shanghai in the Ming dynasty and whose work can be seen in museums today. The stitches they used were few in comparison with those used in western embroidery; but the technique was exquisite as was the colouring and shading produced by changing the lie of the silk thread, sometimes so fine as to be almost invisible.

It is possible to visit silk factories, of which there are many in the Yangtze Valley, and also the embroidery workshops of the four great schools of Chinese embroidery, in Suzhou and Hangzhou, Changsha, Chengdu and Guangzhou. The Suzhou Embroidery Research Institute keeps alive a tradition of a thousand years weaving 'k' o ssu' silk tapestry on small hand looms, where each motif is worked separately with a handheld shuttle. Some of the imperial robes in the Peking Palace Museum are in 'k'o ssu'. It is not to be confused with modern machinemade 'silk tapestry' pictures.

Good quality embroidery can be found in many cities but the best is not cheap. Distinctive fine cross-stitch work is sold in the Minorities areas, where they also make batik. Silk and brocades are very good value in China, but mixtures with manmade fibres are now common and it is important to check before purchase that the fabric is pure silk.

Ivory

As in many other parts of the world, ivory has been carved in China from very early times. It was used in the rituals of the Shang dynasty 1500 years before Christ, and through the centuries it has been made into fans, combs, chopsticks, ornaments, figures and furniture. But it was in the eighteenth century that the most superb work was produced in the workshops of the Forbidden City in Peking, where skilled craftsmen from Peking specialised in stained and engraved pieces, and men from Guangzhou produced complex and delicate work including complete landscapes and the celebrated carved concentric balls. Today master craftsmen can be seen at the Daxin Ivory Carving Studio in Guangzhou carving balls with as many as forty layers. Each ball is detached from the outer one by knives with curved blades inserted through holes in the outer layers; the pierced designs are similarly cut through the same holes.

Cloisonné

Unlike silk and porcelain, the technique of making cloisonne was introduced into China, probably by Arab traders in the fourteenth century. It is made by attaching gold, silver or copper filaments to a metal base following an intricate pattern and creating small separate cells, or cloisons. The design is then made by filling these with coloured enamel paste. The piece may need to be fired several times, as different enamel colours are fired at different temperatures. Special workshops were set up in the imperial palace by the Qian Long Emperor in the eighteenth century to make the court wares ranging from tiny ornaments to huge screens and incense burners, some of which still furnish the halls in the Forbidden City.

Cloisonné can be seen in production at the Arts and Crafts Workshop in Peking.

Architecture

Early Chinese conquerors regularly destroyed the capitals of their predecessors but records and excavations give evidence of a strong attachment to capital cities rectangular in shape, with high walls, a lattice of intersecting streets, an independent enclave for the Imperial City within the outer wall, and a further walled enclave for the Imperial Palace inside that. On such a grand scale was the layout of Changan, the capital of the Tang dynasty (618-907), the capital of the Northern Song (960-1126) at Kaifeng, and Peking under the last three dynasties. But topography sometimes overrode these principles. The irregular outer wall of Nanjing followed the natural defence line. The Southern Song capital at Hangzhou (1127-1279) had to be squeezed between the West Lake and the river and almost all its elements were irregular.

Provincial capitals and the walled towns showed a similar mixture of the regular and irregular. The Zhenhai Lou in Guangzhou was the tower which stood at the highest point of the old wall dominating the nearly semi-circular city below it. River towns had to be protected from attack by boats and their walls naturally followed the shore line. Only when a town became prosperous could it afford the investment of material and manpower necessary to build and maintain a wall, which would have to follow the shape of the town as it then was.

The gate of a Chinese city was the key to its security and a convenient point for the collection of taxes on the commerce passing through. The massive gates of the Imperial Palace had a double significance. They protected the imperial presence and symbolised imperial authority. There is no more impressive gate than the Meridian Gate (Wu Men) at the entrance to the Forbidden City in Peking, and there are fine examples of city gates in both Nanjing and Xi'an. Gates of the smaller provincial cities were more modest. The old city gate still preserved on the banks of the Banyan Lake in Guilin is tiny when compared to its counterparts in the larger cities.

Europeans used to distinctive styles for palaces, cathedrals and mausolea may be surprised to find that in China one type of structure is used for most monumental buildings whether palaces, temples or ceremonial halls at tombs. All were built to a pattern well established by the tenth century and, in its essentials, in use long before that.

In the traditional Chinese building free standing wooden pillars are seated on round stone bosses set at intervals into the ground or on a terrace. The pillars are tied at the capitals by crossbeams, laterally and trans-versely, forming a structural frame which bears the weight of the roof and gives the building its stability. The space between the pillars is then filled in with a combination of wall, doors, windows or latticework as the design requires. To give the roof its pitch, short pillars set on the transverse beams support other beams which decrease in length as the level rises, until a single kingpost at the centre can support the ridge of the roof.

The most important buildings have hipped roofs which sweep down-wards from the roofridge on all four sides, as in the Taihe Dian, the first of the three great halls in the Forbidden City. In buildings of the second order of importance a gable is set in the upper half of the roof at each end, as in the Baohe Dian, the third hall. Lesser buildings have conventional gables. Yellow glazed tiles were reserved for imperial buildings. Temples, palaces and other important places usually had green, turquoise or blue glazed tiles. In very exposed places such as the temple at the top of Mount Tai Shan, iron or bronze tiles were used to minimise breakage.

The third distinctive feature of Chinese architecture was the use of cantilevered brackets at the pillarheads to enable the edge of the roof to be extended outwards well beyond the line of the pillars. In the later buildings the bracket system was developed to a point where the mixture of horizontal, curved and slanting levers with highly ornamented supports was as much decorative as functional.

Experts do not agree on the origin of the graceful curves of Chinese roofs but they could well have been a natural and aesthetic product of the method of roof construction. Nor is there any unanimity of opinion on the origin of the line of animals and birds, some mythical, and the human figure which decorate the corners of the roofs of important buildings, beyond the belief that they had some protective influence, possibly against fire and evil spirits. Those who visit the fortress gate where the Great Wall meets the sea at Shanhai Guan will note that the roof ornaments there are human figures, many in military uniform.

Although the construction and proportions of buildings had in themselves to be aesthetically satisfying, each had to form part of a harmonious whole. The arrangement of the buildings along the main axis of the city was also crucial to the effect. Nowhere in the world is there a finer procession of buildings than the line of gates, towers and palaces running from south to north in Peking.

A pagoda was an almost invariable feature of Buddhist temple architecture. It is commonly held that the pagoda, like Buddhism itself, entered China from India. But some authorities have seen an indigenous and separate origin, particularly for square pagodas, in ancient Chinese watchtowers. The earliest were constructed in wood. Later pagodas were built of brick, and the finest clad in stone. Most had a central staircase but the Liao and Jin dynasty pagodas (tenth to thirteenth century) of north China were solid, usually octagonal, with thirteen stories. (The pagoda of the Tianning Monastery in Peking is typical of the Liao period.) Pagodas were often built to house Buddhist relics or as expressions of devotion to the Buddhist faith. The Great Wild Goose Pagoda (Dayan Ta) at Xi'an was constructed in brick as a safe depository for the sutras and relics brought back from India by the Tang monk Xuan Zang. Other pagodas were built to attract benign influences. The Pagoda of Six Harmonies (Liuhe Ta) at Hangzhou was erected in the hope of protecting the city from tidal waves. The Wenfeng Pagoda in Yangzhou was built with contributions from scholars hoping for success in the official examinations.

Traditionally the streets of Chinese cities would be lined with open fronted shops, the finest with elaborately decorated fronts and distinctive signboards. They are unfortunately now a rarity. Gone too are most of the commemorative archways (pailou), many erected to honour virtuous widows, that once spanned the streets of old China.

Domestic architecture varied widely from region to region. In Peking the typical courtyard house offered to the street only a blank wall and a single gate. Even when the heavy double doors were opened, the view within was obscured by a decorated screen wall originally placed there to prevent the entrance of malign spirits. Inside the first courtyard were the domestic quarters. A central gateway or moongate led into the next courtyard, beyond which stood the main reception area with rooms for the family on each side. In the larger houses there were more courtyards beyond and sometimes a garden with pools, rocks, and pavilions. An easily visited example today is the home of the Chinese writer Lu Xun which is maintained as part of a museum dedicated to him. The Sichuan Restaurant with its numerous courtyards in southwest Peking is an example of a more well-to-do home.

In the loess lands of northwest China cave houses are still hollowed out of the soft hillsides, with decorated doors and windows filling an arched front. The northwest is also the home of the fortified village in which the roofs of the houses slope inwards from the high blind back wall which formed the outer defence of the village against bandits and the bitter weather. Inside the houses, as in many parts of the north, the main rooms are heated by a 'kang', a raised, mat-covered platform usually occupying about one third of the room and kept warm by flues from the kitchen stove. It provides a warm bed at night, and during the day the family work and relax on it, sitting crosslegged round low-tables.

Dwellings in the warmer and damper south have open lattice windows and wide overhanging eaves to throw the rain away from the main walls. Parts of central China south of the Yangtze River have grey brick houses built in short terraces, and separated by tall dividing walls whose curved tops rise well above the level of the roofs on either side, as a precaution against the spread of fire. In the tropical south the large open plan houses built on stilts, with their bamboo frames and palmleaf roofs, are reminiscent of the houses of Southeast Asia.

2. China's Capitals

Through the centuries many cities large and small have served as capitals in China. The ancient capitals were all in the valley of the Yellow River or its tributaries. The Shang dynasty (sixteenth to eleventh century B.C.) ruled first in Zhengzhou and later at Anyang, both in the modern province of Henan. Their successors, the Zhou and the Qin who came from the west, chose towns further upriver, and particularly in the valley of the Wei, a tributary of the Yellow River near modern Xi'an. They were not static. The Qin moved their base no less than eleven times before they united China. The next dynasty, the Han (206 B.C.-220 A.D.) had a capital, Changan, near Xi'an, but after a short interregnum from 9-25, the dynasty was re-established further east at Luoyang on the Yellow River. After the collapse of the Han, China was not united again until 589 A.D. by the Sui who again chose Changan, but the second Emperor rebuilt Luoyang as his eastern capital. The Tang rulers (618-907) too used both cities. In their day Changan was one of the greatest cities in the world.

The Song came to power in the tenth century, and after much debate they decided to abandon the old sites and establish themselves at Kaifeng, further downriver, because of its better communications and food supply. They were under constant pressure from the northern nomads who first occupied the city which is today Peking and made it one of their five capitals. These northern horsemen later drove the Song from Kaifeng. A son of the Emperor escaped south where he established the Southern Song court at Hangzhou. They stayed there for 150 years, leaving the northerners in possession of north China. Both were overwhelmed by the Mongol hordes in the thirteenth century, and Kublai Khan built at Peking the capital Marco Polo knew as Cambulac (Khanbalik). Apart from two short periods, one in the fourteenth century and one in this when it was at Nanjing and Chongqing, the capital has remained at Peking ever since.

Peking (Beijing)

The Peking area has been inhabited since prehistoric times. Zhoukoudian, where the skull of Peking Man was found in 1929, is only thirty miles away on the other side of the Yongding River. A town called Ji grew up on its north banks, and pottery-lined wells of the period discovered since 1965

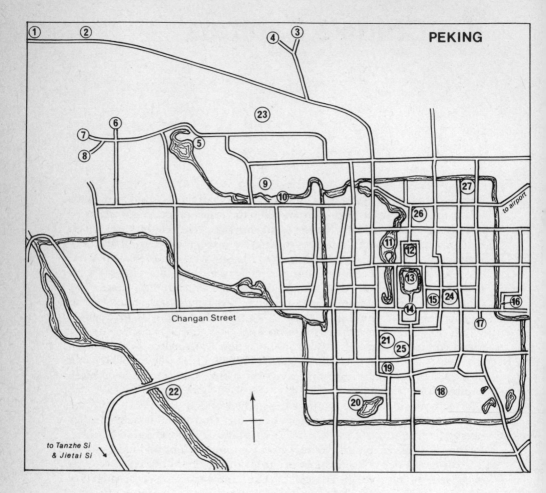

PEKING

Changan Street

to airport

to Tanzhe Si & Jietai Si

1. To the Great Wall
2. Juyong Guan
3. Ming Tombs
4. The excavated tomb, Ding Ling
5. Summer Palace
6. Temple of the Sleeping Buddha
7. Temple of the Azure Clouds
8. Fragrant Hills
9. Five-tower Temple
10. Zoo
11. Bei Hai Park
12. Prospect Hill
13. Forbidden City and Palace Museum
14. Tianan Men Square
15. Peking Hotel
16. Friendship Store and diplomatic quarters
17. Railway station
18. Temple of Heaven
19. Chianmen Hotel
20. Joyous Pavilion Park
21. Liuli Chang
22. Marco Polo Bridge
23. Yuanming Yuan
24. Wangfujing Street
25. Da Zha La'r Street
26. Drum Tower
27. Lama Temple

show that it was located in the southwest quarter of the present city. The town grew in importance because of its strategic position just south of the Juyongguan and Gubeikou passes through the mountains to the north. It was well placed to serve as a trading centre at which furs, hides and other goods from the nomadic northwestern tribes could be exchanged for the agricultural products of the south. In the tenth century the semi-nomadic Khitan Mongols erupted from their homelands outside the Great Wall, took the North China Plain and established their southern capital in Peking, only to be ousted in their turn by their vassals the Jurchen who drove them out in 1125. The Khitan were the people who gave Europe the name 'Cathay' for north China, and the Russians the name 'Khitai' by which they know China today. They took the dynastic title 'Liao', and the Jurchen took the dynastic title 'Jin'.

The great national capitals at this time lay far to the south in Kaifeng and Hangzhou. The history of Peking as a national capital began only in the thirteenth century when the Mongol Kublai Khan, grandson of Genghis Khan, conquered China and built the city so much admired by Marco Polo. This is not the city which remains today. When the succeeding Chinese dynasty, the Ming, expelled the Mongols from north China, they established their first capital at Nanjing on the Yangtze River. The third Ming Emperor decided to remove the capital to his own power base at Peking where he had much of Kublai's city torn down, and spent fifteen years creating a new capital. The best craftsmen from all over the country were summoned to Peking in 1406, and officials despatched to the southern and southwestern provinces to requisition the finest timber, tiles, and other materials. In 1421 the capital was once more established in Peking.

After more than two centuries of peace, peasant uprisings gave the Manchus, ever watchful north of the Great Wall, their opportunity to conquer the whole of China. Admirers of Chinese culture, they took over what the Ming had left behind, repairing, rebuilding and adding to the existing city without much changing its form. Their great contribution was in the construction of the summer palaces northwest of the city, including the Yuanming Yuan, where the court spent much of its time until the British and French forces destroyed it in 1860.

Only after their defeat in 1860 did the Manchus concede the right of residence in Peking to foreign legations. They chose a quarter almost at the gates of the Imperial City. After the Boxer uprising in 1900 it was turned into a foreign enclave which was run by the legations until the outbreak of the war with Japan in 1941.

In 1927 the new Nationalist Government moved the capital back to Nanjing (Nanking), and Peking, the Northern Capital, was renamed Beiping, Northern Peace. Twenty-two years later, after the war with Japan and three years of civil war, the city surrendered to the victorious Communist armies, and on 1 October 1949 Mao Zedong declared the establishment of the People's Republic of China from the Gate of Heavenly Peace, the Tianan Men, at the entrance to the Forbidden City. Peking was the capital once again. A period of rapid expansion began. The city walls were removed, new residential areas, universities and factories sprang up outside the old walled area, and the city grew to many times its original size. The population now numbers over six million.

Cities within Cities and Tianan Men Square

Peking was built as a series of 'cities within cities'. At the centre lay the Forbidden City (now the Palace Museum) with its high red walls and four gates. Surrounding it was the Imperial City whose walls enclosed the Lake Palaces, the Altar of Land and Grain (now Zhongshan Park) and the Ancestral Temple (now the Working People's Palace of Culture). Outside again was the city itself, divided into a northern section, often known as the Tartar City because under the last dynasty it was largely reserved for Manchus, and a southern section often called the Chinese City. The wall which starts near the Peking Hotel and runs west along the north side of the main avenue is the old south wall of the Imperial City.

The hub of Peking is now the Tianan Men Square dominated by the vast gold-roofed Tianan Men Gate to the north; the Great Hall of the People, built in 1959, to the west, and the Historical Museum and Museum of Revolutionary History to the east. The Six Boards of the Metropolitan government, the Boards of Civil Office, Revenue, Ceremonies, War, Punishment and Works stood here in imperial times but disappeared with the fall of the Manchu dynasty. Officials once assembled in the square to hear imperial edicts or the roll of scholars successful in the official examinations read from an Edict Declaration Platform erected in front of the Gate. After the ceremony the edicts were carried in a Dragon Pavilion, a special wooden box, to the Board of Ceremonies to be copied onto yellow paper and despatched to all parts of the empire.

The square has seen many stirring events since then. On 4 May 1919 it was the assembly point for students demonstrating against concessions made to Japan in the Versailles peace treaty. Their protest is now taken as marking a turning point in the history of modern China. In 1967 during the height of the Cultural Revolution hundreds of thousands of students and school children assembled to acclaim Mao Zedong as their hero. On 5 April 1976 an astonished world learned of riots in the square as the now vilified radical members of the Politbureau, known as the Gang of Four, sought to suppress a mass commemoration of the death four months earlier of Premier Zhou Enlai.

The centre of the square is occupied by the Monument to the People's Heroes and in 1976-7 a Memorial Hall to Mao Zedong was built at its southern end. This part of the square is dominated by two huge city gates, both originally part of one gate in the wall of the Tartar City. The Main Gate (Qian Men) nearest the Mausoleum, stood on the city wall. Protecting each main gate of the city was a semi-circular outwork topped by an Arrow Tower; the outer wall has gone but the second gate is the remaining Arrow Tower.

The Forbidden City and The Palace Museum (Gu Gong)

In the Forbidden City (now the Palace Museum) twenty-four Emperors, fourteen in the Ming and ten in the Manchu Qing dynasty, lived isolated from the outside world in a palace forbidden on pain of death to the vast majority of their subjects. This unique and magnificent example of Chinese monumental architecture was first built when the capital itself was laid out from 1406 to 1421. Over the centuries many of its buildings have been reconstructed, enlarged and further embellished. Throughout, the lofty pillars of the rare and fragrant wood, nanmu, which support the roofs of golden tiles on its hundreds of buildings, are richly decorated in crimson and gold, the bronze lions guarding the entrance gate are masterpieces of casting, and the marble balustrades and central ramps are carved with superb imperial dragons.

The southern half of the Forbidden City was called the Outer Court. At its entrance, inside the Tianan Men, stands the fortress-like Meridian Gate (Wu Men). Now the entrance where visitors buy their tickets, the central door was once reserved for the use of the Emperor alone. The striking of a drum and sounding of a bell from the towers above announced his departure to perform sacrifices at the Temple of Heaven or the Ancestral Temple, and also marked his ascending the throne within the palace for one of the Great Ceremonies. A guard of imperial elephants was drawn up outside the gate on ceremonial occasions, and it was the custom to 'present the captives' here when victorious generals arrived from the field of battle.

Crossing the Jade Canal inside the Wu Men and passing through the Gate of Supreme Harmony (Taihe Men) between its majestic bronze lions, the visitor arrives in the vast courtyard before the main ceremonial buildings. Here row upon row of officials in court dress would take up their positions, civilian officials to the east, the position of honour, and military officials to the west. Each stationed himself according to rank with the help of bronze markers set in the ground, waiting in complete silence until, at the moment when the Emperor ascended the throne, all were commanded to prostrate themselves nine times, only the guard remaining standing. They faced the first and most important of the ceremonial buildings, the Hall of Supreme Harmony (Taihe Dian), set high on a three-tiered terrace of marble. The three flights of steps lead up past bronze incense burners on either side of a marble ramp intricately carved with dragons, symbol of the Emperor, over which only his chair could pass. Inside the hall, high in the roof a golden dragon is carved above the gilded throne which the Emperor ascended for his accession, at the New Year and to receive congratulations on his birthday. Between golden columns entwined with dragons, clouds of incense rose from incense burners round the throne, and from great bronze tortoises and cranes, symbols of long life, on the Dragon Pavement outside. The Emperor prepared himself for the ceremonies and read over his texts in the smaller square hall behind, the Hall of Middle Harmony (Zhonghe Dian). The next hall, the Hall of Preserving Harmony (Baohe Dian) still dates substantially from Ming times, although it was repaired in the late seventeenth century. Banquets for visiting vassal princes and ambassadors were given here, and from 1789 the Emperor presided over the highest examinations in this hall. The long ramp leading down the back, with its design of dragons and clouds, is the finest carving in the palace. First worked in the Ming dynasty, it was recarved in 1761. The slab had to be brought from the quarries during the winter along roads specially flooded to provide an ice surface, since only ice sledges could cope with its immense weight of 250 tons.

Returning for a moment to the Meridian Gate, to the east of the Jade Canal a gate leads out to the Hall of Literary Splendour (Wenhua Dian) where the imperial princes studied and the classics were expounded before the Emperor twice a year. Behind it was the Imperial Library (Wenyuan Ge) whose remaining volumes have now been transferred to the Peking Library. In the hall alongside, the Hall of Transmitted Intellect (Chuanxin Dian), the Emperor paid homage to the tablets of the legendary Emperors and of Confucius.

The Inner Court occupied the northern section of the Forbidden City. At its centre was the Palace of Heavenly Purity (Qianqing Gong) where, during the Ming and early Qing dynasties, the Emperors lived and conducted state affairs. Just inside the Gate of Heavenly Purity (opposite the long ramp) was the Office of Tranquil Affairs (Jingshi Fang) or Eunuchs Department, which supervised the activities of the thousands of eunuchs who served in the city and who played such a disastrous role in some periods of both the Ming and Qing dynasties.

Behind the Palace of Heavenly Purity, the first hall, is the square Hall of Supreme Union (Jiaotai Dian) now used for the exhibition of imperial seals. In Ming times many of the Empresses lived in the third of the palace buildings, the Palace of Earthly Tranquillity (Kunning Gong) behind which the gate leads out to the palace gardens. In later years the imperial marriages were conducted here. The last Emperor of the Manchu dynasty, Pu Yi, describes in his autobiography how, when he was sixteen he and his thirteen year old bride were left to spend their wedding night in this awesome bridal chamber. He became oppressed by the overpowering crimson of the decoration, the red bed curtains and pillows, the red dress and wedding skirt of his bride, and her rouged face. 'It all looked like a melted red wax candle', and he abandoned his bride and retreated to his own quarters in the western part of the Forbidden City.

The atmosphere was probably made the more depressing by the knowledge that the western section of the same hall was used for the celebration of shamanistic rites going back to the time when the Manchus were nomads in their wild homelands north of the Great Wall. Each morning between 3 and 4 a.m. a sorceress danced and chanted as she performed the ancient sacrifices. On birthdays and other special occasions members of the imperial guard dressed in animal skins to perform dances commemorating episodes in the life of Nurhachi, the founder of the Manchu dynasty.

In the Imperial Flower Garden behind this palace the members of the Emperor's family enjoyed strolling among the tree peonies, and other flowers, rocks, pools, pavilions and ancient cypresses as old as the palace itself. A path decorated with stones and shells, most colourful after the rain, leads to the Hall of Imperial Peace (Qinan Dian) in the middle of the garden; it has an unusual low pitched roof and has been unchanged since the Ming dynasty. It is dedicated to the Daoist God of Fire, Xuan Wu. At the back two gilded elephants in bronze are a reminder of the elephants once on guard at the Meridian Gate.

The north gate of the garden leads out through the Gate of Divine Military Prowess (Shenwu Men) to the moat, the road and on to Prospect Hill Park (Jing Shan). Tickets to visit the Forbidden City can also be bought at this gate, and a taxi ordered at the office next door.

From each side of the Flower Garden small roads lead south to the Six Palaces of the East and West, the residences of the princes, the Empresses and the concubines. Those on the east are now used for exhibitions of the palace collections of jade and handicrafts, porcelain, and bronzes – not all open every day. The East Road leads south back into the great courtyard separating the Outer and Inner Courts behind the Hall of Preserving Harmony. Turn east through the Jingyun Gate and continue across the open space to a second small ticket office beside a gate leading into a long treclined courtyard. This is the entrance to the paintings and jewellery exhibitions. You need another ticket only for the jewellery. Inside the gateway on the right is the Nine Dragon Screen of brilliant glazed tiles. Constructed in 1772, it protects the gateway to the Palace of Peaceful Old Age (Ning Shou Gong) which leads into a tranquil court bordered with low spreading pines. They shade pavilions where the visitor may rest a while to absorb the atmosphere of this beautiful palace. The Qian Long Emperor restored the buildings in 1772 in preparation for his retirement after sixty years on the throne, believing it to be unfilial to reign longer than his illustrious grandfather the Kang Xi Emperor. At the Hall of Imperial Supremacy (Huangji Dian) in the next court he held banquets for One Thousand Old Men, officials of over sixty years of age, as a mark of the respect in which the Chinese hold the aged. The hall and the surrounding buildings are now used to exhibit the Palace Museum collection of paintings. Ming and Qing paintings are usually shown in the side buildings, and the early paintings, Tang, Song and Yuan in the main halls in October to November; the exhibition dates should be checked each year. A pleasant courtyard to the west offers refreshments and shops for the foreign visitors. Behind the Palace of Peaceful Old Age is a gate guarded by two gilt lions which leads into the Hall of the Culture of Character (Yangxian Dian). Here you have to hand in your ticket. In this part of the palace, with its secluded miniature gardens, were the private apartments first of the Manchu Qian Long Emperor after his retirement, and later for a time of the Empress Dowager Ci Xi and her ladies in waiting. The buildings now house the collection of jewellery, gold and silver ornaments, jade carvings and imperial robes, saddles and weapons. Tradition has it that in 1900, before the court fled to Xi'an to escape the allied forces advancing on Peking, the Empress Dowager hid her treasure here. On her return more than a year later she was fortunate enough to find it intact in spite of the fact that the palace had been occupied by foreign troops. A sad story connected with this same flight tells of the murder of the Emperor's favourite, the Pearl Concubine, by command of the Empress Dowager who resented her influence over the young Emperor. She was drowned in the well which may still be seen just inside the north exit to this part of the palace.

The lofty richly decorated building looking over the eastern wall of the Palace of Peaceful Old Age was the palace theatre, the Pavilion of Pleasant Sound (Changyin Ge).

Returning to the Imperial Flower Garden, a gate in its northwestern corner leads into the Studio of Pure Fragrance (Shufang Zhai). Here at the beginning of each year the Emperor performed the ceremony of the First Writing with the Vermillion Brush, a reference to the red ink which he alone could use. The Qian Long Emperor lived in the next building to the west, the Palace of Mighty Glory (Chonghua Gong) when he was a prince. After ascending the throne he invited his ministers and scholars here in the first month of each year to drink tea and compose poems, two of which he selected to hang in the Hall of Honour (Chongjing Dian) next door.

Like the other palaces in this part of the City, the Palace of Eternal Spring (Changchun Gong) was in later years often occupied by Empresses or by favourite concubines, each of whom might have her own independent establishment. The number of ladies in waiting allowed was laid down by the Emperor, from twelve for the Empress to four for the lesser concubines, but these numbers were generally exceeded and each also had many maidservants. When the Empress Dowager lived here after 1884 the palace was often used for the theatrical performances she so enjoyed.

The later Manchu Emperors worked and lived in the Hall of Mental Cultivation (Yangxin Dian) at the south end of the West Road. In its east rooms is a small throne with a screen behind it. During the minority of her son the Empress Dowager Ci Xi sat behind the screen instructing him on the answers he should give, thus in effect conducting the affairs of state herself. After he attained his majority she still made use of this device because it was contrary to dynastic law for a woman to act for the Emperor. In this same room the last Emperor, a child of six, abdicated on 2 February 1912, although he continued to live in the palace until 1924.

Following the West Road south out into the courtyard behind the Hall of Preserving Harmony, the route west goes past the Offices of the Grand Council, modest apartments for such great officers, on the way to the Longzong Gate. Above the doors an arrowhead lodged in the nameboard recalls the unsuccessful attempt of members of the White Lotus Sect to storm the Forbidden City in 1813. On arrival at the outer gate they became embroiled in a quarrel with men moving coal into the City and showed their swords. The palace guards raised the alarm and after a fight the attack was frustrated.

Through the gate and across the courtyard stand two gilded mythical beasts guarding the imposing gateway to the Palace of Peace and Tranquility (Cining Gong). Empresses lived here in both the Ming and Qing dynasties and the marriage ceremonies of imperial princesses were held in the palace. When the co-Regent of the Empress Dowager died here suddenly in 1881 it was widely believed that she had been poisoned by her jealous rival.

Closely connected with the Forbidden City, although outside the moat, were the Ancestral Temple (Tai Miao — now the Workers Cultural Palace) and the Altar of Land and Grain (Sheji Tan — now the Zhongshan Park). The Ancestral Temple, which lies at the southeast corner of the City, was first built in 1420 and reconstructed in 1544. Here the reigning Emperor paid homage to the tablets of his forebears at the time of his accession and marriage, when his armies achieved great victories, and on other great occasions. In the Main Hall, which matches in size and splendour the buildings in the Forbidden City, the thrones of the Manchu Emperors were set out in order on a dais, each with a stand for the Emperor's spirit tablet. In the third hall were the tablets of the four Manchu chiefs who were raised posthumously to the rank of Emperor when Nuchachi founded the Manchu dynasty in Shenyang in 1616. With a surprising but doubtless conscious sense of continuity, the lying-in-state ceremonies of a number of leading members of the Communist Party have been arranged in the Main Hall where the Emperors of China were honoured before them.

On the opposite side of the Forbidden City at the southwest corner is the Altar where in the second and eighth months of the lunar calendar, the Emperor paid homage to the Gods of the Land and the Grain who in ancient times symbolised the state. The Hall of Worship (Bai Dian) near the three tiered marble altar terrace was made a Memorial Hall to Dr Sun Yat-sen, the father of the Chinese revolution, in 1928. First erected in early Ming times, the hall is one of the best examples of all wood construction in the capital. The Pavilion for Rehearsing the Rites in the south of the park was originally in the Court of Ceremonies (Honglu Si). All officials summoned to attend their first imperial audience had to come to practise the approved ritual in front of the pavilion before being allowed into the palace.

The park with its beautiful flowers, the tree peonies and wisteria in spring and chrysanthemums in autumn, is a favourite place for old and young in Peking. It is now known as Zhongshan Park.

North Lake Park (Bhei Hai)

Water is a vital element in the planning of any Chinese city, not only for domestic use but because lakes, pools and streams are essential to the Chinese concept of landscaping. When the Khitan and Jurchens set up their capitals in Peking in the tenth century they based their cities on a water system flowing from the Lotus Pond (Lianhua Zhi) which still gives its name to a park south of the Military Museum. Kublai Khan needed more water for his city and built his capital around the larger lake system fed from the Jade Spring in the Western Hills, of which the North Lake Park (Bei Hai) and the Summer Palace Lake are both part. The North Lake was at the centre of the city which Marco Polo saw, with the Mongol palaces on either side.

Just inside the entrance to the park on the left is the fortress-like Round Citadel (Tuan Cheng). Before Kublai built his city this was no more than a small island at the edge of the lake. He built a hall there and his successors, the Ming, added the wall. In 1746 the Qian Long Emperor completely rebuilt it reconstructing the hall in the form of the cross with the curved double roof surrounding the main structure as it appears today. In the hall a Buddha, carved from one piece of jade, has a mark on the left arm attributed by Chinese to soldiers of the allied armies who, when they occupied Peking in 1900, tried to split it open in the hope of finding jewels inside. Of greater historic interest is the huge black jade wine vessel, carved with fish and dragons, in a pavilion near the wall. It was used by Kublai Khan in 1265, disappeared when the Mongols were ousted from Peking, and recovered in the reign of the Qian Long Emperor. The last Ming Emperor is said to have sat in the Citadel playing chess with his concubines to take his mind off the success of the peasant leader Li Zicheng, who eventually overthrew him.

From the Citadel a marble bridge leads across the lake to the hill surmounted by a White Dagoba (Baita). On the slopes are a profusion of temples, ornamental halls and pavilions and rockeries, each with a name extolling its beauties, alluding to events in Chinese history or mythology, or recalling a famous quotation from Chinese literature. Of the two main complexes of buildings the first is the Temple of Everlasting Peace (Yongan Si), rising step by step from the end of the bridge up to the Dagoba. In front of it the square building faced with blue, green and yellow glazed tiles, each with a Buddhist figure, once housed a Lamaist god, Yamantaka the Destroyer, who wore a necklace of skulls. The second complex is formed by the buildings and long verandah of the palaces skirting the lake on the northern side of the island. The court came here to enjoy and view and watch winter sports on the frozen lake. The buildings now house an excellent restaurant, the Fang Shan. A ferry crosses the lake from its entrance to the less grand but good Beihai Restaurant on the north shore.

The White Dagoba, a landmark on the Peking skyline, was built in 1651 to commemorate the visit to Peking of the fifth Dalai Lama, and occupies the site of one of the central features of Kublai's capital, the Guanghan Hall which was demolished in 1579. Chinese landscape artists believe that in building the Dagoba and the lofty Hall of Rippling Waves (Yilan Tang) on the north face, the Manchus ruined the previous harmony between the buildings on the hill and their reflection in the lake. But they credit them with bringing into the park the concept of 'a garden within a garden', for example the Clear Mirror Studio (Jingching Zhai) at the north end of the lake. From the Dagoba Terrace there is a spectacular view over the city, and across the lake to the Five Dragon Pavilions (Wulong Ting) near the northwestern shore, to the Studio of the Tranquil Mind (Jingxin Zhai) which has the Clear Mirror Studio within it, and the buildings of the former Buddhist temples and the Pine Hill Library (Songpo Tushuguan) now a reading room. If you have time to walk round the lake you will pass the old Altar of Silkworms, where sacrifice was offered by the Empress or her representative in token of the importance of sericulture to the empire, at the north end of the east shore. It is worth walking round, not only for the beauty of the views back to the island, but to see, among the buildings of the northern shore, another fine Nine Dragon Screen of coloured glazed tiles, similar to the one at the gate of the Palace of Peaceful Old Age in the Forbidden City.

To the south, the terrace overlooks the Middle and South Lakes (Zhong Hai and Nan Hai) which now house the Central Government and Party offices and are not open to the public. On the west side of the Middle Lake is the small bungalow where, in his declining years, Mao Zedong lived and received important visitors. Beyond it, about half way down the lake lies the Palace Steeped in Compassion (Huairen Tang), once the preferred residence of the Empress Dowager, who found the Forbidden City gloomy and lived in it as little as possible. She died in this palace in 1908. Her body was placed in the coffin which she had kept ready for the occasion. Preparing a coffin of good quality was common practice among all Chinese who could afford it and a great comfort to the elderly.

Distance and trees obscure the South Lake and the visitor must rely on imagination to visualise the small island, the Ocean Terrace (Ying Tai) on which the luckless Guang Xu Emperor was imprisoned by the Empress Dowager after the failure of the Reform Movement in 1898, a movement which she rightly saw as a threat to her despotic power. In the far distance the southern gate of the South Lake opens on the main east-west avenue of Peking, Changan Dajie. It was built as a pavilion by the Qian Long Emperor for the concubine of Khozi Khan, a Central Asian chieftain, who was taken into the Emperor's harem after the Khan's defeat by Chinese forces. She became known as Xiang Fei, the Fragrant Concubine, and there are many legends about her. She is said to have resisted the advances of the Emperor even though he had fallen in love with her. Whether she died naturally or was forced to commit suicide on the orders of the Emperor's mother is a matter of dispute. Tradition had it that she was buried in the Joyous Pavilion Park in the south city, but the prosaic fact seems to be that she lived in the court for twenty-eight years, and her burial place has been identified and investigated among the Eastern Qing Tombs.

Prospect Hill (Jingshan)

North of the Forbidden City, Prospect Hill gives a fine view over the sea of golden roofs which crown the palace buildings, and of the crenellated walls and ornate corner towers reflected in the wide moat. Earth dug out when the Peking lakes and the canals in the Forbidden City were dredged was tipped on the hill, substantially increasing its height until it became endowed with the status of a guardian hill (Zhen Shan) protecting the palace against evil influences from the north. The last Emperor of the Ming dynasty hanged himself from a tree near the top as the rebel forces which overthrew him stormed the city gates. In Manchu times the Shouhuang Hall in the north of the park housed portraits of the imperial ancestors. In the Hall of Observing Virtue (Guande Dian) to the east, the bodies of deceased Manchu Emperors and Empresses lay in state before the funeral. The hall is on the site of an old archery pavilion. Archery continued to feature in the examinations for Manchu officers right up to the end of the nineteenth century, long after the defeat of numerically superior Chinese forces by European armies had demonstrated that archery was no match for rifles and artillery.

Looking north from the top of Prospect Hill, two large buildings stand against the skyline, the Drum Tower (Gu Lou) and, behind it, the smaller Bell Tower (Zhong Lou). Both date from the fifteenth century but have been substantially rebuilt since then. The bronze bell in the Bell Tower was cast to replace the original unsatisfactory iron bell which still lies abandoned behind the Drum Tower. The bell and drum were used to mark the time and the change of watches during the night. Further north is one of Peking's last remaining city gates.

Away to the west is another of Peking's landmarks, the Pagoda at Eight Mile Village (Bali Zhuang) which stands beside the Jade Canal that connects the Summer Palace Lake to the city. The pagoda was erected in 1578 beside the Temple of Compassionate Old Age (Cishou Si). The funds for its erection are said to have been provided by the mother of the Wan Li Emperor, whose tomb has been excavated in the Ming Tombs Valley, but the temple was dismantled and its timbers sold by the monks living there.

Life At Court

The world outside could follow the comings and goings of the Emperor and his conduct of state business from the *Peking Gazette*, a combination of government record and court circular. Its compilation and despatch to the provinces was the responsibility of sixteen Directors of the Government Courier Service, normally holders of military rank. Palace life began early. Soon after 3 a.m. the Shaman sorceress performed the Manchu rites in the Palace of Earthly Tranquillity. A typical entry in the *Gazette* read 'His Majesty will proceed at 5 a.m. to the Dagao Hall [near the Beihai] to offer worship. Thence he will proceed to the Prospect Hill where he will offer sacrifice in the Shouhuang Hall. Re-entering the palace His Majesty will ascend the Palace of Heavenly Purity [Qianqing Gong] where he will accept congratulations on his birthday. At 8 a.m. he will take his seat to watch a theatrical performance.' (7 May 1874.) In the Dagao Hall he would have been offering sacrifice to the Jade Emperor, the supreme god of the Daoists, and in the Shouhuang Hall to the portraits of his ancestors.

The Emperor's programme depended a great deal on the government business of the day; on whether there were Grand Ceremonies to be performed at one of the Altars of Heaven, Earth, the Sun or the Moon, or special audiences to be given; whether the court was preparing to pay homage at the Imperial Tombs, or take up residence in the Summer Palaces or at the Summer Retreat at Chengde. The princes had their own programme. The diary of the last Manchu Emperor, Pu Yi, who followed palace routine even after his abdication, records that as a boy he rose at 4 a.m. to practise calligraphy. A eunuch stood outside his door while he

1 Inside the Forbidden City in Peking, marble bridges lead to the Gate of Supreme Harmony and the great ceremonial halls beyond.

2 A gilt bronze lion in front of the Emperor's Inner Palace: lions were believed to suckle their cubs through their paws.

3 A courtyard in the Palace of Peaceful Old Age in the northeast corner of the Forbidden City.

4 The three marble terraces of the Alter of Heaven where the Emperor performed the annual sacrifice.

5 The Hall of Prayer for the Annual Harvest is a masterpiece of Chinese architecture.

6 One of Peking's few remaining memorial arches spans the little street outside the Confucian Temple in the north of the city.

7 Ruins of the European style palaces in the Yuanming Yuan.

8 The Marble Boat of the Empress Dowager and boats for hire at the Summer Palace outside Peking.

9 The entrance gate to the Temple of the Sleeping Buddha in the Western Hills near Peking.

10 The Great Wall at Bada Ling near Peking.

11 *Above left and right*
A general and an official from the Processional Avenue leading to the tombs of the Ming Emperors.

12 An elephant in Chengde, at the Putuo Zongsheng Temple which was built in the Tibetan style of the Potala Palace at Lhasa.

13 Red and white Tibetan style buildings outside the Great Buddha Hall of the Puning Temple at Chengde.

14 The 5th century Great Buddha, carved in the likeness of a Northern Wei Emperor, at the Yungang Caves outside Datong.

dressed, reading aloud the previous day's lesson. His senior tutor arrived at 5.30 a.m. and they read the Classics together until 7.30.

Throughout. the day hundreds of dishes were prepared in the palace kitchens (just south of the Nine Dragon Screen) so that the Emperor and his family could call for food at any time. Normally they ate twice a day, but most of the dishes were consumed by eunuchs and others at the court.

Officials prepared state papers or compiled official records in the Imperial Archives. In the palace workshops along the north wall court painters worked on portraits and other pictures or fans commissioned by the Emperor and Empresses, and skilled craftsmen made jewellery or carved jade and precious stones. Much of the domestic work was in the hands of the eunuchs. They were responsible too for the correspondance of the Household Department, for the recording of the births and deaths of princes and princesses of the Imperial Clan, and controlling the stores and the treasuries. Their favour was essential to anyone seeking to prosper at court despite the efforts of the early Manchu Emperors to curb their power. Their loss of manhood was not matched by any loss of vanity. One observer recorded that one eunuch, although 'under thirty years of age, never made an appearance without his face being entirely painted: his person, as it were made up, and his dress altogether gaudy.' The last of the three thousand or so who served in the palace in Manchu times left only in 1924.

The Empresses, concubines and ladies-in-waiting were busy on their own affairs in their apartments in one of the Six Palaces of the East or West. The choice of concubines was a serious matter of state. Under the Manchus, girls from the Manchu Banner families had to be presented at about the age of thirteen at one of the triennial selections, and could not marry until they had appeared. The girls were carefully examined to ensure that they were free from blemish, and if placed on the short list their family history and circumstances minutely scrutinised. The final choice was made by the Emperor and Empresses. To the families of those chosen it meant preferment and high social standing; to the girls, a lifelong incarceration at court. The numbers of official consorts varied. In the middle of the last century the Xian Feng Emperor (the husband of the Empress Dowager) had a total of ten of various ranks among his 'major personnages of the Inner Court'. A concubine who bore a son would be automatically advanced in rank, and if her son succeeded to the throne she would be promoted to Empress. The promotion could if necessary be conferred posthumously, and she would then be reburied in the tomb of the Emperor to whom she had born the child.

At night the palace fell silent. Apart from the guards and eunuchs, no male other than a resident member of the imperial family could remain within its walls.

The Temple of Heaven (Tian Tan)
The Emperor was the Son of Heaven. From heaven he received his mandate and when he lost it his dynasty fell. Small wonder that when the Ming Emperor Yong Le built his new capital between 1406 and 1421, one of the

most magnificent elements in his plan was an Altar of Heaven, more often called in English the Temple of Heaven. The present marble altar terrace and its connected hall of the Imperial Universe were completed in 1530.

'Heaven is round and Earth is square' in the Chinese tradition. Heaven is open, blue and male (yang), odd numbers are appropriate to the 'yang' principle and nine is the highest single odd number. These beliefs are symbolised everywhere. The altar faces south, so the north walls of the park symbolised heaven and are curved. The south walls are straight. The tiles on the roofs of the main buildings are deep blue. The empty altar terrace is open to the skies. On its three round tiers the circles of flagstones, the steps between the tiers, and the number of finely carved balustrades are all in multiples of nine. There were nine separate rites in the sacrificial ceremony.

The ritual at the altar was the most important in the whole court calendar. On the day before the winter solstice, having fasted for three days in the Palace of Abstinence (Zhai Gong), and escorted by two thousand of his relatives, officials, guards and the royal elephants, the Emperor proceeded in state out of the Meridian Gate, the huge south gate of the Forbidden City, through the Qian Men Gate, whose central doors were opened for him alone, and on to the Altar of Heaven. On arrival he made his way to the Hall of the Imperial Universe (Huangqiong Yu), the exquisite blue-roofed circular building in the enclosure opposite the altar terrace, where he performed 'the three kneelings and nine prostrations' before the tablets of his ancestors.

After inspecting preparations for the following day he passed the night in the Hall of Abstinence near the West Gate. Within this double-moated, heavily defended lodging, a bronze figure held up a plaque enjoining him to 'Fast and Meditate'. Before dawn the Emperor took his place in a yellow silk tent south of the altar. The first of the nine rites began with the 'Welcoming of the spirit' of the God of Heaven, whose tablet was set in a place of honour under a blue brocade canopy near the north steps of the top terrace. The Emperor offered incense to the god and to the tablets of his ancestors which were sheltered by rectangular canopies at each side. He presented in turn silk, and vessels of sacrificial meat and wine. A eulogy was read to the god and the ancestors, musicians accompanying each rite with set music while ritual dances were performed on the terrace below. After the completion of each ceremony the Emperor returned to his station at the foot of the south steps leading to the top terrace, kneeling and prostrating himself as required by the rites. Finally the sacrificial vessels were withdrawn and the spirit of the god bid farewell. The Emperor withdrew to supervise the burning of everything which had been offered in sacrifice, including the complete carcase of an ox, in the furnaces south of the altar. The ceremonies complete he returned in state to the Forbidden City.

As their names indicate, the buildings at the north end of the causeway connecting them to the altar were used for a different ceremony. The original Hall of Prayers for the Annual Harvest (Qi Nian Dian) which stands on the three-tiered Altar of Prayers for Grain (Qigu Tan), was burnt down in 1889 and rebuilt the same year. With its famous triple-tiered blue roof, complex and sumptuously decorated interior roof structure, and triple series of massive wood pillars representing, from the centre outwards, the four seasons, the twelve months, and the twelve 'branches' (similar to zodiacal signs), it is a masterpiece of Chinese monumental architecture. On the fifteenth day of the lunar New Year the Emperor prayed here for a bountiful harvest.

Art shops fill a number of the side buildings once used for storage.

The Altar of Heaven was only one of a number of altars in and around the city. Originally homage was also paid there to the spirits of the earth, but in 1530 a separate Altar of the Earth (Di Tan) based on the numeral six (as the Altar of Heaven is based on nine) was built in the north city. Each year the Emperor performed the ritual ploughing at the Altar of Agriculture (Xiannong Tan) opposite the Temple of Heaven. There were altars for homage to the elements (wind, clouds, thunder and rain) and to the hills, lakes and rivers, at the Tianshan Tan and the Diqi Tan in the same enclosure. Similar ceremonies took place in honour of the sun and the moon at the Altar of the Sun (Ri Tan) in the park next to the British Embassy at Jian'guo Men Wai, and at the Altar of the Moon (Yue Tan) on the opposite side of the city. Female members of the imperial family officiated at ceremonies in honour of sericulture at the Xiancan Tan in the North Lake Park (Bei Hai). In times of drought the Emperor himself would pray for rain at the Altar of Heaven. These numerous altars and the importance attached to the ceremonies performed there reflect the vital role of natural forces in a predominantly agricultural society.

Embassies and Legations
Most embassies in Peking are located in two diplomatic quarters in the eastern suburbs of the city, at Jian'guo Men Wai, or at Sanlitun (Three Mile Village — it is three Chinese miles from the old city wall). The Manchu Emperors would have been pleased with this arrangement. When forced to concede the right of residence to foreign legations in 1860 they tried unsuccessfully to lure them out to the site of the Old Summer Palace (Yuanming Yuan) near the Western Hills. Determined to be near the seat of power, the legations leased palaces and residences from Manchus and Chinese near the Forbidden City. There they remained among the local residents until, in 1901 following the siege of the legations during the Boxer uprising, a Protocol gave them full control of a large area running along the south side of the main east-west avenue (Changan Dajie) in front of the Peking Hotel. The Legation Quarter became a 'state within a state' under foreign jurisdiction and with its resident garrisons until the war with Japan.

Turning right out of the Peking Hotel, and then left at the first traffic lights into a road divided by a narrow park, the visitor will find on his right the tall red wall of the former British Legation. It was first leased in 1861 from the Duke of Liang, a descendant of one of the thirty-three sons of the Kang Xi Emperor. Having fallen on hard times, the duke leased his palace to the British in perpetuity, and it became well known to the Pekinese as the 'English Palace' (Yingguo Fu). The British Embassy moved to the diplomatic quarter at Jian'guo Men Wai in 1959, and the old legation is now occupied by Chinese government offices. It was the command post for the defence of the legations against the Boxers in 1900. During the siege, which lasted from 20 June to 14 August 1900, nearly five hundred civilians took refuge inside its walls, protected by only four hundred and fifty Legation Guards and volunteers of eleven different nationalities who manned the defences until relieved by an allied expeditionary force from Tientsin (Tianjin).

Further down the road, the corner site was occupied by the Russian Legation. The Russians have been resident in Peking longer than any other European power. The Treaty of Nerchinsk in 1689 gave them the right to send caravans trading in furs to the Chinese capital and with them went priests to minister to the Cossack prisoners of war taken when the Chinese captured the Siberian settlement of Albazin in 1685. In 1727 a permanent ecclesiastical mission was established. When over a century later a Russian Minister was appointed to Peking, the Archimandrite gave up his residence to him at the South Hostel (within the Russian Legation) and moved to the North Hostel in the northeast city. Here the descendants of the Cossack prisoners were living on land they had been given to maintain themselves and build a church. During the 1950s when the Chinese began moving all foreign missions from the old Legation Quarter, the Russians built themselves a large new embassy with offices, staff quarters, cinemas and many other facilities at the North Hostel, which explains why they alone are not in the diplomatic quarter east of the city.

The former United States and some other legations lay along Dong Jiaominxiang, known to foreign residents as Legation Street, which runs east and west from the crossroads at the corner of the Russian Legation. The Xinqiao Hotel is at the east end of this street and has good western and Chinese restaurants.

Parks and Pastimes

The resident of Peking has a wide choice of parks for family outings on Sundays and holidays, and there is no nicer way to see Peking 'at home' than to spend some time in the Zhongshan Park near the Forbidden City, in the North Lake Park, or in the Joyous Pavilion Park in the south city which is now graced by the beautiful Cloud Painting Pavilion formerly in the South Lake of the Lake Palaces.

Early risers can watch the exponents of Chinese Shadow Boxing (Taiji Quan) practising their graceful exercises among the trees. Children soon arrive to play; to get in free they have to be able to walk under the bar beside the ticket office. Once inside they play 'kick feather', kicking up a weighted shuttlecock with toe, heel and instep, skipping and rope jumping over linked elastic-bands, and sometimes a diabolo can be heard humming as an enthusiast shows off his skill. In winter Peking goes skating on the lakes, and small boys speed across the ice on homemade sledges, a far cry from the richly ornamented sleighs in which the Peking nobility, wrapped in sable robes, once took the winter air. Chinese babies, bundled in brilliant pink padded silk cloaks and tiger-bonnets are peddled along in bicycle side-cars among the millions of bicycles which are the main means of transport for most of Peking's population. Along the canals, weekend fishermen make themselves boats from two large lorry innertubes lashed to a wooden frame, or even to the bicycle itself if they want to go with the current and still have transport home.

Visitors who have an interest either in modern Chinese literature, or Chinese family houses, will enjoy the museum just off Fucheng Men Street in the north city dedicated to the father of modern Chinese literature, Lu Xun. His house, a single-story courtyard-house with living rooms, bedrooms and kitchen arranged around courts in the style typical of old Peking, is now part of the museum and is furnished as it was when Lu Xun lived there in the 1920s.

One of Peking's oldest shopping streets is in the south city off the west side of Qian Men Street. For three hundred years before the fall of the Manchu dynasty the nobility and wealthy shopped in Da Zha La'r Street. Although much of it was burnt down in 1900, some of the shops can still trace their establishment back to the seventeenth century. The most famous is the Tong Ren Tang Pharmacy which first opened in 1669. It supplied medicine to the Imperial Court and still dispenses Chinese herbal remedies to customers all over the world. Another old shop, the Tian Hui Zhai, was the last to sell snuff, which remained popular with the Minority Nationalities long after most Chinese had turned to cigarettes.

The city's main shopping street, which runs north from the Peking Hotel, took its name, Wangfu Jing, from the Well of the Prince's Palace which once occupied this area. It is fascinating to explore its varied shops; the Peking General Department Store, the China Arts and Crafts Store, the Peking Paintings and Scrolls Shop, seals, fur and toy shops, as well as the East Wind Market are located here.

An even more interesting shopping area for many people is the Glazed Tile Factory, Liuli Chang, named after a pottery which in Ming times produced glazed tiles for the roofs of the Forbidden City. It has been famous for centuries for its old book shops, for pictures, rubbings, jewellery, bronzes, porcelain and other antiques. At the time of writing the street is being restored and a number of the shops have found a temporary home in the Temple of Heaven Park. But the Rong Bao Zhai Painting and Calligraphy Studio, whose history goes back to the seventeenth century is still in Liuli Chang. It is renowned for its watercolour woodblock printing process, by which it produces fine — and modestly priced — reproductions of classical and modern paintings, for its artists materials, including fine papers, as well as for original, and expensive, modern paintings, and even more costly reproductions of classical masterpieces. Rong Bao Zhai are also at the Marco Polo Shop on the west side of the Temple of Heaven.

Eating Out
In Peking the most typical dish is Peking Duck which is served in duck restaurants (Kaoya Dian) specialising in a meal based largely on dishes

made from all parts of the duck. For roasting, the duck carcase is filled with water, and sewn up before being hung in an extremely hot oven. This produces meat which is tender inside with a crisp and golden skin on the outside. The duck is carved into small pieces and eaten rolled in a thin pancake with sauce and spring onions. At the Donglai Shun Restaurant in the Dongfeng Market they specialise in Mongolian Hotpot, paper thin slices of mutton and other meat, vegetables and noodles are cooked at the table in stock kept boiling round a small charcoal stove. At the small Kaorou Wan you cook your own main dish of sliced meat, vegetables and egg on a table-size iron griddle. Two restaurants specialising in northern Chinese food are Fengze Yuan in the south city, and Cuihua Lou in the north city. Those who like hot food will enjoy the Sichuan Restaurant in Rong Xian Hutung, both for its excellent cooking and delightful surroundings in an old Chinese mansion with many courtyards. The Fangshan Restaurant in Beihai Park takes pride in producing dishes in the imperial style in part of the old Lake Palace; on the other side of the lake is the less grand but good Beihai Restaurant. A meal at the Tingli Guan is one of the highlights of a visit to the Summer Palace. Its fish comes fresh from the lake; try squirrel fish (songshu huoyu); or in summer, lotus leaf fish (he ye huang yu). The setting is a palace theatre, whose name, the Hall for Listening to Orioles, evokes memories of the Peking Opera singers who once performed here.

Temples
There were once many temples and monasteries, large and small in the Peking area. A few of the older ones still exist but have not yet been restored. Two lie in the area in the southwest of Peking where the Jin and the Liao had their capitals in the tenth to the thirteenth century. The temple of the White Cloud (Baiyun Guan) was once Peking's biggest Daoist establishment (see p.25). Another is the Buddhist Temple of Heavenly Peace (Tianning Si) with its typical Liao style pagoda. Among the temples which are open is the Temple of the Source of the Law (Fayuan Si). It owes its existence to a Tang Emperor who in 645 dedicated it to the memory of the soldiers who fell in his campaigns against Korea. It seems ironic that centuries later in 1127 the deposed Song emperor was imprisoned here by the Jin armies after they had swept across north China and captured his capital at Kaifeng. The Temple of the Source of the Law was an ordination temple for monks of the Legalistic School. As hundreds of novices would sometimes present themselves for the ceremony, the Temple of Universal Salvation (Guangji Si) in the northwest of the city, which was under the jurisdiction of the Fayuan Monastery, was required by imperial decree to receive and conduct the ordination of those who could not be accommodated at the superior monastery. The Fayuan Monastery is now the home of the Buddhist Academy where new monks are trained, and of the Chinese Buddhist Museum which has among its exhibits a number of statues of Buddhas of different periods, including the oldest ceramic statue, dated to the Eastern Han dynasty (25-220 A.D.).

On the north side of Fucheng Men Street up a narrow lane, the White

Dagoba Temple (Baita Si) looms over the surrounding houses. The temple was built to celebrate the accession of the Liao Emperor Shou Chang in 1096, but most of its buildings are much later. A Nepalese architect put up the dagoba for Kublai Khan who enlarged and embellished it in 1271. Workmen repairing it after the 1976 earthquake discovered some boxes under its 'umbrella mast'. Inside were a number of relics presented by Qian Long in 1753, including a small Buddha of pure gold, the Tripitaka sutras, and a monk's robe and hat which may have been worn by the Emperor at some Lamaist ceremony. They are on display in the temple.

One of the finest temples in Peking, and the largest Lama temple, is the Yonghe Gong in the north city. A Manchu prince who succeeded to the throne as the Yong Zheng Emperor lived there after it was built in 1694, but custom decreed that it could not be used as a palace after his accession. In 1744 his son converted it into a lamasery. It has been magnificently if garishly restored, and still boasts an unusually complete collection of Buddhist figures in its main halls. These include the huge statue of Maitreya, the Buddha of the Future, standing 75 ft high and carved from a single tree, presented to the Qian Long Emperor by the Dalai Lama, which fills the Pavilion of Myriad Happiness (Wanfu Ge) at the north end. The pavilion is linked by flying bridges to the side buildings. In front of it, the Hall of the Wheel of the Law (Falun Dian) is distinguished by the striking Tibetan style pavilions on its roof. Among the peculiarly Lamaist artifacts are the images, including in the side halls, Yama the bullheaded God of Death, and the gods locked in embrace with their consorts; a bronze statue of Tsongkapa (1357-1419), the founder of the Tibetan Yellow Sect, in the Hall of the Wheel of the Law, and the 'thangkas', painted wall hangings portraying the deities. The Yonghe Gong is one of the most unusual and interesting temples in Peking and well worth a visit.

The Confucian temple across the road, whose gate is in the small street going west, is a complete contrast to the extravagant flamboyance of the Lama temple. Here the Confucian cult is represented by a fine group of classical buildings in the grounds of the temple and the Imperial College. The Confucian temple, founded in 1306, was the scene of elaborate ceremonies attended by the representatives of the Emperor, which were held here on the 27th day of the eighth lunar month to celebrate the Emperor's official birthday. The main hall, the Hall of Great Perfection (Dacheng Dian), rebuilt in 1906, housed the tablets of Confucius and his four chief disciples, including Mencius. The tablets of his other disciples were in the side buildings, and those of his forebears in the Hall of Reverence (Chongsheng Dian) at the back.

Next door is the former Imperial College (Guozi Jian) which is now the Capital Library. A college was established on this site in 1287 by the Mongols. When their successors, the Ming, drove them out, their need for officials to govern the new empire was so urgent that they greatly expanded it. Soon there were ten thousand students at the Peking College and another six thousand at the Southern Imperial College at their old capital in Nanjing. Although the number of students gradually declined, the Imperial

College remained the highest seat of learning in the land. The Emperor himself delivered an annual lecture on the Classics. In 1728 the college received the first European students granted permission to reside in Peking when the Russians were allowed to send a few students to study Chinese administration. The recently restored buildings date only from the reconstruction of the college in 1784 when the Qian Long Emperor added the Biyong Hall. Instead of walls, it has doors on all sides which could be thrown open during the Emperor's lecture, allowing the assembled student body and officials to gather round the building to hear him. It was during the reign of this same Emperor that the Thirteen Classics were inscribed in the one hundred and ninety stone tablets kept in the Taixue Gate.

North of the city, outside the Anding Gate, is the Yellow Temple (Huang Si), once another centre of Lamaism. It was rebuilt in 1652 as a residence for the Dalai Lama when he came to visit Peking. More than a century later it was restored for the visit of the sixth Panchan Lama, who died there of smallpox. The fine gold topped octagonal marble stupa with a pagoda at four of its corners was erected by the Qian Long Emperor in his memory and as a reliquary for his robes.

Just north of Peking Zoo, with its famous pandas and Manchurian tigers, the jagged spires of the Five Towers Temple (Wuta Si) rise above the trees bordering a quiet canal. In the early fifteenth century the Indian monk Pandita came to Peking and presented the Emperor with five golden Buddhas and a plan, probably of the great Buddhagaya Pagoda in India. Sixty years later the Temple of True Perception (Zhenjue Si) was built following this plan with the five towered stupa that remains today as its focal point. More than five hundred Buddhas are carved on the stupa walls. Stone staircases inside lead up through a round roofed Chinese style pavilion and out onto the terrace with five marble pagodas commemorating the five gold Buddhas. The whole building is covered with fine Ming carvings of lions, elephants, horses, peacocks, and human headed garuda birds together with prayer wheels, the eight Buddhist symbols and quotations from the sutras.

Just off the North Ring Road a tall temple roof can be seen above the surrounding buildings. This is the Great Bell Temple (Dazhong Si) built in 1733 to house the 46 ton Garland Bell. This enormous bell has the text of the Garland Sutra cast on its surface, and the custodian may invite you to stand inside it if you dare risk being deafened by its great voice. From the fifteenth century the bell hung in the Temple of Longevity (Wanshou Si) near the canal west of Purple Bamboo Park. It was probably brought over on ice sledges and winched up to the right height on an artificial mound, which was remoed after the bell was secured. The temple now has a collection of antique bell.

There are many beautiful temples in the Western Hills beyond the Summer Palace, and one of the nearer ones is the Temple of the Sleeping Buddha (Wofo Si) about ten miles from the city. It is a Tang foundation, and houses a large statue of a reclining Buddha originally cast in 1331. A pretty walk along a stone path leads up the wooded valley to a stream behind the temple.

In the next valley is the Temple of the Azure Clouds (Biyun Si) which was founded in the fourteenth century but has been much restored since then. It is known for its Hall of 500 Lohan and for the high marble terrace and five pointed stupas which tower over the temple. The Yunnan marble terrace and stupas, with fine carving, were erected during the rebuilding in 1748. There is a memorial hall in the temple to Dr Sun Yat-sen, the father of the Chinese republic, who died in March 1925. His coffin lay in state here while his mausoleum was being built in Nanjing. The Soviet Union presented a metal coffin which arrived too late for his burial and it remains on display in the memorial hall.

Just west of the entrance to Biyun Si is the east gate of the Fragrant Hills Park. Adventurous young people like to climb its precipitous 1500 ft peak whose name is also translated as Incense Hill (Xiang Shan). It has been a popular scenic area for seven hundred years, and takes its name from the two large rocks on the peak, often shrouded in swirling mists, that give an illusion of clouds of incense rising from an incense burner. In autumn the western slopes are ablaze with crimson leaves.

Over the centuries many temples were built on its slopes, but all are in ruins except for the green and yellow tiled Porcelain Pagoda which crowns a small hill not far from the East Gate. It overlooks the Zhao Miao, a Tibetan style temple built by the Qian Long Emperor for the visit of the Panchan Lama in 1780. The temple is closed but the glazed tile marble archway decorated with the 'dragon sporting in the clouds' motif in front of it is a splendid sight. Close by, behind a high wall, is the Studio of the Heart's Perception (Jianxin Zhai), an enchanted place where traditional buildings surround a tranquil lotus pond in the southern style. On calm days the buildings are mirrored so perfectly in the pool as almost to deceive the eye, and certainly to deceive the camera. There is a good restaurant and a guesthouse in the park.

Further into the hills, about twenty miles from the city, two early monasteries lie in beautiful secluded valleys. The site of the Monastery of the Pool and Mulberry Oak (Tanzhe Si), founded in the third century, was considered as a possible location for the Ming tombs. The monastery grew into one of the great establishments of the area and thousands of monks have been ordained on the terrace in the rear of the lefthand courtyard. The daughter of Kublai Khan (1260-95) who became a nun here and is said to have worshipped in the Hall of the Goddess of Mercy (Guanyin Dian) is buried in the temple area.

The Monastery of the Ordination Terrace (Jietai Si) founded in the seventh century, takes its name from the carved marble ordination platform dating from the Ming dynasty (1368-1644) that stands in the northwestern courtyard. It was one of the most important centres for the ordination of monks of the Legalistic School of Buddhism and the ceremony held here annually no doubt justified the permanent ordination platform. Some other large monasteries conducted ordinations only once every three years, erecting temporary platforms for the purpose.

The Summer Palace (Yihe Yuan)

The Summer Palace, seven miles northwest of Peking, is the only survivor of a succession of such palaces which stretched from the Western Hills to the present sites of Qinghua and Peking Universities, and which went under the general name of the Yuanming Yuan. Although the use of the area for country retreats goes back to the eleventh century, the palace as it is today was developed in the reign of the Manchu Qian Long Emperor in the eighteenth century. He channelled the waters from the Jade Spring Hill (Yuquan Shan) to the west to enlarge the lake, naming it the Kunming Lake after a lake near the old capital of Changan. The buildings in the palace park were twice looted by allied forces who occupied Peking in 1860 and again in 1900. They were restored by the Empress Dowager in 1888 and 1902.

The palace is built on the Hill of Longevity (Wanshou Shan) a beautiful hill rising from the north shore of the lake. Buddhist temples climb steeply up to the peak, and residential courtyards flank the northeast lake shore. The lake itself with its islands, causeways and ornamental bridges evokes an atmosphere of elegant country living. Even though the court retired to the Summer Palace for relaxation there were still ceremonies to be conducted, and the first Great Hall facing the entrance at the East Gate, the Hall of Benevolence and Longevity (Renshou Dian), provided appropriately formal surroundings. The bronze incense burners in the courtyard are in the form of both mythical and real animals including dragons and phoenixes, symbols of imperial majesty.

To satisfy her love of theatre, in 1892 the Empress Dowager built the large three-storey stage in the courtyard to the north of the Great Hall. Like the playgoers of eighteenth century Europe, the Chinese enjoyed elaborate effects, and the theatre's floors and ceilings hide trap doors to allow the apparition of immortals and demons. The Empress Dowager's private apartments were beyond the theatre near the lake. The path from the Great Hall to the lake passes the Hall of Jade Ripples (Yulan Tang). In this small courtyard the reigning Guang Xu Emperor was often confined after his abortive attempt to introduce reforms and overthrow the Empress Dowager. Her vindictiveness is made manifest by the brick walls concealed within the side rooms which, even today, block every view of the lake.

From the Hall of Pleasure and Longevity (Leshou Tang) where she spent much of her time, the Long Covered Gallery (Chang Lang) follows the lake shore to the central temples. Once famous for the five hundred scenes of West Lake in Hangzhou painted on its beams, its decorations now include many scenes from Chinese stories and legends. It leads to the focal point of the palace park where a group of temple buildings dominates the centre of the hill, rising from a magnificent archway on the lake side through the Hall that Dispels the Clouds (Paiyun Dian) up steep steps to the towering Pavilion of Incense (Foxiang Ge) rebuilt in 1892 to house an enormous statue of the Goddess of Mercy, and finally to the Hall of a Myriad Buddhas (Wanfo Dian) on the peak. Built in 1750, its walls are completely faced with green and yellow glazed tiles inset with small Buddhas. A panoramic view rewards the climb to the top. On the way up it is worth making detours to the west to the Pavilion of Precious Clouds (Baoyun Ge) constructed in 1750 entirely of bronze, and to the east to see the twin pavilions housing huge revolving prayer drums.

Continuing along the lake, the Long Gallery passes the Pavilion for Listening to the Orioles (Tingli Guan). Originally a palace theatre, it is now an excellent restaurant whose entrance is across the stage. Further west is the Marble Boat (Shi Fang). Its fanciful superstructure was erected by the Empress Dowager on a stone hull carved in the eighteenth century. From here a boat will take you to visit the picturesque bridges along the western causeway and the Seventeen Arch Bridge which links the eastern lakeshore to the island Temple of the Dragon King (Longwang Miao). Now used as a rest house, it was one of the ten temples of the Western Lake in Ming times. The Dragon King was believed to control the rivers and lakes, helped no doubt by the Bronze Cow (Tong Niu) at the entrance to the bridge. Cast in 1755, it was credited with the power to prevent the lake overflowing, and to keep water spirits from invading the shore.

Away from the lake, north of the Hill of Longevity, the path winds quietly along the banks of the Suzhou Canal, the haunt of azure winged magpies, overlooked from the hilltop by ruined temples in the Tibetan style. It ends at the Garden of Harmonious Interest (Xiequ Yuan). In this gem of the elegant southern style a lotus pond is surrounded by verandahs and pavilions in a garden hidden behind high walls and entered through a moongate. It was copied by the Qian Long Emperor from the Jichang Garden in Xihui Park in the Yangtze valley town of Wuxi. It can also be easily reached from the main east entrance by following the path north past the large three-storey theatre.

The Yuanming Yuan
In the middle of the eighteenth century the Manchu Qian Long Emperor commissioned the Jesuits at his court to build palaces in the European style as a curiosity to fill one corner of his Summer Palace gardens. It took from 1747 to 1759 to complete the buildings, which by an irony of history were burned and looted a century later by the British and French forces who occupied Peking in 1860. Their action was in retaliation for the illtreatment of emissaries they had sent to parley with the Chinese forces. The ruins have gradually disappeared and today only a few decorated marble pillars and arches remain to mark the site. Although the buildings have been destroyed, a set of etchings preserved in the Bibliothèque Nationale in Paris show in detail the elaborate design of the ornate buildings, reminiscent of Versailles, which must have looked so exotic to the Chinese eye. Contemporary paintings show members of the court visiting the palaces dressed up in European clothes. A society has been formed in Peking to restore some of the extensive gardens of the old Yuanming Yuan, of which the Jesuit palaces were only a small part.

The Ming Tombs (Shisan Ling)

Both the Ming and the Manchu Qing dynasties sought out secluded valleys in the nearby mountains for their imperial tombs. The sites had to conform to strict geomantic principles concerning location, protection from the north, and the availability of water. Having rejected the Western Hills valley in which the Monastery of the Pool and Mulberry Oak (Tanzhi Si) is located, the Mings chose a site on the way to the Great Wall. All its inhabitants were evicted and the whole area surrounded by a wall.

The tombs of thirteen Emperors, beginning with Yong Le, the architect of Peking, can be seen dotted around the once secluded Valley of the Thirteen Tombs, many of them in a state of romantic ruin. The finest, that of Yong Le himself, has been completely restored. It is approached by a long Processional Way running the length of the Valley, the beginning of which is marked by an impressive white marble archway, now just off the road, built in 1540 when the Jia Jing Emperor lengthened the Way. The reliefs of lions and dragons on the bases of the pillars are full of life. A road paved with marble led on to the great Red Gate, the original entrance built by Yong Le which commands the valley and the way to the Avenue of Animals and Officials. This is lined with statues of animals, unicorns, camels, elephants etc., sitting and standing in groups of four, followed by majestic figures of four generals in full armour, four civilian officials carrying the jade tablet used at court audiences, and four officials of the Imperial Household. The route passes through the Spirit Star Gate (Lingxing Men) over a marble bridge and on to the entrance of the red walled tomb enclosure. Just inside, the building to the east was the Spirit Kitchen where sacrificial meats were prepared, and on the west the Spirit Store for the sacrificial vessels. Inside the next gateway the white silk and other offerings were burnt after the completion of the rituals in the glazed tile furnace just off the path. The ceremonies at the burial, and later of homage, were performed in the Hall of Sacrifice (Lingen Dian) a building which matches in grandeur those of the Forbidden City. Like the other great ceremonial buildings it stands on a three tiered marble terrace with carved balustrades. Its vast double roof is supported by massive pillars of fragrant 'nanmu', a rare wood from southwest China, which are 12 ft in circumference and more than 30 ft high. Behind the Hall beyond another gate, a marble altar with replicas of the sacrificial vessels stands before the Precious Wall (Bao Cheng) encircling the burial mound. Crowning the wall and dominating the whole tomb is the tower, the Ming Lou, which protects the huge stele engraved with the posthumous title of the Emperor buried in the vault below.

Yong Le's tomb has not been excavated. The only excavated tomb is the Ding Ling, tomb of the Wan Li Emperor who ascended the throne in 1573 at the age of ten and reigned for forty-eight years. He paid little attention to state affairs — except for the building of his own tomb which was designed to be one of the most splendid in the valley. The tombs were badly damaged during the wars which brought the dynasty to an end. When the Manchu

Qian Long Emperor came to the throne he restored the surface buildings, on a somewhat smaller scale, in the hope of diminishing the hostility of Chinese loyal to the memory of the Ming dynasty. The Ding Ling was damaged again by fire in 1914.

When looking for the way into the tomb in 1956 the excavators were fortunate enough to find a small stone pillar which told them exactly where to find the entrance; it was probably put there to facilitate the reopening of the tomb, which had been completed in 1590, for the burial of the Emperor who did not die until thirty years later. The tomb vault was guarded by an imposing arched gateway of white marble, sealed with heavy studded doors each carved from a single block of marble with handles in the form of lion heads. The doors were secured on the inside by a self-locking device, a small stone pillar propped against the inside of the door which fell into sockets as the door closed. The pillar and the diagram of how it worked are displayed just inside the vault door.

When the tomb was opened two marble thrones each carved with phoenixes, the symbol of the Empresses, stood against the walls of the outer burial chamber. Before the inner door was the superb marble throne of the Emperor himself, vigorously carved with a powerful five-clawed dragon clambering over the back. In front of each throne stood an incense burner, two candle holders, and a pair of large porcelain urns, known as Eternally Bright Lamps, which still contained a residue of congealed lamp oil.

The coffin of the Emperor, flanked by those of his two Empresses, was lying on a low dais in the inner chamber. Strips of wood on the tomb floor still showed the marks of the wheels of the carriage on which the enormous imperial coffin had been brought into the tomb. The Empress Xiao Duan had died just three months before the Emperor himself. The second Empress, Xiao Jing, was originally a palace maid-servant who had borne the Emperor a son at the age of seventeen. She had been buried at the Eastern Well in the same valley, but was posthumously raised to the rank of Empress Dowager because her son became the Tai Chang Emperor. But he reigned only a few weeks, and it was her grandson who had her reburied in the Ding Ling in accordance with custom.

On the dais and on the floor were the remains of large boxes containing the imperial crowns, robes, brocades, swords, vessels in gold and silver, and wooden models of houses, horses and attendants. Some of these may be seen in the museum at the tomb or in the Palace Museum in Peking.

The Qing Eastern and Western Tombs (Dong Ling and Xi Ling)
The Manchu Qing dynasty, the last to reign over China, was first established in Manchuria, and the tombs of the early rulers are there (see Shenyang, page 82). Once established in Peking, they adopted the same pattern for their tombs as their Chinese predecessors, the Ming, with avenues of animals, archways, marble bridges and even more magnificent ceremonial halls and tomb mounds. They chose a valley eighty miles east of Peking at Zunhua Xian, within which there were once fifty-four tombs of emperors, empresses, members of the imperial family and concubines,

including the two greatest of the line, the Kang Xi and Qian Long Emperors, and the notorious Empress Dowager Ci Xi. The tombs were plundered in 1928 by the warlord Sun Dianying.

Part of the Qian Long Emperor's tomb has fallen into disrepair, but the tomb chambers with their four sets of marble doors still contain magnificent Buddhist carvings, including representations of the Four Heavenly Kings, Buddhas, and texts in Tibetan and Sanscrit.

The tomb of the Empress Dowager is splendid in every way. A feature of its carving, particularly on the ramp in front of the main hall, is the reversal of the normal pattern. The usual design, called The Dragon Sporting with the Phoenix, shows the dragon (representing the emperor) above the phoenix (representing the empress). The Empress Dowager, more than a match for any Emperor, reversed the pattern so that the phoenix appears above the dragon.

The Yong Zheng Emperor (1723-35) the third in line, chose a different site, a valley near Yi Xian about eighty miles southwest of Peking, ostensibly because the geomancers of the time advised him that no suitably auspicious site remained at the Eastern Tombs. Two other Emperors, the fifth and sixth, followed his example, and the illfated Guang Xu Emperor who suffered so much at the hands of the Empress Dowager is also buried here, far from the influence of his tormentor. His tomb, begun in 1909 a year after he died and finished in 1915, was the last imperial tomb to be built in China. Nearby, a smaller tomb protects the remains of the equally unhappy Zhen Fei, his beloved Pearl Concubine.

A second explanation of why the Yong Zheng Emperor moved away from the Eastern Tombs is connected with the strong Chinese tradition, not universally credited, that he altered the testament of his father, the Kang Xi Emperor, so that the succession should fall to himself, the fourth son, instead of to the fourteenth son, and in consequence he wished to be buried well away from the spirit of his father.

Ceremonies of homage at the Eastern and Western Tombs continued until the flight of the last Emperor Pu Yi from Peking in 1924, some thirteen years after the fall of the dynasty.

The Great Wall

Traces can still be found in north and northwest China of defensive walls built by small states who fought among themselves as early as the fifth and fourth centuries B.C. The first Emperor of the Qin Dynasty (221-206 B.C.) linked some of these fortifications into one continuous barrier running from what is now Liaodong province in northeast China, westward to the bend in the Yellow River, and southwest to Lintao near Lanzhou. The Han (206 B.C.-220 A.D.) substantially extended the system of fortified areas out into Xinjiang province to provide both a springboard for campaigns into Central Asia, and to protect Chinese settlers, their grain stores, and traffic on the old Silk Road. The latest, and among the greatest, wall builders were the Ming Emperors. It was they who built the section most often visited forty miles north of Peking. The Qin wall lay a long way to the north.

The Ming wall is part of a defensive system which begins at Nankou, the southern entrance to a strategic pass through the mountains. Further up lay the garrison town of Juyong Guan, some of whose massive walls still stand today. The white marble Cloud Terrace just beyond the town gate was originally the base for three stupas built in 1345. Below it is a superb marble arch carved with animals and Lamaist figures, and, inside the tunnel, with the Four Heavenly Kings of Buddhism, mystic formulae, and the record of the building of the stupas in six languages, Sanscrit, Chinese, Uighur, Tangut, Mongol and Tibetan.

From Juyong Guan the road climbs sharply to the fortified gateway of the Great Wall itself at Bada Ling. Here the wall can be seen snaking across the surrounding hills. Constructed of a core of rammed earth and rock, it is faced with stone and brick and reaches a height of 23 ft, with a width of 18 ft at the top, on which ten soldiers could march abreast. Two-storey garrison posts housed ten or more guards. At vantage points there were Battle Terraces (Zhan Tai) with stores of bows, arrows, and in later dynasties, cannon and ammunition. The topmost tower also served as a beacon tower. According to military regulations of 1468, one column of smoke and one gun salvo were the signal for an attack by a force of a hundred men, two of each for five hundred, three for a thousand, and four for five thousand or more.

The section of the Great Wall at Shanhaiguan, the Pass where the Mountains Join the Sea, and the point where it reached the coast, was begun in 553. The imposing gate which spans the main street, with its inscription 'The First Pass in the Empire', was the eastern gate of the Ming garrison city and was built in 1381. It was one link in an extensive chain of defences and outworks over which there is a good view from the top of the wall. Figures of military heroes and weapons decorate the roof of the great tower above the gate.

The flaw in the theory of static defence was demonstrated when the Ming dynasty collapsed. After Peking fell to the Chinese rebel leader Li Zicheng in 1644, the Ming commander at Shanhaiguan enlisted the aid of the Manchu forces, who passed through the wall unopposed and conquered the whole of China.

Some way outside the gate is the Temple of Meng Jiang. A folk tale tells how her husband was conscripted to labour on the building of the Great Wall in the Qin dynasty (221-206 B.C). When, after a long search for him, she learned of his death, her tears caused part of the wall to collapse and reveal his body. In fact the wall built by the First Qin Emperor ran some hundreds of miles to the north of Shanhaiguan.

Shanhaiguan is usually visited on a day's excursion from the popular seaside holiday resort of Beidaihe.

The western outpost of the Great Wall, the Ming walled garrison town of Jiayu Guan in Gansu province, has also been restored.

Marco Polo Bridge (Lugou Qiao)

Perhaps the most famous bridge in the world, described in detail by Marco Polo, crosses the Yongding River just over ten miles south of Peking. With a few exceptions the bridge today corresponds closely with his description of it, although the river is now silted up and no longer carries 'much merchandise' to the ocean. Begun in 1189 and completed in 1192, the bridge is distinctive for its fine arches, paved marble surface, and for the hundreds of stone lions, each one different, which crown the balustrades. At the west end a carved elephant pushes with his great head against the balustrade which is supported by a lion at the opposite end. Many of the small lions have been replaced over the centuries, but some remain as Marco Polo saw them in the thirteenth century.

The stone pillars at each end record repairs to the bridge in 1668 and 1785. A second pillar at the east end, protected by a richly carved marble canopy, is inscribed in the calligraphy of the Qian Long Emperor with the title of one of the Eight Scenes of Peking — 'Moonlight at Dawn on the Lu Gou'. The Chinese name for the bridge is the Bridge over the Lu Ditch, the Lu Gou Qiao.

A short climb to the top of the wall of the old garrison village of Wan Ping will give an excellent view over the bridge and the village houses.

Zhoukoudian and Peking Man

On 2 December 1929 a fragment of the skull of an early man was found on Dragon Bone Hill near the small town of Zhoukoudian, about thirty miles southwest of Peking at the foot of the Western Hills. The discovery excited paleoanthropologists throughout the world. Peking Man (homo erectus pekinensis) who lived about five hundred thousand years ago, had emerged to provide a new link in the chain of evolution from the ape to homo sapiens.

Later discoveries have produced evidence of hominids in China earlier than the Zhoukoudian discoveries. Sites in Lantian county in Shaanxi province excavated between 1963 and 65 have produced a skull fossil of Lantian Man who predated Peking Man by two to three hundred thousand years. In the last thirty years many other sites in China have produced evidence of early man in the form of skull fragments, bones and artifacts, but the Zhoukoudian site has remained important both for the number of discoveries made there — it has produced the remains of more than forty people — and because it provides the first evidence of the use of fire by early man in China.

The original skull fragment discovered by Dr Pei Wenzhong, now regarded as the founder of the study of paleolithic archaeology in China, disappeared during the war with Japan. Fortunately casts of it have been preserved. A small exhibition at the site illustrates the origin of man and the relationship of Peking Man to other early hominids. There is a more comprehensive exhibition in the Peking Historical Museum.

The path to the Monastery of Eternity on Emei Shan, the Buddhist sacred mountain.

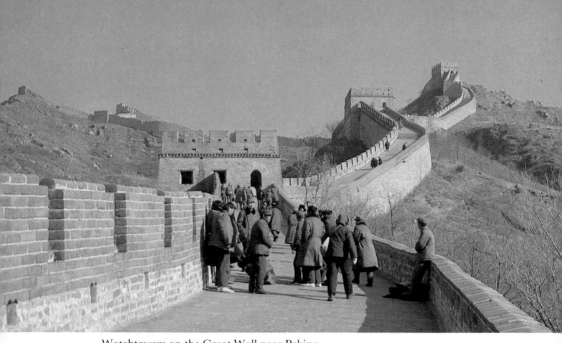

Watchtowers on the Great Wall near Peking.

The Palace of Heavenly Purity in the Inner Court of the Forbidden City in Peking.

Chengde (Jehol)

In the second half of the seventeenth century the Manchus were firmly established in Peking, but the Emperors were determined that they should not become effete nor lose contact with their homelands. They continued to encourage competitions in military skills such as riding and archery, and mounted great hunting parties north of the Great Wall. To accommodate these expeditions they established Royal Lodges, one of the most important of which was on the Luan River in Jehol where the Kang Xi Emperor stayed on his first expedition to the north in 1677. One winter's day in 1701 he chanced to ride along the banks of the Wulie River, also known as the Warm River (Rehe) at Chengde, and found it so beautiful that he decided to have a Royal Lodge there. Work began in 1703, continuing over a period of eighty years until in scale and splendour the Lodge matched the Summer Palaces in Peking. It is now being carefully restored and can be reached from the capital by a comfortable five-hour train journey with occassional views of the Great Wall, or a short flight by air.

The lodge became known as the Summer Mountain Retreat and remained a summer residence until the Jia Qing Emperor died there on 2 September 1820, possibly struck by lightening but more probably of apoplexy. Because of this bad omen the retreat remained unused for nearly forty years, until the Xian Feng Emperor, husband of the notorious Empress Dowager, fled to Chengde in 1860 to escape the British and French forces advancing on Peking. The court were confirmed in their fears that Chengde was an unlucky place when Xian Feng died there a year later.

The main palace buildings, which are Chinese in style, are approached through the Lizheng Gate, the south gate of the walled enclosure. The principal ceremonial hall, the Hall of Simplicity and Sincerity (Danbo Jingcheng Dian) is also called the Nanmu Hall because it is built in 'nanmu', the same fragrant southern laurel used in the great pillars of the Forbidden City and the Ming Tombs in Peking. The private apartments were in the halls behind, and the Refreshed by Clouds and Water Hall (Yanpo Zhishuang) where the Xian Feng Emperor died in still furnished as it was when it was his bedroom. The Pine Stork Studio (Songhao Zhai) beside the main palace was once occupied by the mother of the Qian Long Emperor. In 1793 this Emperor received Lord Macartney, the first British Ambassador to China, in the Eastern Palace nearby, but this building has now disappeared.

Behind the main palace is a large lake and a beautiful park which combine to make the retreat the biggest of the former imperial gardens remaining in China today. The Forest Garden (Wanshu Yuan) where the Emperor entertained Lord Macartney is to the north of the lake. The Manchus were admirers of the Yangtze Valley scenery, and even here six hundred miles to the north they recreated lake scenes, pagodas, pavilions and gardens from famous southern cities. The Gold Mountain Pavilion on the east bank of the lake is a copy of the Gods' Pavilion (Shangdi Ge) at

Gold Mountain Temple (Jinshan Si) at Zhenjiang, a town on the Yangtze River near the junction of the Grand Canal; similarly the Misty Rain Tower (Yanyu Lou) on an island in the lake is a copy of another building of that name in the South Lake at Jiaxing, south of Shanghai.

On a path running north along a spur of the lake is the Palace Library, the Wenjin Ge. It is said to have been built in the style of China's oldest existing library, the Tianyi Ge, the private library of the Fan family founded in the sixteenth century near Ningbo, not far from Hangzhou. The Fan Library was jealously guarded. Keys were held by different branches of the family and all had to be available before it could be opened. There were severe penalties for any member of the family who misused it. The Chengde Retreat Library was built to house one of the four original manuscript copies of the Complete Library in Four Branches of Literature, the Siku Quanshu, a collection of the major approved works of Chinese literature extant at the time compiled by command of the Qian Long Emperor; the Chengde copy is now in the Peking Library. Later three extra copies were made for provincial libraries.

The pavilions on the hills in the park look out over the Eight Temples Without, of which seven now remain. The building of these temples is connected with an important chapter in Chinese history. During the second half of the seventeenth century the Russians and Chinese jostled for position on the Amur River until, in 1689 they signed the Treaty of Nerchinsk which demarcated much of the frontier between the two empires. The Kang Xi Emperor's interest in an accommodation with the Russians was in part motivated by his wish to be free to concentrate on securing the allegiance of the Tibetans and the Mongols following the completion of the Manchu conquest of the rest of China. He was particularly troubled by the activities of Galdan, Khan of the western Mongols of Sungaria, who, having conquered large parts of present day Xinjiang province, advanced his forces close to Chengde. Helped by cannon cast by the Jesuits in Peking, the Kang Xi Emperor defeated Galdan at Urga (now Ulan Bator) in 1696, but it took another sixty years before Manchu power was established right across Xinjiang to the Pamirs. The Manchus were similarly concerned with Tibet, the centre of Lamaist Buddhism, a religion with an increasing following among the Mongols. By a series of interventions they established the Dalai Lama as the temporal ruler of Tibet under their own protectorate.

Chengde played an important role in the diplomatic effort which the two great Manchu leaders, the Kang Xi and Qian Long Emperors, used in support of their campaigns. Mongol princes were invited to join them on hunting expeditions and great banquets were given here in their honour.

Paintings by the three Jesuit artists, Attiret, Castiglione and Sickelpart in the Palace Museum in Peking, and in museums abroad such as the Musée Guimet in Paris, give a vivid impression of the colourfulness and scale of these great hunts and military manoeuvres.

The Eight Temples Without were built for the same purpose. The Puren Si, the earliest of them, was constructed in 1713 when loyal Mongol princes came to celebrate Kang Xi's 60th birthday. The Anyuan Miao, also called the Ili Temple, was built in 1764 for a small tribe of Sungar Mongols who moved from their traditional grazing grounds near Ili in Xinjiang close to Chengde. As their temple north of the distant Ili River had been destroyed during the Manchu campaign of 1755, the Qian Long Emperor had this copy built for them. The Pule Si was built in 1766 for the use of the Khazaks and Buriat Mongols on their visits to Chengde. Its Round Hall with double tier of circular roofs has a magnificent ceiling.

In building the Puning Si in 1755 as a copy of the Samye Monastery in Tibet, Qian Long had his eye on the Tibetans as well as the Mongols. 1755 was the year in which he began his most successful campaign against the western Mongols, and two stele in the temple record his expeditions. A third stele commemorated the occasion on which he received the princes of the Eleuth Mongols and bestowed Manchu titles on them. This temple is also known as the Great Buddha Monastery because its Mahayana Hall (Dachengzhi Ge) houses a gigantic many-armed Avalokitesvara, carved in wood and standing nearly 70 ft high.

The two largest monasteries are the Putuo Zongsheng and the Xumi Fushou. The first was built between 1767 and 1771 in the style of the Potala in Lhasa, to commemorate the sixtieth birthday of the Qian Long Emperor, which fell in 1770, and the eightieth birthday of his mother, which fell in the following year. A stele in the monastery celebrates the return of the Turguts, a western Mongol people who in 1630 had migrated from Xinjiang to the Volga River. In 1770, deciding that they could tolerate Russian rule no longer, they returned to Xinjiang bringing with them a jade seal given to them by the Ming Yong Le Emperor four hundred years before.

The second, the Xumi Fushou Temple, was built in 1780 in honour of the visit of the sixth Panchan Lama who came to Chengde to congratulate Qian Long on his seventieth birthday. It is in the style of the Panchan Lama's seat in Tibet, the Tashilumpo Monatery at Shigatse. These Tibetan style monateries with their fortesslike flat roofed buildings sited to take advantage of the most imposing heights are architecturally in stark contrast to the Chinese style buildings inside the retreat and the park. The architecture of the Pule Si with its double-tiered rectangular base topped by the circular roofed hall is an example of the Sino-Tibetan style.

Zhengzhou and Anyang (Henan province)

Zhengzhou was one of China's earliest capitals. The Shang dynasty (sixteenth to eleventh century B.C.) established itself here before moving north to Anyang, and the outline of their city's rammed earth walls can still be traced. Among the finds from the Shang period made in the area are some of China's oldest known bronzes and earliest primitive porcelain.

It is possible to arrange a day's excursion from Zhengzhou to the Shaolin Monastery about fifty miles away in the Dengfeng Mountains. In the Main Hall is a unique painting of monks practising the martial arts (kong fu). Martial exercises were known in China long before the establishment of the

Shaolin Monastery in 478 A.D., but the monks here developed their own famous school. Another interesting building is the Hall of the First Ancestor (Chuzu An) in which the Four Heavenly Kings, the guardians of the temple, are depicted on pillars. The hall was erected in 1125, before the practice of providing a separate building for statues of the Kings became widespread.

Probably during the fourteenth century B.C. the Shang moved their capital north to Anyang. At the end of the dynasty the town fell into obscurity, from which it did not emerge until in 1899 a Chinese scholar identified it as the source of 'dragon bones'. These were the shoulder or leg bones of animals, or tortoise shells, which had long been used in powder form in Chinese medicine. The 'dragon bones' bore strange markings which, when they were eventually deciphered, were recognised as an early form of writing used in oracle consultation. In 1929 systematic excavation began to produce hundreds of magnificent bronzes, and firm confirmation that this was indeed the capital to which the Shang had moved from Zhengzhou. The excavations, known as the Yin ruins, lie a few miles north west of the town. The royal tombs contained many sacrificial victims as well as horses and chariots, and some very early examples of marble sculpture.

Today a quiet provincial town, Anyang has a wellknown landmark in the unusual tenth century Wenfeng Pagoda which is considerably wider at the top than at the base.

Xi'an

The historic city of Xi'an lies on the south bank of the Wei River in a fertile plain wedged between a high loess plateau to the north and the Qinling Mountain range to the south. To the east the Wei flows into the turbulent Yellow River as it leaves the province of Shaanxi at Tong Guan, the Yellow River pass. It is to this easily defended pass that the province owes its name, West of the Pass, and the city of Xi'an its strong strategic position.

Evidence of early settlements in the area were discovered in 1953 with the excavation of a number of Neolithic villages dating from 4000 B.C. at Banpo a few miles east of Xi'an. A museum has been erected over the site to preserve the remains of the village houses, and the tools, ornaments and pottery found in them. The funerary vessels interred with adults reveal their belief in an afterlife. Children were buried in large pottery jars.

The capital of the Zhou rulers (c.1027-256 B.C.) was in the Xi'an area. Excavated Zhou tombs were found to contain the remains of chariots and horses as well as of servants sacrificed in the belief that they would continue to serve their masters in death as in life.

In 246 B.C. a new young king ascended the throne of the State of Qin which had its capital at Xianyang on the Wei River. Twenty-five years later his forces had subdued all rival states and unified China for the first time. Determined to create one empire that would endure he decreed one code of law, one written language, one system of weights and measures, and one standard for axle widths.

When the Confucianists criticised his administration he had hundreds of them buried alive, and their classics burned. To protect his empire from the nomadic armies of the north, he decreed the linking of a series of existing defensive walls into one Great Wall along the northwestern and northern frontiers. Many Chinese folk tales survive of the million conscripts and convicts who died miserably in the building of this wall.

Another army of labourers was employed on the construction of palaces and pleasure gardens, including the huge A-Fang Palace with its covered bridge across the Wei River. The third great monument built by this ruler, who took the title of the First Qin Emperor (Qinshi Huang), was his own tomb. A Chinese historian writing a century after his death records that 700,000 people worked for thirty-six years to build it. It was filled with untold treasure, including models of his palaces and a map of the empire with the rivers flowing into a quicksilver sea. Those of his wives who were childless were immured with him, and the coffinbearers sealed into the tomb to keep its secret safe. Traps and mechanical crossbows were set to kill intruders, and a great mound was raised over it. In spite of all precautions the tomb was plundered when the dynasty was overthrown in 206 B.C. At the same time the conquerors destroyed the Qin capital and set fire to the A-Fang Palace; it burned for three months. An earthen mound remains to mark the site.

Although they had described the tomb, historical records had given no hint of the magnificent army of terracotta and bronze figures that guards the approaches to it. It was only in 1974 that farmers digging a well about a mile to the east of the tomb mound at Lintong, an hour's drive from Xi'an, discovered the first of what proved to be vast pits containing thousands of lifesize figures, each with its face individually sculpted, of infantry, archers, crossbowmen, cavalrymen and charioteers with their horses. Officers are recognisable by their distinctive armour and headgear. When the tomb was plundered the pits were looted for the genuine military equipment with which this terracotta army was supplied, but sufficient weapons, harness and other trappings survived to enable Chinese archaeologists to reconstruct the scene. Traces of pigment on the figures remained to show the original rich colours of their uniforms. A site to the west of the tomb mound has recently produced two chariots each with four horses and a driver, half lifesize, all in bronze, possibly replicas of chariots used by members of the Royal Family. The tomb itself has not yet been excavated.

Part of the terracotta army is now protected by a vast hangar and presents a breathtaking sight. Warriors and horses from the pits may also be seen in the museum in Xi'an, and in other cities including Peking and Shanghai.

The first Emperor of the succeeding Han dynasty began the building of a new capital near the old Qin city in c. 200 B.C. He named his capital Changan, Eternal Peace, and his dynasty Han. Han China was comparable in power and influence with the almost contemporary Roman empire and Changan became a great and prosperous city; but only the foundations of palaces and gates and the remains of earth walls survive to mark its site five miles northwest of the present town.

About twenty of the Han dynastic tombs lie thirty or so miles west of Xi'an. The biggest is the Mao Ling, the tumulus of the Han Emperor Wu Di (140-86 B.C.). Stone carvings in the exhibition halls of the nearby tomb of his general Huo Qubing, who was killed on the western frontier in 117 B.C. at the age of twenty-four, include an impressive representation of a war horse trampling a Hun soldier. Changan was destroyed when the dynasty fell in 220 A.D., and it was not until the seventh century that it was restored to its former glory.

Changan in the Tang dynasty (618-907 A.D.) was again the capital of one of the great empires of the world whose boundaries stretched from the Pamirs to Korea, but like its predecessors it has largely disappeared. Only a large mound in the northeast suburbs remains to mark the foundations of a once magnificent palace, the Daming Gong.

The Imperial Palace was in the north of the city. South of it lay the Imperial City where government business was carried on. Enclosing these two inner cities on the east, south and west were the residential districts with straight, wide, tree-lined streets with markets to east and west. The whole was surrounded by high city walls with massive gates crowned by lofty towers. The layout of this carefully planned city had a strong influence on other cities in China and abroad. In Japan the city of Kyoto was laid out on the plan of Changan.

The Xingqing Park in the east city, where the Emperor held court at the Xingqing Palace, contains two copies of Tang buildings. Peonies like those in the park were first introduced into Chinese gardens during Tang times.

Life in Tang Changan as depicted in the paintings, writings, tomb murals and poems of the time was brilliant, hedonistic and cosmopolitan. Many of China's painters and her greatest poets, including the hard drinking Li Bo, and the younger, brilliant but disillusioned Du Fu, came to enjoy and describe the life of the capital and the court, which divided its time between the pursuit of pleasure and the enjoyment of music, dancing, superb food, and the writing of poetry and elegant calligraphy. For the energetic, both men and women, polo, introduced to China from Persia, was a favourite game. Crown Prince Li Xian (654-84 A.D.) was a keen polo player, and the game is illustrated in murals in his tomb outside Xi'an. Visitors from Central Asia and Persia were often to be seen on the streets of the city and trade along the Silk Route produced a vogue for foreign luxuries, for Central Asian and Persian dress, jewellery, makeup, food and music. The court had its scandals and affairs to which the poets delighted in alluding in language veiled but easily intelligible to those in the know. But with affluence went poverty, and Du Fu highlighted in his poems the stark contrast between the careless opulence of the court and the misery of the poor.

The splendour of the empire was reflected in the decoration of the tombs of its rulers, about fifty miles northwest of Xi'an. The famous bas-relief carvings of the Emperor's favourite horses came from the Zhao Ling, the tomb of the second Tang Emperor, Tai Zong (629-49); four are now in the museum in Xi'an, with replicas of the other two which are in the United States. The museum at the Zhao Ling contains a collection of Tang tomb figurines and murals from other nearby tombs.

The most impressive tomb is that of the third Emperor Gao Zong (649-83) and his Empress Wu Zetian who, after his death, became the only woman to rule China as Emperor in her own right. She had been concubine to his father. In 650 the new Empress arranged for her release from the nunnery to which, as was the custom, she had been sent on the death of the old Emperor, hoping that out of gratitude the girl would help her recover the new Emperor's affections from a rival beauty. Wu Zetian ruthlessly supplanted her benefactress in the affections of the new Emperor, and following his death in 683 she seized power and was herself proclaimed Emperor seven years later, invoking the authority of the Buddhist Great Cloud Sutra to justify a woman's right to rule. She was a devout Buddhist and embellished the cave temples at Longmen with many beautiful figures. But gossip also credited her with a succession of lovers to which she no doubt felt entitled as would a male Emperor to his harem. When she died the Emperor Gao Zong's tomb was opened at vast expense to receive her body. The tomb has not yet been excavated, but along its Imperial Way is a stately procession of stone carvings — tall pillars, huge winged horses, lions, birds and a double row of generals, ten on each side and more than twice life size. The figures in a group of sixty-one lifesize representations of the 'Guest Princes' are now unfortunately mostly headless. The 'Guest Princes' were the leaders of the border people who owed allegiance to the Tang Emperors and the special envoys from Central Asia and Persia; their names and status can in some cases still be discerned from the inscriptions on their backs.

Almost the whole wallspace of the tomb of Li Xian, who was given the posthumous title of Crown Prince Zhang Huai, is devoted to scenes of hunting in the hills and forests, of polo, one of the Prince's favourite pursuits; of court scenes showing officials receiving foreign guests, and of court ladies in the palace garden watching a hoopoe in flight and catching cicadas.

The tomb of Li Zhong-run, grandson of Wu Zetian who was given the posthumous title of Crown Prince Yi De, was built in 706. His royal status can be discerned from the architecture and figures depicted in the remarkable series of murals which cover a wall area of 400 sq. metres. One shows a guard of honour drawn up in front of gate towers which by their magnificence and form must have represented an entrance to imperial precincts. The guard of honour of nearly a hundred men would probably have been used on important state occasions, perhaps when the Crown Prince took a consort or paid homage to the tombs of his ancestors outside the city. Another indication of his status is the row of twenty-four halberds displayed in ceremonial racks. Sumptuary laws defined rigorously the number of such emblems appropriate to each rank of nobility and officialdom.

The tomb of the Princess Yung Tai, grand-daughter of the Empress Wu, is entered by a long sloping tunnel with niches on each side that were filled with hundreds of pottery tomb figures, including attendants, horsemen, grooms and animals. On the walls further into the tomb copies have been made of the original murals of her ladies-in-waiting carrying her fan, bowls, boxes and candles, and what is probably a head scratcher for the elaborate, high-piled coiffures. Their clothes are in the popular Central Asian vogue with tight sleeves, high waists and long stoles, their long curved shoes holding up their hems. Inside the tomb chamber the large black stone sarcophagus is finely engraved with designs of young women in a garden, feeding the birds, and adjusting a stole. Her epitaph says that the Princess died in childbirth at the age of eighteen. But another version of her death asserts that she was put to death by order of her grandmother who believed the Princess had dared to criticise her.

Another woman famous in Tang history was Yang Gui-fei, the Precious Consort who died tragically in 756. Much admired for her 'plump round cheeks, almond eyes and ample breasts' she introduced a vogue for the voluptuous figure so apparent in the Chinese art of the period. She was taken into the harem of the Emperor Xuan Zong, then in his fifties, who became completely infatuated with her. For many years they spent the winters together at the Huaqing Hot Springs at Black Horse Hill, not far from the tomb of the First Qin Emperor, where the bath she is said to have used is still preserved today. Her ambitious brother's bitter rivalry with the Emperor's favourite general An Lushan ended in disaster. The general rebelled, and when he marched on the capital from his base in Yuzhou (now Peking) the Emperor fled to Sichuan province taking Yang Gui-fei with him. Not far along the road his guard mutinied, killed Yang Gui-fei's brother and forced the Emperor to have her strangled with a white silk scarf in front of a Buddhist shrine. The heartbroken Emperor never recovered and abdicated in favour of his son.

About two miles south of the present city the square brick Great Wild Goose Pagoda (Dayan Ta) rises seven stories and more than 200 ft high, a monument to the supremacy of Buddhism during much of the Tang period. In 629 the Buddhist monk Xuan Zang, in spite of an imperial prohibition on foreign travel, had slipped away to journey to India to study Sanscrit and Buddhist philosophy, and to collect relics and scriptures to bring back to China. He was away for fifteen years. On his return he was personally welcomed by the Emperor, who was much impressed by his knowledge and wisdom. The Great Wild Goose Pagoda was built in 652 to an Indian design as a fireproof repository for the relics and scriptures which Xuan Zang had brought from India. It stood in the grounds of the Temple of Great Benevolence (Cien Si) which was then within the city walls. This temple was much grander than the modest but still beautiful monastery within which the pagoda stands today.

The fine engraving on black marble over the west door of the pagoda of Buddha preaching to the Boddhisattvas provides a rare opportunity to see a contemporary representation of wooden Tang buildings; and on each side of the south door two fine black marble stele are inscribed with prefaces to Xuan Zang's translations of the sutras by the Emperors Tai Zong and Gao Zong in the hand of the famous calligrapher Chu Suiliang.

The small Wild Goose Pagoda (Xiaoyan Ta) south of Xi'an was built in the grounds of the Daqian Fu Temple in 707 to house a collection of Buddhist scriptures brought back from India by the monk Yi Jing, the first important pilgrim to have made the journey by sea. He was greatly honoured on his return to Changan in 695 by the Empress Wu Zetian herself. In the mid sixteenth century it was cracked from top to bottom by an earthquake and the top two stories fell.

Buddhism did not, however, continue unchallenged. In 845 the Emperor Wu Zong decreed its suppression and bronze images and bells were required to be surrendered to the Salt and Iron Commission to be smelted into coin. Wooden or clay images were spared. Nearly four thousand monks and nuns were required to leave the monasteries. This anti-Buddhist movement had been inspired by the Daoists who had achieved equal prominence for their religion in court ceremonial as early as 711. The supremacy of Daoism was shortlived, and there is no Daoist monument in Xi'an to match the two pagodas. The suppression was also directed against the foreign religions represented in Changan, including Manichaeism, Nestorian Christianity and Zoroastrianism. There were many Moslems in Tang Changan, and although the existing buildings are much later, the Great Mosque in Huajue Gang dates its foundation back to this time.

After the fall of the Tang dynasty and the destruction of Tang Changan, the city was never again the national capital. But when the Ming dynasty came to power in the fourteenth century they built up its defences once more. The massive walls, gates and corner towers constitute one of the best surviving examples of Chinese military architecture of the time.

The Bell Tower, a conspicuous and colourful landmark in the town centre, and the Drum Tower, a little to the west, are from the same period. When the Manchu dynasty replaced the Mings in the mid seventeenth century they built themselves a special walled enclave known as the Manchu City. The Bell Tower became a gate at its southwest corner from which new walls ran north and east to meet the main city walls.

Xi'an came back into the news in 1900 when the Manchu Dowager Empress Ci Xi, and the Emperor fled to the city from Peking during the Boxer uprising. Peking had been occupied by the allied armies in order to raise the siege of the legations. The Empress Dowager and her party left the Forbidden City disguised as peasants, but once safely away from the capital they proceeded on their way in state. On arrival in Xi'an the court was set up in the old official residence of the Governors of Shaanxi. Installed in this Temporary Palace she continued to rule the empire from Xi'an until the court returned to Peking in 1902. The old Chinese families of Xi'an, many of whom could trace their ancestors back a thousand years, looked askance at the brash Manchu court and were heartily glad to see it go back to Peking. Their deep dislike of the Manchus became manifest when the revolution of 1911 overthrew the dynasty and the Manchu city was completely destroyed. A number of Christian missionaries living in and near the city were caught and killed in the fighting.

Early in the 1930s the forces of the Manchurian general Zhang Xueliang arrived in the city, having been driven from their homelands by the Japanese occupation of Manchuria. The Nationalist leader Chiang Kaishek hoped to use them, and the forces of the local warlord Yang Hucheng, in his campaigns against the Communists instead of against the Japanese. They refused to accept his orders, and when Chiang flew to Xi'an to re-establish his authority he was arrested at the Huaqing Hot Springs Park. When he heard shots during the night he tried to escape through a window but was captured on the mountainside. The place where he was taken is now pointed out to visitors to the park.

The Communist leader Zhou Enlai, who later became prime minister, came from the Red Army base at Yan'an to negotiate with Chiang, the price of his freedom being an alliance with the Communists against the Japanese. The dispute was settled and Chiang released on Christmas Day 1936. From that time on until the outbreak of fullscale civil war in 1948 the Communists maintained a Red Army Liaison Office in Xi'an which has been reopened as a museum.

In the last three decades Xi'an has developed into a modern city with important machine building, textile and electrical equipment industries, universities and technical colleges. Its population of two and a half million now far exceeds the population of ancient Changan in its heyday.

The Shaanxi Provincial Museum occupies the site of the former Confucian temple. The main building of the temple has disappeared but ironically the seven pavilions which housed the records of each of its reconstructions, together with some side buildings, have survived. The exhibits in the museum illustrate the history of the province and include a fine collection of bronzes, stone sculpture, Buddhist and Daoist figures, Han and Tang tomb figurines, and the bas-relief carvings of horses from the tomb of the Tang Emperor Tai Zong. But it is most famous for its Forest of Tablets (Bei Lin), an ancient library engraved on stone in which the whole history of Chinese calligraphy can be studied. The library was begun in the eleventh century by a member of the Imperial Academy, and through the ages it has grown into a great national collection of more than a thousand tablets, dating back to the Han dynasty. Of great interest to visitors from the west is the Nestorian Tablet erected to record the arrival of a Nestorian Christian priest in Xi'an in 781. A cross is engraved on the pointed top of the stone, and the text, in Chinese and Syriac, describes the Nestorian doctrine.

Luoyang

Luoyang has had both a brilliant and a tragic history. Alternately a great metropolis and a wartorn ruin, it was the capital of nine dynasties. A Zhou ruler built the first planned city with walls, palaces and temples in the eighth century B.C. where the Wang Cheng Park now stands. Trade and manufacturing flourished here. Two thousand years ago its successful merchants were already being criticised for ostentation and outdoing their betters. Foreign traders came by land and water importing and exporting ideas as well as merchandise. Among the distinguished scholars who made the city their home during the first and second centuries A.D. were the Han historian Pan Gu, Zhang Heng who devised the first seismograph, Cai Lun the inventor of paper and Ma Jun who designed the irrigation wheel.

After the collapse of the Han empire a period of turmoil ensued, and early in the fourth century the Huns destroyed Luoyang. During the next century a tribe of Mongol origin conquered north China. Their rulers, the Northern Wei Emperors at first kept their capital at Datong near the northern border, but after peace was established, they moved down to Luoyang which they decided to rebuild in the style of Nanjing, then the beautiful capital of a southern state. Architects were sent there to draw up plans for the construction of a magnificent new capital at Luoyang. Before long the citizens were so prosperous again that even their servants were dressed in gold and silk brocades. Being foreigners themselves the Northern Wei rulers favoured the foreign religion of Buddhism. In addition to creating another complex of cave temples outside the city at Longmen, they built more than a thousand temples in and around the city, among them the splendid Jingming Temple where every year all the Buddha statues in the city were gathered before being carried through the streets with music and singing; and the lovely nunnery, the Yaoguang Si, with its towering pagoda, which was the butt of ribald jokes about the wild but dashing horsemen who had once raided the convent. The most magnificent of all was the Yongning Temple, built by the fierce but amorous Dowager Empress Ling who handled a bow with as much vigour as she handled her court.

As the city grew, enormous supplies of grain were needed to feed the people and the garrison. To this end the Sui Emperor Yang Di (605-18) built large granaries and improved the waterways connecting the Yellow River near Luoyang with the riceproducing Lower Yangtze Valley. In 1971 the Hanjia Granary, one of the largest, was discovered just west of the old city; built to resist damp and insects it could hold 250 thousand metric tons.

Because of its many gardens Luoyang also became known as the Flower City, and since the seventh century has been famous for beautiful tree-peonies as well as for azaleas and chrysanthemums.

Although the Song did not choose Luoyang as their capital it continued to be a town of some consequence, and it was only after the Mongol hordes under Kublai Khan swept across China in the thirteenth century and removed the capital to Peking far away in the north that Luoyang was finally abandoned by the literati and became a minor provincial city.

Modern Luoyang, with its tractor factory, mining equipment and ball-bearings factories is an industrial centre with a population of over a million. Little of its ancient glory can now be found above ground and visitors come primarily to see the cave-temples at Longmen, and the ancient White Horse Monastery just outside the city. The Luoyang Museum has a good regional collection including objects discovered since 1965 during the museum's investigation of three hundred Tang tombs in the vicinity which contained a wealth of figurines.

The city's artistic traditions are continued in local handicrafts, and its potteries produce excellent reproductions of Tang designs, assisted by a research institute which gives advice on the techniques employed in the Tang dynasty.

The recently restored White Horse Monastery (Baima Si), eight miles east of Luoyang, was founded in 68 A.D. The present buildings date mainly from 1556. Although reputed to be the first Buddhist monastery in China, it was probably only one of the first, just as Luoyang was only one of the three early centres of Buddhism. The white stone horses standing outside the main gate symbolise the two horses which, in the first century, carried Buddhist scriptures over the long road from India, arriving with their masters, two Indian monks, just after the Chinese Emperor had dreamed of a golden god coming from the west. He welcomed them and built them this monastery, which became an important centre for Buddhist studies. The monks, Kasyapa-Matanga and Dharmaratna, are buried inside the first courtyard, and halls are dedicated to them in the temple. The Main Hall contains a Ming Sakyamuni with his two disciples Kasyapa and Ananda, the Bodhisattvas Manjusri and Samantabhadra, and fine Yuan dynasty Lohan. On the east of this courtyard are guest-rooms and on the west the Hall of Founders with statues of the first six abbots. The next hall, the Thousand Buddha Hall, also has Ming Sakyamuni, Vaidura and Amitabha Buddhas with five thousand small Buddhas in wall niches; behind the next hall, steps lead up to the Cool Terrace (Qinglian Tai), on which stands a graceful pavilion shaded by gnarled cypresses where the Han Emperor Ming Di came to study the sutras with the Indian monks.

The tapering square pagoda rising southeast of the monastery, the Cloudkissing Pagoda (Chiyun Ta), was built in the late Tang period but substantially restored in the twelfth century. Although Luoyang was sacked again and again as dynasty after dynasty fell, successive Buddhist Emperors restored and cared for the White Horse Monastery, which fared better than the city. It was known for its great bell, for the delicious grapes grown in its gardens, and in the seventh century for a notorious abbot, a favourite of the Tang Empress Wu Zetian. Formerly her cosmetics supplier, he was made a monk so that he could have easy access to her apartments, but once installed as abbot he gathered around him an unruly gang who soon brought about his downfall.

South of Luoyang is a temple built in honour of the God of War. It takes its name from its ancient cypress trees and is called the Forest of Guan, Guanlin. The God of War was Guan Yu, a hero of the Three Kingdoms period of the third century, whose head is said to be buried in the tomb behind the temple. A well known story from the popular historical novel *The Story of the Three Kingdoms* tells how his murderer sent Guan Yu's head to Cao Cao, the leader of the rival state of Wei, hoping to be rewarded. His hopes were dashed when Cao Cao, suspecting a trap, gave Guan Yu an honourable burial here.

Longmen Caves
The Buddhist cave temples at Longmen, Dragon Gate, eight miles south of

Luoyang, form one of the most famous groups of Chinese stone sculpture, and rank with the great complexes of cave temples at Yungang in Shanxi, and Dunhuang, Binglingsi and Maijishan in Gansu. They are sited in limestone cliffs mainly on the north bank of the Yi River; the name 'Dragon Gate' is used to describe a place where a fast stream forces its way between steep cliffs. In 494 the Northern Wei Emperors moved south from their former capital, Datong, where they had created the Yungang cave temples. In addition to their magnificent new city at Luoyang, they began work on the new cave temples in about 500. The fact that they were now near the ancient centres of Chinese artistic inspiration is reflected in the increasing Chinese influence in design and workmanship in the complex, where new caves continued to be carved for about four hundred years, only gradually declining during the eighth century. The most creative periods were at the height of the Northern Wei prosperity between 500 and 540, and between 650 and 710, at the time when Buddhism was under the patronage of the Tang Empress Wu Zetian.

The innumerable caves and niches on the mountain have been estimated to contain more than 100,000 carved figures, some huge, some tiny. The many inscriptions, invaluable for the study of history and the art of calligraphy, tell of the princesses and nuns who had statues carved in memory of beloved members of their families, of great men who commissioned work to honour the Emperor or to fulfil a vow, and of groups of the faithful who joined together to carve their own Buddhas.

Unfortunately many carvings and the heads of many of the Buddhas have been removed over the years and found their way into private collections and western museums.

There is rarely time for the visitor to see all the caves, but a visit to the better known ones below will provide an insight into the development of Chinese Buddhist sculpture during the period.

The caves are listed from east to west.

Qianqi Si
In the first large cave, carved in 641 during the Tang period, the Buddha is flanked by his two favourite disciples, Ananda and Kasyapa, by two fine Boddhisattvas and two guardian Kings.

The Binyang Caves
The North Cave is the first of a group of three which formed one temple and spans the period from Northern Wei to Tang, the fifth to seventh century. The central cave is the most famous of the three and according to the Wei history was one of the first constructed. Sponsored by the royal family it is one of two begun in 500, built by the Emperor Xuan Wu to honour his predecessor the Emperor Xiao Wen and the Dowager Empress Wen Zhao. It took twenty-three years and the labour of more than 800,000 workmen to complete. Below a magnificent ceiling the central smiling Sakyamuni Buddha, 26 ft tall, again sits between Ananda and Kasyapa, flanked by

Maitreya and Prabhataratna. They have the typical Northern Wei long heads and sharp noses, wear heavy draped robes and are backed by flaming bas-relief haloes.

The beautiful bas-reliefs in this cave used to include the Northern Wei Empress coming in procession to worship, but this is now in a museum in the U.S.A.

The Myriad Buddhas Cave (Wanfo Dong)
This cave was finished in 680, and illustrates the current popularity of the Pure Land School of Buddhism, which promised that simple faith and devotion would be rewarded by rebirth in a Pure Land of jewelled trees and lotus blossoms. In front of the entrance a graceful Guan Yin, with damaged head, holds a vase and a flywhisk. 15,000 Buddhas on the walls surround the central Buddha on his lotus seat, flanked by disciples and Boddhisattvas; on the wall behind him lotus flowers support Bodhisattvas and attendants, and above them spreads a huge lotus inscribed with the date of the cave. At the base of the north and south walls an orchestra plays as dancers swirl around in long floating costumes.

Lotus Flower cave (Lianhua Dong)
Dating from the late Northern Wei it takes its name from the huge lotus carved on the roof. There are reliefs of flying apsaras, flowers and scenes from Buddha's life story.

The Fengxian Temple
The largest cave, finished in 675, is a superb example of Tang art. Today a huge open space stretching 115 ft from east to west and more than 100 ft from north to south, it was built by the Tang Empress Wu Zetian. The holes in the cliff behind the figures were made for the beams of the temple that once protected this area. The great Vairocana Buddha is 51 ft high, with a head 12 ft high and ears 5 ft long. The two fiercely protective Heavenly Kings and a guardian provide a striking foil to the calm Boddhisattvas and the spiritual Buddha who appears here as the saviour of mankind.

The Medical Prescriptions Cave (Yao Fang Dong)
Over a hundred medical prescriptions for herbal remedies of the sixth century are carved round the door.

Gu Yang Dong
This cave shares with the Binyang Cave a position of great importance in the Longmen complex. Of particular interest are its many inscriptions, which were commissioned by noble families, officials, monks, nuns and religious societies. It was the earliest cave, begun when the Northern Wei came to Luoyang in 494, and has walls covered with relief carving and rows of niches, each containing Buddhist figures.

Dong Shan Kan Jing Temple

This is one of the few caves on the other side of the river. Built during the time of the Empress Wu Zetian, it contains relief carvings of lohan.

The poet Bo Juyi (772-846), who loved this place and spent his declining years in Luoyang, is also buried on this side of the river. He was so popular in Luoyang that a famous beauty is said to have put up her price because she could recite his poetry. Stone steps on the hill, built for the visit of the Manchu Emperor Qian Long in the eighteenth century, lead up to Fragrant Mountain Temple where Bo Juyi made his home from 832. Higher up, in the Temple of Nine Old Men, the poet and eight of his famous contemporaries met to enjoy wine and compose poems together. In 846 he died on the mountain and lies buried beside the monk who had been his friend and companion in retirement.

Gong Xian

About halfway between Luoyang and Zhengzhou, an enjoyable two hours drive from Luoyang, there is a group of five small Northern Wei cave temples a few miles east of Gong Xian. Carved in sandstone mainly between 517 and 534, they form a harmonious group. Apart from the Buddhist figures the sculptors have portrayed an imperial procession and groups of musicians.

Near the hotel at Gong Xian are the tombs of the first seven Emperors of the Northern Song dynasty (960-1126) and of the first Emperor's father. They were damaged by the northern invaders who captured the Song capital at Kaifeng early in the twelfth century, but processions of striking dark stone sculptures still stand sentinel along the Spirit Ways leading to the royal tombs. Massive animals and mythical birds and beasts, stout foreign emissaries, tall commanding figures of officials and warriors guard the remains of the tumuli once enclosed by high walls. As the tombs were built not by the Emperors themselves but by their successors, and as Song practice required completion of the work within seven months of the Emperor's death, less care was lavished on these tombs than on those constructed by living Emperors for their own glorification.

Kaifeng

Sadly there is little left in Kaifeng to recall that it was the splendid capital of the Northern Song dynasty from 960 until 1126, when the Khitan armies swept down from the north, sacked the city, and captured the emperor and his entourage. Seventy years later a change of course brought the silt-laden waters of the Yellow River close to the city walls, and for eight hundred years the ever present danger of flood discouraged its development. The fate of Kaifeng is still linked with the Yellow River, held in check by constantly tended dykes 22 ft above the level of the surrounding country.

The site of the Song imperial palaces is marked by the seventeenth century Dragon Hall in the northwest city. The tapering Iron Pagoda (Tie Ta) has towered 180 ft above the northeastern corner since the mid eleventh century; it takes its name from the metallic colour of its glazed bricks, each one decorated with Buddhist figures, animals and plants. The oldest Song relic is the squat square three-storied stump in the southeast city, all that is left of the once graceful Fan Pagoda, built seventy years before the Iron Pagoda. In the park nearby, the Yuwang Temple, a Ming foundation dedicated to the Great Emperor Yu, Controller of Floods, occupies the site of the old Flute Terrace (Guchui Tai) where the famous musician Shi Kuang played more than 2500 years ago. The Xiangguo Monastery, also in the south city and founded in the sixth century, grew into one of the most important Buddhist temples in China. The original buildings were destroyed by flood and the existing ones date only from 1766.

Another site of interest is the ornate tower, with green tiled roofs and balustrades, of the old Yuan dynasty (1271-1368) Daoist temple, Yanqing Guan, dedicated to the legendary Jade Emperor.

The story of Kaifeng would not be complete without a reference to the controversy about who was responsible for the destruction of the old city in 1642. As the Ming dynasty neared collapse the armies of Li Zicheng, who if the Manchus had not intervened might well have become the next ruler of China, laid siege to the city. Official records claim that Li breached the Yellow River dykes to flood out the city's defenders, but other sources assert that it was the Ming commanders who did so while attempting to fill the city moats and inundate Li's forces. Whatever the truth of it, the swollen river engulfed the whole city, drowning a quarter of a million people.

Kaifeng is the home of one of China's foremost schools of embroidery. In the Bian Embroidery Workshops they have on show an exquisitely embroidered copy of the famous handscroll painting of life in twelfth century Kaifeng, the 'Riverside Scene at the Qingming Festival' by Zhang Zeduan, the original of which is in the Palace Museum in Peking.

Tall statues of court officials line part of the Processional Way to the tomb of a Song emperor at Gongxian.

The southern style Garden of Harmonious Interest in the Summer Palace outside Peking.

The Smiling Bodhisattva in the 11th century library of the Lower Huayan Monastery —
a treasure house of early sculpture in Datong.

3. The North and Northeast

The three provinces of northeast China, Liaoning, Jilin and Heilungjiang, stretch north and east of Peking for nearly a thousand miles. Within this vast area, once known as Manchuria, a wide central plain separates the Greater Hingan Mountains in the west from the mountainous border with Korea, the Changbai Shan or Everwhite Mountains. The basin of the Sungari River which flows through the heart of the region forms one of the more fertile areas. The climate is extreme with a growing season of from two hundred days in the south to only a hundred and sixty days in the north and a low mean winter temperature of -1° F in January at Harbin. But with the help of the summer rainfall in June, July and August, the agricultural areas produce large crops of corn, sorghum, soya bean and cotton.

Many of its cities such as Shenyang are highly industrialised and in total Manchuria accounts for a larger proportion of China's industrial production than any other area. Its forests are China's largest source of timber. The mountains are the home of the biggest tigers in the world and of the rare Handa moose, as well as bears, wolves, snow leopard, marten, foxes and hare. Sika deer are raised in large numbers for their antlers, an essential ingredient in many Chinese medicines. Ginseng, the tonic and supposed aphrodisiac, grows wild in the Changbai Mountains. It was once reserved for the use of the Imperial Household.

The Zhalong Nature Reserve on the Wuyur River near Qiqihar is the home of the red crowned crane (grus japonensis) and of the egret, swan, mandarin duck and grebe. Some of the mountain slopes are now the setting for winter sports, and the big northeastern cities are fielding rapidly improving teams of skiers, speedskaters and ice hockey players.

Manchuria was the home of both the Khitan and the Jurchen who in the tenth to twelfth century in turn took over north China. Three hundred years later a new Jurchen leader, Nurhachi, again united the peoples of the northeast and in 1586 refused to pay tribute to the Chinese Ming Emperor. In 1625 he set up his capital in Shenyang where he maintained a court strongly influenced by Chinese customs which attracted many Chinese to his service.

Shenyang

The walled Imperial Palace in Shenyang was finished in 1636. With its seventy-odd buildings it is a Manchu version on a smaller scale of some of the palaces in Peking. In the eastern section two lines of low grey-tiled pavilions, five on each side, line the approach to the octagonal Great Ceremonial Hall (Dazheng Dian). These are the Ten Pavilions of the Princes (Shiwang Ting), one for each of the Eight Banners, the military and jurisdictional units into which all Manchus were organised, and the other two for the conduct of state business. The first ceremonial hall in the central section is the Chongzheng Hall where Nurhachi's son Abahai was enthroned and later proclaimed the change from the old dynastic title of 'Jin' (Golden) to 'Qing' (Pure). The private apartments of the Emperor and the Empress were in the Qingning Gong inside the Rear Palace which is approached through the fine three-storied Phoenix Tower (Fenghuang Lou). The Manchu court did not remain long in Shenyang. By the middle of the seventeenth century an uprising was shaking the Ming empire south of the Great Wall to its foundations and in 1644 Peking fell. The Ming general, Wu Sangui, guarding the frontier against Manchu incursions appealed for their help in driving out the rebels. They responded with enthusiasm, pouring south of the Great Wall to take not only Peking but the whole empire for themselves.

Imperial visits to Shenyang were rare after the move of the capital to Peking and the palaces were often neglected. But the Emperors did come to pay homage to their ancestors and in the eighteenth century the Qian Long Emperor built a theatre in the west section of the palace and also a library, the Wensu Ge. This building was specially constructed to house a copy of the Siku Quanshu, the Complete Library in Four Branches of Literature, a compilation of all the major approved works of Chinese literature extant at that time. Because it was seldom consulted by the Emperor much less care was lavished on the Shenyang copy than on the copies deposited in Peking and at the Summer Mountain Retreat in Chengde.

Although they had transferred their capital to Peking, the Manchus strove to preserve their own national identity. They retained the Manchu dress which sprang from their once nomadic way of life. The cut of their garments originated in the traditional use of skins rather than the textiles used by the Chinese, and the style reflected the demands of an active outdoor life and the need for both men and women to ride astride. The free lifestyle of the Manchu women precluded foot-binding and their wide-winged hairstyle followed the tradition of the nomads. The distinctive pig-tail of Manchu men was forced on the whole male population of China as a symbol of subjection to the Manchu Emperor. The Manchu homeland was kept as a special preserve largely closed to Chinese immigration, and a Willow Palisade maintained to delimit the area where Chinese might live. But in the nineteenth century the need for agricultural labour proved stronger than the Palisade and from that time on the number of Chinese in Manchuria steadily increased.

Nurhachi (1559-1626) is buried with his Empress, Yehonala, at the Eastern Tomb (Fuling), seven miles east of Shenyang. The tomb built in the Chinese style was begun in 1629 and his remains were brought there in 1634. It was enlarged in 1652 by the first Manchu Emperor to reign in Peking, the Shun Zhi Emperor who built the ceremonial hall, the Longen Dian, and the Longen Gate, and was further embellished by the two greatest of the Manchu rulers, the Kang Xi and Qian Long Emperors. Nurhachi's son and successor Abahai is buried with his Empress at the Northern Tomb (Zhao Ling) built between 1643 and 1651 about three miles northeast of Shenyang.

The tomb of the earlier Manchu rulers, the Yong Ling, is eighty miles east of Shenyang near the city of Xinjing, where the Manchus had previously had a capital. The tomb houses the remains of two sixteenth century rulers who were posthumously introduced into the imperial line in 1648. The arrangement of this tomb reflects the Manchu tradition in that more than one ruler was buried there. Only one ruler, accompanied as appropriate by his consorts, was buried in each of the Chinese imperial tombs.

Fifteen miles east of Anshan, China's steel centre, the Thousand Peaks (Qian Shan) an area of wooded mountains and picturesque valleys is renowned for mountain flowers and birds. The largest and most impressive of its Buddhist temples, which date back to the eleventh century, is the Dragon Spring Monastery (Longquan Si), closely rivalled by its Daoist counterpart, the Wuliang Monastery one of the twenty Daoist temples founded here from the seventeenth century onwards. On the eastern border the Everwhite Mountains (Changbai Shan) also offer spectacular mountain scenery and a variety of flowers and birds that are likely to attract increasing numbers of nature lovers as accommodation in the mountains is developed to receive them.

North China: Taiyuan

Taiyuan, the City of the Great Plain, lies west of the Taihang Mountains which separate the North China Plain from the rugged northwest provinces. The area is rich in coal and minerals which provide raw materials for a major iron and steel, chemical and engineering centre. The fertile surrounding plain is famous for its grapes and fruit. Southwest of the city is Xinghua Cun, the home of one of China's most famous drinks, Fenjiu, a spirit which has been distilled here for nearly fifteen hundred years.

The original site of the city was twenty-five miles away on the banks of the Fen River. Remains of the walls of the old city, then called Jinyang, can still be seen at the village of Jinyuan. Jinyang was a strategic border town, a walled city twelve miles in circumference and comparable in stature to other large cities in China. But in the tenth century, because it dared to resist the authority of the first Song Emperor, the city was razed to the ground and the Fen River diverted in order to wipe out all trace of it. Fortunately the Jinci Temple east of the old city was spared. Four centuries later the Ming built a new walled city with eight gates, but it never rivalled the prosperity of its predecessor, Jinyang. During the Boxer uprising in 1900 the name of the city burst into the world news. One Sunday morning, in accordance with an edict of the Empress Dowager so courageously ignored by some other provincial governors, the notorious governor of Shanxi, Yu Xian, had fifty-four men, women and children of western missionary families led into the yard of his official residence and put to death. Once the allied forces had secured Peking, Yu Xian was 'allowed' to commit suicide. As a gesture of conciliation he was replaced by one of the few Chinese who had received a western education (in England at Cambridge). He was hastily summoned from an obscure town near the Mongolian border to which he had been exiled for friendliness to foreigners.

A number of streets in old Taiyuan, some of which remain today, formed T-junctions, a feature attributed by some to a wish to hinder the passage of any invading troops through the city. Others have seen a connection between the Chinese word for such a junction and its homophone 'ding' which means 'to nail', with the implication that, with the razing of old Jinyang, the inhabitants of the area had been 'nailed down' for ever.

The finest temple in the city is the Temple where Goodness is Venerated (Chongshan Si). It was built in 1381 on the site of an earlier temple by the Viceroy in honour of his mother, the Empress. An illustration by a Ming artist showing its great size at that time is still preserved there, but much of it was destroyed by fire in 1864. One of the surviving buildings became a Confucian temple. Another part, the Hall of Great Compassion (Dabei Dian) remained dedicated to Buddhism and is an outstanding example of early Ming architecture. The central figures in this hall are three tall gold Bodhisattvas with 'a thousand arms and eyes to watch over and succour all mankind'. The temple library was stored in wall cupboards, but its valuable eleventh century editions of early sutras printed in Fuzhou have been moved to the Shanxi Provincial Museum. The museum is housed in the former Daoist Temple of the Ancestor Lu, and has an outstanding collection of calligraphy, Buddhist statuary discovered on the site of the old city of Jinyang and in derelict temples in the area, and of local pottery and porcelain.

Another familiar landmark in Taiyuan, the twin pagodas of the Temple of Eternal Happiness (Yongzuo Si), were built in the reign of the Ming Wan Li Emperor (1573-1620).

About fifteen miles southwest of Taiyuan lies one of the most attractive and oldest collections of temple buildings in China, the Jinci. Its origins are lost in history. By tradition it was founded in honour of a brother of the second Emperor of the Zhou dynasty (eleventh century B.C.), Prince Shu Yu of the district of Tang. Although there is still a temple dedicated to him in the northern part of the park, it is not the original building nor is it likely that the original was on that site. From the eleventh century A.D. the cult of Tang Shu Yu was overshadowed by that of his mother, in whose honour the main feature of the temple, the Hall of the Sacred Mother (Shengmu Dian) was erected between 1023 and 1032 and rebuilt in 1102.

The first building inside the gate on the eastern side of the park is the

Water Mirror Terrace (Shuijing Tai), built as a theatre in the Ming dynasty (1368-1644). The building recalls the entertainments which took place at festivals in Chinese temples.

Following the central axis west, a bridge crosses an ornamental stream to the Terrace of Metal Statues (Jinren Tai). Of the four warrior figures, the one in the southwest corner has an inscription showing it was cast in 1097.

The fame of the Jinci owes much to the next buildings, which complete the central axis. First is the Hall of Offering (Xian Dian) where lay pilgrims made their offerings in front of the Main Hall.

The lower structure built in 1168 is typical of the Jin period; the roof was rebuilt in the sixteenth century in the Ming style.

Fifth century records refer to a Flying Bridge at the Jinci, but it is not known when it was built nor where it was in the Temple grounds. The existing Flying Bridge which links the Hall of Offering with the Hall of the Sacred Mother was probably built in the eleventh century and is the only surviving example of an early bridge in cruciform style still existing in China.

The Hall of the Sacred Mother, with its peacock blue tiles, is an architectural masterpiece. By an economical use of pillars the builders achieved an unusual sense of space on the front terrace and in the hall itself, and by careful adjustment of the height of the corner pillars and of the bracketing supporting the roof, a graceful curve has been given to the line of the eaves. Spirited wood carvings of dragons coil round the front pillars. Inside, the statue of the Sacred Mother in full regalia is seated under the central canopy, accompanied by forty-two charming statues of ladies-in-waiting, a few dressed in official robes and a few in men's robes. They carry seals, ink, toilet articles, musical instruments and refreshments, and in spite of the fact that they have been repainted, their natural poses and informal air make them outstanding examples of Song sculpture.

There are also fine Ming statues of women in the upper story of the Hall of the Water Mother (Shuimu Lou) nearby. This hall is dedicated to the legend of a peasant girl who had to go a long way to the well to fetch water for the family where she worked. Returning home one day she met an old man who asked for water. To thank her he gave her a magic riding whip which filled her bucket when she waved the whip over it. This typical folk story is no doubt connected with the stream running through the temple grounds which is fed by a spring nearby.

Chinese visitors to the temple particularly appreciate a stele inscribed in the calligraphy of the second Emperor of the Tang dynasty in 646 A.D., which is one of the earliest examples still extant of an inscription in the 'running script' (xingshu). Beside the Hall of the Sacred Mother are the Zhou cypresses said to be three thousand years old; another ancient tree is a pagoda tree (sophora japonica) planted in the sixth century in the grounds of the Temple of the God of War (Guandi Miao) in the northern section of the park. This temple was only one of a number of similar halls dedicated to Daoist deities within this unique temple park.

Wutai Shan

The sacred Mountain of the Five Terraces (Wutai Shan) eighty miles north of Taiyuan is held by some believers to be the most holy of the four sacred Buddhist mountains in China. The Chinese also call it 'Clear Cold Mountain' because of the severe cold on its peaks which so impressed the Ming dynasty geographer Xu Xiake who described 'huge icicles hanging down several thousand feet in the shadow of the crags'. It had snowed on the mountain in August in 1633, the year he visited it.

Wutai Shan, which is not one mountain but five, has been a place of Buddhist pilgrimage almost from the introduction of Buddhism to China from India in the first century A.D. Of the monasteries which grew up on its peaks and slopes in the early centuries we know little, but by the time of the Tang dynasty (618-907) the mountain was becoming famous all over Asia. The Japanese traveller, the monk Ennin, came in 838 to stay at the Dahua Yan, a monastery dedicated to the Tendai version of Buddhism which he professed. During the succeeding centuries a strong strain of Lamaistic Buddhism crept into both the faith and architecture of some of the temples. The Bodhisattva Manjusri (Wenshu), the patron saint of the mountain, is often found in the temples, seated on his lion.

At the beginning of this century there were over a hundred temples spread over the five peaks. It is one of the ironies of history that the peak temples were held in most esteem and in consequence they were rebuilt and redecorated right up to the present century. But one of the more secluded temples, the Temple of Buddha's Glory (Foguang Si) escaped such constant reconstruction, and its Great Hall is a fine example of Tang architecture. The small Nanchan Si temple in southeast Wutai Xian was equally fortunate, and its Great Hall is the earliest known wooden building in China. A dated repair of 782 A.D. and its style place it between the mid seventh and eighth century. The hall contains seventeen contemporary statues, including Sakyamuni, two disciples, Bodhisattvas, Manjusri (Wenshu) and Samantabhadra (Puxian) and guardians and guardians). It its remoteness protected it from the great Buddhist persecutions of 845.

Datong

Datong, famous both for the temples in the town and the Yungang Buddhist cave temples outside, is an industrial and coal mining town and important railway junction on the route to Mongolia. Railway enthusiasts can visit the steam locomotive works, and there are traditional workshops in the city producing handmade rugs in traditional local patterns.

To reach Datong the railway from Peking follows the northern arm of the Great Wall west through wild scenery for nearly two hundred miles across the dry dusty Shanxi plateau. Originally a trading post with Mongolia, it first became a capital at the end of the fourth century when the Northern Wei, a tribe of Mongol descent, conquered north China and established

The North and the North East

0 100 300 miles
100 400 km

U.S.S.R.

Da Hingan Mountains

HEILONGJIANG

● Qiqihar

Nen River

Songhua (Sungari) River

● Harbin

U.S.S.R.

JILIN

Songhua River

● Changchun

Fushun ●

Shenyang ●

LIAONING

Anshan ●

Changbai Mts

NORTH

KOREA

Chengde ●

◉ **Peking** (Beijing)

Datong ●

● Dalian

Tianjin ●

SOUTH

KOREA

HEBEI

Yellow River

Taiyuan ●

Yellow River

Jinan ●

△ *Tai Shan*

Qingdao ●

Yan'an ●

SHANXI

Anyang ●

Qufu ●

SHANDONG

YELLOW

SEA

Kaifeng ●

Luoyang ● ● Zhengzhou

Gongxian

Xi'an ●

HENAN

SHAANXI

87

themselves at Datong. Soon after their arrival they started work on the Yungang Buddhist cave temples a few miles from the city. For strategic reasons the Northern Wei at first stayed close to the northern borders, but after nearly a century of peace they moved the capital south to Luoyang, and the importance of Datong declined.

After China was reunited at the end of the sixth century the city became an important garrison and frontier town, but not until the tenth century was it again a capital. This time it became the western capital of Khitan Mongols from Manchuria. They took the dynastic title 'Liao' and built a magnificent complex of Buddhist temples in the west city, the Upper and Lower Huayan, and the Shanhua Monasteries. The Upper Huayan Monastery was first built in the tenth century by the Liao (947-1125) and rebuilt by the Jurchen, also from Manchuria, who took the dynastic title 'Jin' (1126-1234). It faces east in accordance with their custom instead of south as is more usual in Chinese temples. The twelfth century Great Hall, one of the two largest early buildings remaining in China today, is strikingly different from later Chinese architecture. It has a massive plain roof with a deep 11 ft overhang supported by cantilevered brackets, and three huge separate and undecorated doors. Inside, the five great gold Buddhas and other statues are fifteenth century, but the wall paintings of Buddhist stories and the brilliant roof decoration were restored in the nineteenth. The other halls were rebuilt in the original style also during the time of the Qing dynasty.

The Lower Huayan Monastery is part of the same eleventh century foundation. All the buildings were rebuilt in the Ming and Qing dynasties with the exception of the Bhagavat Library (Boqie Zangdian) which stands behind the Hall of the Heavenly Kings and dates from 1038. Inside this beautiful building, undisturbed for almost a thousand years, sit three large Buddhas, surrounded by a gathering of superb figures, Buddhas, Bodhisattvas, attendants and guardians, some standing and some sitting on lotus thrones, their original gold leaf softened by the centuries to a soft brown. The unusual expression of one Bodhisattva so attracted the contemporary Chinese scholar Guo Moruo that he dubbed her the Smiling Bodhisattva. The architecture of the hall, the delicately painted beams and coffered ceiling with roundels of flowers are famous throughout China. The monastery collection of Buddhist scriptures is housed in wooden cupboards running along the walls on each side and at the back of the hall; these are exquisitely carved in the form of small scale models of two-storied buildings in the eleventh century style. In the centre of the rear wall, behind the Buddhas, the two lines of buildings meet at an arched bridge on which is poised a graceful model of a Celestial Palace. The ends of its roof ridges, in the form of a fishtail combined with an owl's beak, demonstrate the 'owl-tail' style that is even earlier than the 'owl's beak' roofridge ends used on the roof of the hall itself. During the Ming dynasty the roof of the hall was carefully restored following the original design.

The Shanhua Monastery is of almost equal interest to students of early Chinese architecture. The Great Hall, the Hall of the Three Sacred Ones

(San Sheng Dien) and the gateway were all built between 1128 and 1143: The Samantabhadra Tower (Puxian Ge), built in 1154, was once balanced by a companion tower, the Manjusri Tower (Wenshu Ge) but it was burnt down earlier this century.

By comparing these monasteries with the manual on architecture (Yingzao Fashi) of the Song, the Chinese dynasty which controlled the rest of the country when the Liao and Jin were in power in the north, Chinese architects have been able to trace the development of style and construction methods during this early period.

In the fourteenth century the Ming Emperors walled and fortified the town as a key point in their frontier defences, a role it continued to fulfil during the succeeding centuries.

The early Ming Nine Dragon Screen in the centre of the town once stood in front of the residence of the viceroy. On calm days the nine dragons rising from green waves into dark blue-green clouds are reflected in a long narrow pool. They have the four claws appropriate to princes; the emperor's dragons had five claws. Faced with glazed tiles and standing 20 ft high and 150 ft long, the screen was moved to its present site in 1954.

Outside Datong on the way to the Yungang Caves there is a smaller but similar blue-green tiled Ming screen with three golden dragons, in front of a little eleventh century temple to the Goddess of Mercy, Guan Yin. An old style standing statue of Maitreya Buddha is in the rear hall, but the temple may not be open. The old road still passes between the screen and the temple and under the small temple theatre.

The Yungang Cave Temples

The Buddhist cave temples at Yungang, about ten miles west of Datong, contain one of the earliest and most important groups of Chinese stone sculpture. They rank with the other great cave temples of China at Dunhuang, Binglingsi and Maijishan in Gansu, and Longmen near Luoyang. Cave temples originated in India and spread with Buddhism through Afghanistan and Central Asia to China, picking up Persian and Greek influences along the way. The site of the Yungang caves is beside the old Wuzhou Pass which once controlled the road between Datong and the former Northern Wei capital at Horinger in Inner Mongolia. Early in the fifth century the Emperors came to offer prayers at Wuzhou Mountain, and it was because of its sanctity that the sandstone cliffs beside the Wuzhou River were chosen for the temples.

The Northern Wei used the foreign religion of Buddhism to counter the influence of the Chinese faiths of Daoism and Confucianism. But in 446 the Emperor Tai Wu was converted to Daoism and, persuaded by Daoist priests alarmed by the growing popularity of the new religion, he proscribed and cruelly persecuted Buddhism. When suddenly struck down by a dangerous illness, he panicked and recanted. His successor, full of zeal for Buddhism, authorised the head of the church, the monk Tan Yao, to begin work on five cave temples to commemorate the first five Emperors of

Northern Wei; statues of Buddha in the likeness of Emperors were acceptable as they were considered to be divine themselves. In 460 Tan Yao
began work on the first caves. They were carved out by making an entrance
high up on the cliff and then cutting downwards to separate from the
surrounding walls of rock the great blocks from which the huge Buddhas
were carved. Many of the workers were prisoners of war, and from just one
district, the western outpost of Dunhuang famous for its painted cave
temples, the Northern Wei armies transported thousands of monks and
citizens to Datong. Work on the temples continued for thirty-six years before
the capital was moved south to Luoyang, and later several more important
caves were added. Chinese travellers described the beauty of these 'incense
shrouded temples' with their halls and pavilions beside the water, filled
with thousands of worshippers. Sadly the ten large monasteries added
during the eleventh century have all disappeared, and today only one
seventeenth century building, in front of caves 5 and 6, remains. From the
clifftop pavilion above there is a panoramic view. In this century many
sculptures were removed and sold to collectors and museums abroad, and
the caves suffered years of neglect. In 1973 when Premier Zhou Enlai came
here with the French President, he initiated the complete restoration of the
caves which was completed in three years.

The twenty most important of the fifty-odd caves remaining today fall
into three groups: the five early caves with huge Buddhas, numbered 16 to
20 (the caves are numbered from east to west); the caves with rectangular
floor plans and two chambers; and the square caves with a square central
pagoda-pillar. Space allows a description of only a few of the most interesting caves.

Caves 1-15 (mainly 465-494 AD)
Cave 3 is the largest cave, begun in Northern Wei but left unfinished. Here
Tan Yao is said to have preached to a congregation of a thousand. The three
figures in the inner chamber, believed to be early Tang (seventh century)
have plump round faces and rounded bodies, noticeably different from the
early Northern Wei figures with their square nomad faces and pointed
noses. The Northern Wei court adopted Chinese dress in 486, a change
which is reflected in the appearance of robes and belts on Buddhas, and the
capes and skirts of Bodhisattvas that sometimes flare out into exaggerated
points at the hem.

The Manchu dynasty building protecting the elaborately carved Caves 5
and 6 has galleries for viewing the sculptures, most of which are restored
and elaborately painted.

Cave 6 is considered the finest at Yungang. The huge central pillar is
divided in two, with Buddhas in niches on all four sides above and below,
the corners of the upper part being supported by nine-storied pagodas on
the backs of elephants. A series of Jataka tales of Buddha's life is carved on
this pillar and on the east, south and west walls of the cave; the emphasis in
Yungang is on the life of Buddha, and Buddha as a teacher, which makes it
an easy step to accept as divine the Emperor, the teacher of his people.

Caves 7 and 8 are two of the earliest of the middle period caves, Cave 7 being noted for the six Worshipping Bodhisattvas kneeling above a row of musicians over the inside of the doorway, and for the flying celestial beings (apsaras) on the ceiling; and Cave 8 for the carving, unusual at Yungang, of the Indian subject of Vishnu with many heads and arms, seated on a peacock on the west of the inner entrance arch, opposite Siva seated on a bull on the east.

Caves 9 and 10, probably carved between 484 and 489, are distinguished by their finely designed ceilings. Here are early examples of motifs from Chinese architecture and elaborate flower and plant designs from Central Asia.

Caves 11, 12 and 13 form another group. Cave 11 is dated to 483 by an inscription on the east wall which says that it was constructed by a group of monks and faithful believers as a chamber suitable for offering prayers for the happiness of the Emperor and his family. The painted clay figures along the walls are late additions.

In Cave 12, on the west wall the capitals supporting the eaves of the Chinese roof over three Buddhas are surmounted by animal heads in the Persian style. In Cave 13, the central figure is Maitreya the Buddha of the Future, sitting with his right arm supported by a figure standing on his leg; this figure is a four-armed Vajra, the God of Thunder, and is the only such figure at Yungang. The animated line of Buddhas over the doorway wear widely flaring pleated skirts.

The Early Period: Caves 16-20
These are the Five Caves built by the monk Tan Yao which contain the huge Buddhas carved in the likeness of the first five Northern Wei Emperors. The Indian influence in these early caves is revealed in the oval floor plan and in the central position of the massive square-faced Buddha; the caves are covered with carvings.

In Cave 16, Sakyamuni Buddha standing on a lotus throne represents the Emperor Wen Cheng who authorised Tan Yao to build the caves.

In Cave 17 the central figure, a cross-ankled Maitreya shown as a Bodhisattva, represents an heir apparent who died before succeeding to the throne.

Cave 18 is the most famous of the early caves. The Buddha, visible through the opening over the door, stands 50 ft high, between two fine Bodhisattvas. The folds of his robe, which skim his right shoulder, are decorated with 'a thousand' small Buddhas.

The front of Cave 20 has fallen away and the great seated Buddha by which Yungang is so well known is in the open. This is the Emperor Dao Wu, the founder of the dynasty, who had the strong features of the northern nomads. The statue has been skilfully restored.

As you leave Yungang by the Stone steps leading down to the road, you have a good view across to the small theatre with an open gallery where plays were once peformed for the crowds of pilgrims who flocked to the cave temples for religious festivals.

Tianjin (Tientsin)

Many of the north China towns have been developed as industrial centres. Apart from Peking the largest is Tianjin (Tientsin), a city on the Hai River about thirty miles from the sea and roughly seventy from Peking.

Before the arrival of the Europeans in 1860 Tianjin was a market town (its earlier name Zhi Gu means Purchase and Sale) and a transhipment point for tribute grain brought up the Grand Canal and destined for the capital in Peking. After the Europeans had forced the opening of the city to western commerce, foreign concessions were established, first by Britain and France and later by the Japanese, Germans, Italians, Russians and others. The city's foreign origins are still evident in some of its architecture. The concessions were restored to the Chinese on the defeat of Japan in 1945.

Since 1949 the Tianjin area has become China's third industrial centre. Its development has been stimulated by the proximity of the Kailan coal mines to the northeast, the newly discovered Shengli oilfield to the south, and the salt pans along the coast which support its chemical industries.

The city itself has no ancient monuments but the Tianjin Museum contains a collection of ceramics and Chinese paintings. Antiques for export and reproductions can be bought in the Pavilion of Arts (Yilin Ge), the main antique shop. Many people go to see the high quality Tianjin cutpile carpets being made, and another local speciality are the clay figurines produced by the Zhang family, descendants of 'Clay-figure Zhang' who was famous for his skill in modelling figurines in the last century.

Jinan and Shandong Province

Jinan, the capital of Shandong province, was known as 'The City of 72 Springs'. Not all are still flowing, but of those which remain the best known are the Jet Springs (Baotu Quan), made the theme of one of the poems by the Song poetess Li Qingzhao who lived nearby; the Pool of Pearl Springs near which the provincial governor once had his residence; and the Black Tiger Springs feeding a small river that was part of the city moat. In the north of the city the Daming Lake has a number of small temples on its shores.

The Temple of the Iron Duke (Tiegong Si) was built in memory of a Ming general. Tradition has it that the North Star Temple (Beiji Miao) to the east of it was founded in the Mongol Yuan dynasty to commemorate the visit of a Crown Prince. East again is the Nanfang Temple built in honour of a Song official who improved the local irrigation system. The Xin Qiji Memorial Temple is named for a Song scholar-poet. Xin and the poetess Li Qingzhao are known to the Chinese as the two 'Ans' of Jinan since both have the word 'an' (peace) as part of their pen names.

Just south of Jinan the Xinguo Temple, damaged during the Cultural Revolution but now restored, clings to the side of the Mountain of the Thousand Buddhas (Qianfo Shan). The mountain takes its name from the hundreds of Buddhist carvings on its cliffs dating from the sixth to tenth century. About twenty miles to the east is China's earliest surviving pagoda, popularly known as the Four Door Pagoda (Simen Ta). It is square with only a single storey and was once part of the Shentong Monastery built in 544.

The provincial museum in Jinan has a well known collection of early bronzes and of pottery from the Neolithic cultures of Dawenkou and Longshan which take their names from type sites in the province.

Shandong province's largest port, Qingdao, once a German concession and still famous for beer, is also a popular seaside resort. Laoshan mineral water comes from the beautiful hills nearby.

Tai Shan

In ancient China prominent peaks were regarded as divinities and the origin of the worship of mountain spirits is lost in antiquity. Tai Shan, towering more than 4000 ft over Shandong province, is such a mountain. Sacrifice has been offered on it at least since 219 B.C. when the Qin Emperor who built the Great Wall came to worship here. In time Tai Shan became accepted as the first of the five sacred mountains of Daoism.

At the foot of the mountain in the town of Taian stands the Temple of the Peak (Yue Miao). In its Main Hall, restored in 1956, enormous murals depict a long procession escorting the image of the Spirit of the Peak. There are many stories in Chinese mythology about the identity of this spirit. One names Huang Feihu, a general who performed great deeds during the wars which brought about the downfall of the Shang in 1121 B.C. Another names Yan Wang, the King of Hades and Judge of the Dead. To add to the confusion, the temple on the summit is dedicated to the Daoist deity, the Jade Emperor, who was elevated to the rank of supreme god only in the tenth century A.D. Preserved in the temple is a fragment of what is believed to be one of the oldest carved inscriptions in China, dating from the reign of the second Qin Emperor (209-207 B.C.)

The ascent, which takes about six hours even for a good walker, begins at the Yuezong Gate about half a mile north of the city. One of the first temples on the way up is the Pool of the Empress of the West (Wangmu Chi), a former nunnery which houses a number of images of the Daoist immortals including the Patriarch Lu. He was an eighth century scholar who, among other things, is worshipped as the patron of inkmakers. Higher up, also on the righthand side, stands a former convent dedicated to the Daoist Goddess of the North Star (Doumu Gong), an old foundation rebuilt in 1542 and recently restored. A little further on a path leads over to the Valley of the Sutra Stone, an enormous flat slab of rock on which the Buddhist Diamond Sutra is carved in large and vigorous calligraphy. Higher up again a gateway is inscribed with the words 'The Peak where the Horses turned Back'. At this point the Song Emperor Zhen Zong is said to have been forced to dismount from his horse by the steepness of the slope. There is then a stiff climb to the Second Gate of Heaven. The weary can rest or stay the night at the nearby Zhongtian Men Resthouse, but the intrepid press on to the Pine with the Rank of Official of the Fifth Degree. Legend has it that on his visit to the mountain, the first Qin Emperor, thankful for the shelter of a pine tree at this spot, showed his gratitude by granting it an official rank. The steeply rising path finally reaches the last great ascent, a staircase of nearly two thousand steps climbing to the South Gate of Heaven which stands silhouetted against the sky.

Beyond the gate and just below the highest peak is the temple dedicated to the Goddess of the Dawn (Bixia Yuanjun), the daughter of the mountain god. Its roofs are protected by bronze and iron tiles heavy enough to withstand the fierce winds. This temple was the goal of countless pilgrims who toiled up the mountain, many on their knees, to pay homage to the statue of the goddess in the main hall. A spartan guesthouse has been established in one of the halls nearby. The peak itself is crowned by the temple dedicated to the Jade Emperor, and a rock marking the summit lies inside its courtyard. But the best place to watch the sun rise is on the Riguan Feng, a flat rock down the path to the east. Looking down from the peak to the south, the traveller may pause to remember that below him lies the country where the great sages Confucius and Mencius were born and taught and formulated the philosophy which conditioned Chinese thought, society, and administration for two thousand years.

There are numerous inscriptions all over the mountain, and many other temples, including at the foot the Temple of Universal Light (Puzhao Si) with its ancient pines, and the Lingying Gong within which the Bronze Tower (Tong Lou) now stands. The tower, whose main columns and roof are of bronze, was originally in the Temple of the Goddess of the Dawn at the top of Taishan, but was brought down in about 1770. The halls of the Lingying Gong itself contain a number of bronze figures brought here, it is said, when their original home, a Daoist temple west of Taian, was pulled down at the turn of the century.

Qufu

The small town of Qufu, fifty miles south of Taishan, has for centuries been dedicated to one man and his philosophy. Confucius (Kong Fuzi) was born here in 551 B.C. and returned from his travels to die here seventy-three years later. The name by which he is known in the west is a latinised form, derived from his Chinese family name 'Kong' combined with 'Fu-zi', a title of respect for a great teacher. Qufu was the capital of the State of Lu in which he lived and taught, and which with the neighbouring State of Qi, occupied much of present day Shandong province. Over the centuries, as Confucianism became the dominant cult on which the whole organisation of the state was based, successive dynasties rebuilt and enlarged the Temple of Confucius and the Palace of the King Family, which now occupy the greater part of the town. Between them they rank with the Forbidden City in Peking and the old Manchu summer retreat at Chengde as one of the three largest collections of monumental architecture in China.

Within the temple, one of the most beautiful main buildings is the temple library (Guiwen Ge) which dates from 1190. Even more impressive is the Hall of Great Perfection (Dacheng Dian) rebuilt after a fire in 1724. Coiling dragons entwine the marble pillars which support its massive roof. The courtyard in front of this hall was the scene of the Sacrifice to Confucius, a stately ceremony of ritual music and dancing. To the accompaniment of solemn chanting and music performed on ancient musical instruments, male dancers in silk embroidered robes, 'mortar board' hats and thick white soled boots, the formal attire of those serving in the temple, gracefully manipulated wands tipped with long pheasant feathers. Their number, thirty-six or sixty-four dancers in each group, depended on the rank of the Imperial Prince attending the ceremony. The hall still has a collection of ancient musical instruments which survived the Cultural Revolution.

A stele on the eastern side of the temple commemorates the discovery of the Lu Wall. The story is that when the First Qin Emperor burned the Confucian Classics in 213 B.C., a descendant of Confucius hid some of the texts in the wall. More than a century later, during the reign of the Han Emperor Wu Di great efforts were made to reconstruct the texts of the Classics, and by lucky coincidence the hidden texts were discovered just at this time.

Alongside the main temple lies a modest courtyard and buildings known as the House of Confucius. It stands on the site that the original dwelling of the sage was reputed to occupy, and contrasts strangely with the enormous mansion beside it, the Kong Family Palace (Kong Fu). Over the generations the descendants of Confucius became highly privileged. In 979 A.D. the Song Emperor Tai Zong bestowed posthumous honours on forty-four generations of the Kong family, and in 1055 the Emperor Ren Zong conferred on them the title of Duke. The Duke ranked with the Grand Secretary at Court immediately below Imperial Princes. The Kong Palace was enlarged and embellished until it contained hundreds of rooms used for private apartments, and offices for the large bureaucracy responsible for administering the great family estates as well as arranging the rites and ceremonies performed in the temple. The private apartments were as opulent as those of any princely household. Generations of the Kong family built up by gift and acquisition large collections of bronzes, ceremonial robes, seals, carvings and other objects connected with the Confucian cult, which have made the palace a museum in its own right.

Confucius is said to be buried in the Cemetery of the Kong Family just to the north of the town. This extensive park with its ancient gnarled cypresses is filled with memorial halls, carved stone figures of officials and animals, and the tombstones of generations of the sage's descendants.

4. The Valley of the Yangtze

The wide valley of the Yangtze River, including the area round Shanghai and Hangzhou, is one of the most fertile and intensively cultivated in China. Hot humid summers and temperate winters have encouraged an abundant production of rice, tea and silk on which successive regimes in the north have drawn throughout the centuries. Hangzhou, and the towns of the lower Yangtze, Suzhou, Yangzhou and Nanjing (Nanking) were envied for their elegance and the luxury of their lifestyle. During this century the Yangtze towns became the textile centre of China, and Shanghai has grown into one of its largest industrial cities. There are still areas of great natural beauty to be enjoyed round the West Lake at Hangzhou, in the hill resort of Lushan overlooking the Poyang Lake, and in the wild mountains of Jiangxi province, where until fifty years ago tigers roamed, and whose remoteness provided an ideal base for the Communists in the early stages of the revolution which eventually brought them to power in Peking.

Shanghai

When Shanghai was walled in 1554 to keep out marauding Japanese pirates, it was a modest city which had grown up as a textile centre and natural port. Although the walls have all gone, the old houses and narrow streets lined with tiny shops, selling everything from fans to dumplings, still distinguish the old town from the modern city which surrounds it. It still has its Temple of the City God, one of the few such temples in China today, even though it is now in a market, and a walk through the traditional Yu Garden nearby will provide a glimpse of the life of old Shanghai. This beautiful southern garden once covered twelve acres and took eighteen years to complete. It was created in the mid sixteenth century by Pan Yun-duan, a native of the city who was governor of Sichuan province, in honour of his father. He called it 'The Pleasure Garden' (Yu Yuan), a quotation from the phrase 'to give pleasure to one's elders'. Two hundred years later, it was rescued from neglect by local garden lovers. Reduced in size over the years, today it encompasses only the northeast corner of the old Ming Garden. But inside its high walls, some crowned with dark grey dragons whose scaly bodies undulate along their length, the visitor will find most of the elements of a classic southern garden: a small lake; a hillock constructed on the principle that only rocks may be seen, and not the earth beneath from which the trees and flowers grow; elaborate pavilions for resting in, or for looking out over the walls to the river not far away; walls pierced by decorative openings to frame the constantly changing scenes; ornamental rocks from Lake Tai Hu like the tall Jade Pendant Rock; and skilfully carved tiles like the one depicting the Daoist Moon Palace, a superb example of this branch of art. The rock and tiles are near the south wall. The largest hall in the garden, the Hall which Heralds the Spring (Dianchun Tang) was for a time the headquarters of the Small Sword Society which, in 1853 rose against the Manchu Qing Emperor and captured the old city; it now houses an archaeological and historical exhibition.

Outside the garden, the Pavilion in the Lake (Huxin Ting) with its zigzag bridge was believed by many of Shanghai's foreign residents to be the model for the popular Willow Pattern china; in fact this is a European pattern engraved by Thomas Minton about 1780 and later copied by Chinese potters.

Shanghai's only surviving pagoda is outside the old city at the Longhua Temple, well to the south. It was first erected in 977.

The Jade Buddha Monastery (Yufo Si) on Anyuan Road is entirely modern. It was built in 1918; the jade Buddhas for which it is famous were brought from Burma in 1882. The sutras in the library include manuscripts dating from the Tang and Ming dynasties, and the temple collection includes carvings of Boddhisattvas in stone and wood of the same periods.

In 1843, following the opening of Shanghai to foreign trade after the Opium War, the first British Consul arrived in the port and negotiated the lease in perpetuity of about 150 acres by the river north of the Chinese city. In 1849 the French Consul established a concession to the south of the British; and in 1854 the American Consul raised his flag north of the Suzhou Creek. Nine years later the British and American Settlements were amalgamated to form the International Settlement. With the separate French Concession, the Settlement became a 'state within a state'. Foreign residents were subject to their own consular courts, and the foreign rate-payers elected their own Municipal Council. But the Settlement was never able to isolate itself from the surge of events around it. When in its early years it was threatened by the Taiping Uprising against the Manchu Government the imperial forces were assisted in defeating the Taipings by a small foreign mercenary force from Shanghai led first by an American, Frederick Ward, and then by Major Charles Gordon of the Royal Artillery (Chinese Gordon). The safety of Shanghai itself was assured by the presence of British and French forces recently returned from occupying Peking to enforce the ratification of the treaty which opened Peking to Legations and more ports to foreign trade. Such was the extraordinary attitude of the foreign powers to China at that time that no one found it strange for them to be attacking the capital at Peking and assisting the Imperial Army to suppress the Taipings at almost the same time.

The settlements remained under foreign control until the middle of this century. In 1943, during the war with Japan, the western powers signed treaties returning them to Chinese sovereignty and relinquishing the extra-territorial privileges previously enjoyed by their citizens.

There are still many European style buildings, particularly along the waterfront, to remind the visitor of the International Settlement. The Friendship Store is in the grounds of the old British Consulate-General. The Peace Hotel on the corner of Nanking Road was the Cathay Hotel. A block further south the old Customs House is easily identified by its tall clock tower, and next to it is the distinctive dome of the former Hongkong and Shanghai Bank. Two blocks further on was the Shanghai Club built in 1901, which boasted one of the longest bars in the world. In the French Concession the Cercle Sportif Français opposite the Jinjiang Hotel, the scene of many a fashionable the-dansant, is now the Jinjiang Club for foreign and overseas Chinese visitors. Nanjing Road is still the main shopping street where China's most up to date merchandise is on sale to the smart Shanghai shoppers and Kieslings Café still sells coffee, pastries and icecream sodas.

From the beginning of this century Shanghai and the Settlements proved to be attractive to Chinese revolutionaries of many persuasions, and the growing workforce drew Shanghai deep into the political maelstrom of the 1920s and 30s. On 1 July 1921 the first National Congress of the Chinese Communist Party was held in a house in what is now Xing Ye Road. The house is preserved as a national museum. During the congress the delegates, who included Mao Zedong, were forced to move to a houseboat on a lake in Jiaxing, sixty miles away, to avoid discovery; a similar boat is preserved as a museum there. In 1927 the Nationalist leader Chiang Kai-Shek, having co-operated with the Communists in a campaign to overthrow the warlord regimes, turned on his erstwhile allies, and his forces hunted down every Communist they could find in the Chinese part of the city.

When the Communists took over the city in 1949 they greatly expanded its industries. It is now one of the largest industrial centres in the world with a large port area, shipyards, oil refineries, heavy engineering, heavy electrical industries and a growing electronic and precision industry sector. Six million people live in the city proper, and Shanghai is so important that it is one of the three great municipalities directly controlled by the Central Government.

Such a powerful city is bound to play a major role in political life. The Cultural Revolution which led to the ousting of so many leaders of the Communist Party was launched from here in the mid 1960s. The extremist faction, now known as the Gang of Four, tried to make the city a secure base for themselves by appointing their own city leaders and arming the factory militia. But following the death of Mao Zedong in 1976, the other members of the Politbureau moved against them and they were outmanoeuvred. The city, surrounded by regular army forces loyal to Peking, abandoned them and quickly rallied to the new leadership in the capital.

Apart from a few glimpses of the old city and of the foreign settlements, Shanghai offers the visitor an opportunity to see something of modern

China through visits to its factories and communes, the industrial exhibition and, most enjoyable, a boat-trip on the busy Huangpu River. Equally worthwhile is a visit to the Shanghai Museum on Yenan Road which has one of the best collections in the country of early bronzes and paintings from the Tang and Song periods onwards. Two of the famous lifesize pottery horses and a warrior from the tomb of the first Qin Emperor (221-209 B.C.) at Xi'an can be seen there.

There is a popular excursion to Songjiang, twelve miles to the southwest, to see the eleventh century square brick pagoda, and the fourteenth century screen wall of the former Temple of the City God decorated with a large bas-relief of carved clay brick depicting the Monster of Avarice.

The position of Shanghai enables it to draw on an abundance of seafood, fresh water products and a wide variety of vegetables. The cooking is good at the Shanghai Mansions, the Peace Hotel and Jinjiang Hotel, especially if ordered in advance.

If you want to go out for a meal, the Xin Ya, 719 Nanking Road East has Shanghai style Cantonese food, and a menu in English; try sweet-sour pork, beef with oyster sauce, and Shanghai eels. For excellent Shanghai food go to the Old Shanghai Restaurant at 242 Fuzuo Lu in the Old City. Your interpreter will have to order the meal as there is no English menu. The adventurous who do not want a full meal will enjoy the Shanghai specialities sold in the small openfronted snack bars that line the narrow streets. In season do not miss the softshell crabs.

Hangzhou (Hangchow)

Hangzhou, the capital of Zhejiang province, with a population of 980,000, is a beautiful lakeside resort on the north bank of the Qiantang River. It stands in a fertile agricultural area famous for tea, with silkworm cocoons, sugar cane, rice, bamboo and mandarin oranges among its other crops. The whole process of silk production, from silk reeling to the weaving of the finished fabrics, which in Hangzhou goes back to the seventh century, may be seen by visiting one of the silk textile factories. The many handicrafts for which Hangzhou is famous include sandalwood fans, silk parasols, bambooware, bamboo chopsticks, scissors, silk brocade pictures and silk embroidery. Of all its beautiful flowers, perhaps the most admired are the chrysanthemums exhibited in the autumn flower shows which include hundreds of varieties, many well known for their use in herbal teas and other remedies.

By the closing years of the sixth century Hangzhou had become sufficiently prosperous and important to require the protection of walls, and to produce the funds and corvée labour to construct them. It was linked to the capital at Luoyang by the Sui Emperor Yang Di who extended his Grand Canal south of the Yangtze River in order to tap the area's plentiful supplies of grain. In the ninth century one of China's renowned governor-poets, Bai (or Bo) Juyi, improved the waterways and dykes to increase the water available for irrigation; the Bai Causeway which crossed the West

Lake from east to west is named in his memory. When China later split into a number of independent kingdoms, the city became the capital of the Wuyue rulers who enlarged the city walls and built many temples and pagodas. At that time the lake was a shallow bay connected to the sea by the Qiantang estuary. Over the years the sand bar at its entrance silted up, and the Wuyue Princes constructed an embankment to keep out tidal waves, thus forming the West Lake much as it is today. It was another governor-poet, Su Dongpo, who developed the lake as the city's main reservoir, using the dredgings from the lake to build the Su Causeway across the lake from north to south.

Even while the Song dynasty still had its capital at Kaifeng in the north, Hangzhou was one of the great cities, the first among the prefectures in the southeast and famous for the beauty of its mountains and lakes, the prosperity of its commerce and its fleets of seagoing ships. When Kaifeng was captured in 1126 by invaders from the north, the survivors of the Northern Song court were driven south and established a temporary capital in the city, safe from the nomad cavalry who could not fight effectively among the myriad lakes and waterways of the area. At first a Temporary Palace was set up on Phoenix Hill, but later the court moved to a new imperial palace within the city walls. The new capital attracted great families and rich merchants, bringing further wealth to a city already prospering from its thriving silk and tea industries and busy port. One contemporary writer complained that, seduced by Hangzhou's splendour and sophistication, the dynasty had lost much of its incentive to recapture the northern plain; another lamented the fact that the youth of the great families thought of nothing but their own pleasure.

The tall many-storied wooden houses that sprang up to accommodate the rapidly increasing population were a constant fire hazard, but in spite of destruction by fire and war, enough of its splendour remained after its capture by the Mongols in 1276 to impress visitors from the west. For if Friar Odoric, who was in China in the fourteenth century, is to be believed, Marco Polo was by no means the only Venetian to have visited Hangzhou, 'I have met in Venice people in plenty who have been there. . . . For 'tis the grandest and noblest city and the finest for merchandise that the whole world containeth.'

The popular saying 'Above are the Halls of Heaven, Below are Suzhou and Hangzhou' dates from this time, and it seems probable that it was this that led Marco Polo to mistranslate the name by which he knew the city, 'Qinsay' (Temporary Capital) as 'City of Heaven'.

Hangzhou retained its fame and prosperity through the succeeding Ming and Manchu dynasties. The two great Manchu rulers, the Kang Xi and Qian Long Emperors both admired the city, which remained in Chinese eyes the model of poetic beauty. But in 1860 and 1862 disaster struck when the Taiping armies, who came close to overthrowing the Manchus, sacked it. Despite the terrible destruction in this war, production was soon restored, and the records of the Imperial Manufactory at Hangzhou for the late nineteenth century show that the city was again providing the court with large amounts of silk, satin and brocade.

Only a few old houses remain today, but Hangzhou's beautiful setting makes it still one of China's most popular resorts.

The West Lake (Xi Hu)

The West Lake is about nine miles in circumference. On the green, wooded hills which rise to a height of a thousand feet on three sides of it are many temples with panoramic views, and clear streams wind down to the lake through tea gardens and bamboo groves.

One of the most enjoyable things to do is to take a boat on the lake. Almost in the centre is the Island of the Three Pools that Mirror the Moon, at its most beautiful when the lotus bloom in summer. Constructed between 1607 and 1611 it is really an embankment enclosing four small lakes, arranged as a traditional Chinese garden with pavilions, decorative rocks, and a nine-bend bridge added in 1727. The three little seventeenth century stone pagodas to the south of the island replace ones which the poet-governor Su Dongpo had built when he was dredging and cleaning the lake in 1089. The pagodas were believed to seal off three deep pits full of evil spirits to prevent the spirits from coming up to harm boats that passed by. On autumn nights the reflections from lamps placed in the pagodas shine in the water like nine full moons.

In the eighteenth century a member of Lord Macartney's Embassy to Peking, John Barrow, described an excursion on West Lake: 'We had a splendid yacht, and another made fast to it, to serve as a kitchen; the dinner began the instant we went on board, and ceased only when we stepped ashore. It consisted of at least a hundred dishes in succession, among which were excellent eels, fresh caught in the lake, and dressed in a variety of ways; yet the water was as clear as crystal. Vast numbers of barges were sailing to and fro, all gaily decorated with paint and gilding and streaming colours; the parties within them apparently all in pursuit of pleasure. The margins of the lake were studded with light aereal buildings, among which one of more solidity and of greater extent than the rest was said to belong to the Emperor. The grounds were inclosed with brick walls and mostly planted with vegetables and fruit trees; but in some there appeared to be collections of such shrubs and flowers as are most esteemed in the country.'

Parallel with the north shore the mile-long Bai Causeway runs from east to west cutting off the small northern part of the lake. The Causeway is broken by the Interrupting Bridge (Duan Qiao) and the Brocade Belt Bridge (Jindai Qiao). The Interrupting Bridge is a favourite place to enjoy snow scenes, and an old story tells how once upon a time an enchanted White Snake Maiden met and fell in love with a young scholar here. They were parted by a monk who imprisoned the White Snake under Thunder Peak Pagoda on the south side of the lake. The unhappy pair and their maid, the Blue Snake Maiden, are immortalised in a popular Peking opera called 'The Story of the White Snake'.

On the north shore, not far from the Interrupting Bridge, a path leads up the hill to the tall Needle Pagoda. Last restored in 1933, the pagoda is a famous landmark, once much admired as a foil to the now fallen Thunder Peak Pagoda (Leifeng Ta) on the south shore. The pagoda, whose real name is Protect the Prince of Chu Pagoda (Bao Chu Ta), was built in the tenth century by the Prime Minister of the State of Wuyue in the pious hope of ensuring the safe return of his Prince, Qian Chu, who was detained at the court of the Song Emperor in Kaifeng. When the Prince was finally permitted to leave Kaifeng, the Emperor is said to have handed him a parcel full of rejected petitions urging the Emperor never to allow the Prince to return to Hangzhou.

There is a beautiful walk along the path leading west from the pagoda following the crest of the hill past pavilions, caves and sculptures; it comes down to the lake at the Yuefei Temple near the Hangzhou Hotel. The path toward the back of the hill leads to the Yellow Dragon Cave where the rare 'square bamboo' grows.

Returning to the Bai Causeway, the road leads across the lake to Solitary Hill (Gu Shan), the largest of its four islands. Jutting out into the water is the Pavilion of the Calm Lake and Autumn Moon (Pinghu Qiuyue Ting) where the Kang Xi Emperor sat to enjoy the moonlight outside his palace nearly three hundred years ago. The palace, noticed by John Barrow, which lay along the foot of Solitary Hill, was badly damaged during the Taiping uprising. One of the most famous buildings destroyed was the Wenlan Ge, one of seven libraries specially built towards the end of the eighteenth century to house copies of the great compilation of Chinese learning, the Siku Quanshu (see Chengde). The Wenlan Ge, now part of the Zhejiang Museum, was rebuilt in 1880 and the remaining volumes of the Hangzhou copy of the Siku Quanshu reassembled here.

From this point two small islands can be seen in the larger Outer Lake. On one stands the Pavilion at the Heart of the Lake; and on the other a tall concrete cenotaph built in 1929 in memory of a general who fought against the Japanese pirates in Ming times. Further along the lakeside road a pleasant tree shaded path leads up to a little stone pagoda and a garden laid out by the Seal Engravers' Society of Zhejiang (Xiling Yinshe). Originally a group of literati who met here early in this century to study and collect ancient seals, the society is still active and there is a small studio where ink, seals and seal impressions may be purchased.

From the pagoda a path winds down the back of the hill through bamboos and azaleas to the lakeside Pavilion where the Crane was Sent Out (Fanghe Ting) and the tomb of the Song poet-painter Lin Hejing (967-1028). He is said to have looked after his many plum trees as well as he would have cared for a wife, and his crane as he would have cherished a son. Plum trees and cranes have a special significance for Chinese scholars, as symbols of long life. If guests arrived when the poet was out, his servant sent the crane out from the pavilion to summon him home, and it would fly round happily as he entertained his friends. When the poet died the crane pined away and the plum trees withered.

A lakeside path leads from the pavilion back to the Xiling Bridge (Xiling Qiao) which connects the west end of Solitary Hill with the north lake shore. At the end of the bridge a pavilion marks the tomb of the fifth century beauty Su Xiaoxiao, who fell in love with a handsome stranger riding by on his black horse as she passed this spot in her painted chair. The road runs on beside the lake, past the Hangzhou Hotel and the Yue Fei Temple, then turns south onto the Su Causeway which runs from north to south for about 1¾ miles across the lake. It has six bridges and is a perfect place to walk in the early morning to see the devotees of 'shadow boxing' (taiji quan) beginning their day with graceful exercises. Towards the end of the Causeway on the west is the Huaguang Pond for Viewing Fish, a pleasant park with pavilions and winding bridges from which to look at the goldfish.

On the south side of the lake at the foot of Nanping Hill the Monastery of Pure Compassion (Jingci Si) founded in 954 and recently restored, is one of the two most famous monasteries in Hangzhou and balances the Monastery of the Soul's Retreat (Lingyin Si) on the northwest shore. To the left of the main gate a small pavilion shelters a tablet inscribed with the words 'Nanping Hill where the evening bell resounds'. The unforgettable sound of the great bell of this temple, struck with a wooden beam and reverberating across the still lake has been lauded by poets through the ages.

Opposite the Monastery on Sunset Hill (Diezhao Shan) stands a column marking the site of the Thunder Peak Pagoda (Leifeng Ta), erected in the tenth century for the Lady Huang, a consort of Prince Qian of Wuyue. For centuries it was a famous landmark, but in the sixteenth century Japanese pirates set fire to it because it was used as a watchtower to give warning of their raids. After burning for three days all the woodwork was destroyed. The tall column of brown burned bricks that remained stood for nearly four more centuries until, one quiet September afternoon in 1924, it suddenly collapsed in a heap of rubble. For years the bricks at the base of the pagoda had been chipped away by superstitious pilgrims who scattered the brickdust on their fields to ensure a good crop, or sprinkled it in their tea to promote good health. Gradually the base became too slender to support the huge pagoda and it collapsed. Inside many of the bricks were silk scrolls inscribed with Buddhist scriptures that had been written and placed in the building in 975 by command of Prince Qian. One of these bricks with its scroll may be seen in the Zhejiang Museum on Solitary Hill.

Returning along the lake and following the road towards the Qiantang River a path on the left climbs up the Jade Emperor Hill (Yuhuang Shan). A pleasant climb to the top gives fine views over the river and the Pagoda of Six Harmonies (Liuhe Ta), over the West Lake, and down into the valley where the fields were planted in the pattern of the Eight Trigrams (Ba Gua) of Daoism. It was here that the Southern Song Emperors performed the annual ploughing ritual.

On the other side of the road a path leads to the Monastery where the Tigers Ran Off (Hu Bao Quan). Local legend tells of a monk in the ninth century who, wishing to build a monastery, prayed for water. He had a vision in which two tigers were called by Buddha to claw a spring from the ground. After it began to flow they ran off. This spring is now in the courtyard of the small restored temple. Water from it has great surface tension. Coins will float on it and they can be added to a bowl of spring water without making it overflow. For centuries connoisseurs have come here to enjoy Dragon Well tea made with water from the spring.

The Pagoda of Six Harmonies (Liuhe Ta) rises nearly 200 ft on Full Moon Hill (Yuelun Shan) overlooking the Qiantang River Bridge. In the middle of the tenth century, Prince Qian was persuaded by two monks of the temple here to build the pagoda to protect Hangzhou from the tidal bore which surges up the river. The great brick pagoda with its wooden galleries must have been a magical sight when lit for a festival with lamps hung at every window and corner of its thirteen stories. It also served as a navigation mark for ships, and every evening lamps were lit on the top. It was destroyed during the wars of the twelfth century, but was rebuilt when the Southern Song established their capital at Hangzhou and most recently repaired in 1971. A magnificent view rewards the long climb to the top. Not far away is the White Pagoda with nine stories which also dates from the tenth century.

The Qiantang River bore, against which it was hoped the Pagoda of Six Harmonies would give protection, is caused by the sixty mile wide mouth of the river narrowing to only two miles at Zhakou, the port of Hangzhou, thus forming an enormous funnel. When a strong tide flows in against a fast underflow downriver an immense wall of water is built up over the shallow riverbed. It reaches its greatest height (over 20 ft) about forty miles from Hangzhou at Haining where the funnel narrows. The roar of the approaching bore can be heard for forty-five minutes before it comes into sight. It occurs every month to some degree but is at its most impressive during the autumn equinox when thousands of people throng to watch it at the Haining Pagoda. An ingenious system of buttresses was constructed at Haining to protect junks from the bore. These were built over thirty feet from the sea-wall, and along each buttress a shelf was made, six to eight feet above the riverbed and extending out about twenty feet. At high tide the junks tied up to the buttresses and when the tide went out they were left on the shelves. When the tide turned the buttresses broke the force of the incoming bore and the fleet of junks, floating off the shelves, could then ride safely upriver on the after rush.

A few miles beyond the Six Harmonies Pagoda is the Five Cloud Mountain (Wuyun Shan) where the Path with 72 Turnings, leading to the Zhenji Monastery, gives superb views over West Lake and the Qiantang River. The monastery, founded in the tenth century, is known for its two wells which are always full, in spite of being at a height of more than a thousand feet. There is a beautiful half-day's walk from here across the hills south of West Lake to the Monastery of the Soul's Retreat.

In the valley west of Five Cloud Mountain is the Cloud's Rest (Yun Chi), where a path winds through bamboo groves. Many different varieties, including the small bamboo used for making the famous Hangzhou chopsticks, and the rare square bamboo, flourish in the groves. The little tenth century temple was recently restored and made into a teahouse.

On the north shore of West Lake, just west of the Hangzhou Hotel is the tomb and memorial temple dedicated to Yue Fei, a national hero and great general of the twelfth century. He valiantly defended south China against the Jin invaders from the north who had captured the Song court and capital at Kaifeng, and driven the survivors south of the Yangtze River. But Yue Fei had jealous enemies at the effete Southern Song court in Hangzhou, and the success of his campaign against the Jin armies provoked a rival general to engineer his recall from the battlefield, his trial on trumped up charges, and his murder in prison. Twenty years after his death the next Emperor had his body reburied with honour, bestowing on him the post-humous rank of Prince in recognition of his loyalty and devoted service. In 1221 the temple was raised to his memory. Inside the Great Hall is a statue of Yue Fei, made by the Hangzhou Art College. During his trial Yue Fei revealed that his mother had four characters tatooed on his back meaning 'Protect your country with the utmost fidelity', the words which are now inscribed on either side of the hall. Yue Fei's faithful generals and his family are commemorated in the temple halls. The smaller tumulus covers the body of his adopted son who was killed with him. His betrayers are depicted in iron statues kneeling in the courtyard.

The south fork of the road going west from the lake leads to the Monastery of the Soul's Retreat (Lingyin Si) and the Peak that Flew Over from India (Feilai Feng). A tree-shaded path follows a stream running along the foot of the peak, which was so named in the fourth century by Hui Li, a monk from India who claimed that this was one of the peaks of a famous Indian mountain. Hui Li's tomb is marked by a small sixteenth century stone stupa by the path. The cliff beside the path has caves at the east end and the largest collection of Buddhist rock carvings in Hangzhou, comprising some 300 figures dating from the tenth to fourteenth centuries. The cave furthest to the left, the Cave of Green Woods (Qinglin Dong), has the earliest surviving sculptures on the hill, three carvings of Buddhas made in 951. A panel carved in 1022 shows the Buddhist Rocana Festival with Sakyamuni Buddha seated on a lotus pedestal; on his left is the Bodhisattva Manjusri (Wenshu) on his lion, and on his right is Samantabhadra (Puxian) on his elephant, with two apsaras flying above them; they are attended by four Heavenly Kings, four Bodhisattvas and worshippers. Along the way to the temple, the Dragon's Roar Cave (Longhong Dong) has fine thirteenth century (Yuan) Buddhist statues in niches at the en-trance; below are reliefs of Buddhist figures, including one of the Chinese monk Xuan Zang showing him bringing the Buddhist scriptures from India to China and the white horses that carried them. The sculptures inside the cave include Guan Yin, the Goddess of Mercy, and pilgrim inscriptions with one by the poet-governor Su Dongpo. Further along the cliff, a benign thirteenth century Laughing Buddha (Maitreya), with eighteen Lohans is a favourite with photographers.

The path leads on to the Great Gate of the Monastery of the Soul's Retreat, the largest and most famous monastery in Hangzhou. Founded in 326 by Hui Li, the monk from India, it has been destroyed and rebuilt several times in the original style. Inside the Main Hall, a triple roofed building rebuilt in the nineteenth century and recently restored, is a 60 ft high Sakyamuni Buddha made in 1956 as a replica of the Tang original. At the back Guan Yin, the Goddess of Mercy, is represented as Guardian of the Sea. The finely carved Sutra Pagodas outside the hall stood in this courtyard since the tenth century when more than three thousand monks lived in the monastery. Its fame is due more to its history and beautiful setting than to the present buildings, and also to the fact that a number of temples elsewhere in China copied its halls and statues.

The path outside the monastery leads on west, up through trees and bamboo groves to the little Hermitage of Dao Guang (Dao Guang An), named for the Buddhist monk and poet, Dao Guang, who often was visited here by his friend the Tang poet Bai Juyi, prefect of Hangzhou from 822-4. The golden lotus add to the beauty of the hermitage pond and there is a fine view across to the West Lake and Qiantang River.

From the car park at the entrance to the Monastery of the Soul's Retreat a path leads into the hills to the old Three Monasteries of India, through the tea gardens and small villages.

The north fork of the road leading west from West Lake goes to the Hangzhou Botanical Gardens. Over the last twenty years the gardens have been extended to cover nearly 500 acres. The bamboo groves contain more than a hundred varieties, and the well organised grounds have extensive areas of fruit and flowering trees arranged according to families.

The Jade Spring is in the Gardens on the site of the fifth century Monastery of Clear Ripples (Qinglian Si). The spring still feeds a large pool where visitors come to see the large grey and gold carp and relax over a bowl of tea or lotus root in the modern tea house.

From the southwest corner of the West Lake a path leads into the hills to the Three Yanxia Caves; first to the Stone Chamber Cave, through groves of osmanthus fragrans to the Water Music Cave, and on to the Yanxia Cave itself. The most famous of the Buddhist figures in the caves are the Song carvings of Guan Yin and the Boddhisattva at the entrance to Yanxia Cave.

The Dragon Well Monastery (Longjing Si), now a teahouse, and its famous spring are on a hill about a mile above Dragon Well Valley, to the south of West Lake. The Dragon Well Commune tea gardens grow one of China's four great green teas, famous for its beautiful leaves, fragrance, flavour and fine colour. In season it is possible to see the tea being picked and then dried in shallow heated iron basins; traditionally the leaves were turned by hand to dry them evenly. According to Chinese tradition, tea was being used as a medicine as early as 2000 B.C. In 780 A.D. Lu Yu wrote the *Tea Classic,* a treatise on the growing, processing, preparation and correct drinking of tea, which was by then a popular beverage and an export commodity. Through centuries refinements were made, aromatics and flowers added, and by the sixteenth century fermented or black tea was being produced. The Dutch first brought tea to Europe at that time. Though extremely expensive it soon became fashionable and in time came to be regarded as a necessity. The Chinese believe tea to be stimulating, cooling and good for the eyesight and the digestion.

Going on towards the Qiantang River, the Valley of Nine Streams and Eighteen Rivulets has lovely walks and a welcome teahouse at the Nine Streams.

While you are in Hangzhou try to eat at Lou Wai Lou on the lakeside which specialises in dishes made from the fish and waterplants in the lake (especially 'sheng cai' in soup) — it is expensive.

Less expensive is Hangzhou Jiujian on Yan'an Road — try their Dragon Well tea shrimps (Longjing xiapian) and a mixed dish of pork, shrimp and vegetables (sibao caixin), and chicken cooked in Shaoxing wine.

Shaoxing

Less than an hour's journey southwest of Hangzhou through an area renowned for rice and fish lies Shaoxing, an attractive small town of whitewalled timbered houses with dark tiled roofs which back onto stone bordered canals and lakes. One of the oldest and most widely drunk wines in China, Shaoxing Yellow Rice Wine is still produced here from glutinous rice and the exceptionally pure water drawn from Mirror Lake (Jian Hu) between November and March when it is at its best. Traditionally families buried stone jars of this wine a month after a daughter was born, recovering it for her wedding celebrations.

The home and school of one of China's greatest modern writers, Lu Xun, who was born in Shaoxing in 1881, are open to visitors. A large temple dedicated to the legendary Emperor Yu who is reputed to have controlled the Great Flood, is about two miles from the town.

Suzhou (Soochow)

The ancient city of Suzhou on the old Grand Canal in south Jiangxu province was once one of the two most beautiful cities in China, celebrated in the saying 'Above is Paradise, below are Suzhou and Hangzhou'. It lies about fifty miles west of Shanghai and twelve miles east of Tai Hu, one of the biggest lakes in China, in flat countryside interlaced with waterways and thickly populated. Rice, winter wheat, rape and cotton are grown, as well as mulberries for silk production, and fruit. For centuries people have flocked from the city each spring to enjoy the brilliant yellow of the fields of rape, and the soft purple of the clover.

Suzhou is known for its gardens, canals, silk, embroidery, printing and handicrafts. In the modern city local industry includes mining, metallurgy, chemicals and electronics as well as light industry and handicrafts, and supports a population of half a million people.

The long story of this famous city fills 150 volumes of the official Chinese Histories. It begins in the sixth century B.C. when He Lu the King of Wu cut canals, drained the land and built a moated and walled capital with well laid out streets and palaces. The cultural and commercial life of the city was constantly enriched by the arrival of scholars and wealthy merchants who came seeking refuge from the fighting which plagued the north and northwest of China. There was a huge influx in the twelfth century when the Jin invaders captured the Song capital and court at Kaifeng, and the survivors fled to the south to set up a southern capital at Hangzhou.

When Marco Polo came here a century later as an official of the Mongol court he described Suzhou as a 'noble city' of six thousand bridges, with quantities of silks and cloths of gold, producing rhubarb and ginger, and with inhabitants who were clever, cunning of hand, and wise.

Five hundred years later a member of Lord Macartney's Embassy was amazed by its luxury and sophistication, 'a town . . . of the greatest artists, . . . most wellknown scholars, the richest merchants, . . . and the home of delicately made women with tiny feet . . . .Canals thronged with gondolas cross it in all directions: it is a delightful place to walk in, both inside and outside the walls.' Suzhou women were in fact so noted for their beauty and musical voices that they were imitated by fashionable women all over the country, and women as well as men appeared in the renowned Suzhou opera companies. During the Manchu dynasty (1644-1911) one of the three Imperial Manufactories was sited in the city and supplied the government and court with silk fabrics and the famous Suzhou embroidery. Records of the last century show that the Manufactory was filling enormous and varied orders from the court that included such items as green and white jadestone seals of state, satin book-wrappers with dragon patterns and silk linings, lute strings and silk-lined lutestring wrappers, as well as silk braid and chased ivory tags for fastenings.

Suzhou was also a centre of the book trade. Bibliophiles collected libraries of rare books, discussed and copied works with friends, and printed catalogues and facsimiles of rare editions.

It was not surprising that a succession of Chinese rulers should wish to draw on the wealth of such a prosperous area. For this purpose the Grand Canal was extended to Suzhou and Hangzhou in the seventh century. Later it fell into disrepair, but the Mongol Emperor Kublai Khan improved and rebuilt it adding a paved roadway alongside, along which the 1200 mile journey from Hangzhou to Peking could be accomplished in forty days. European Ambassadors travelling along the canal in the eighteenth and early nineteenth centuries have described the winching of their barges through the great sluices, the magnificent vessels of officials travelling on business, the boats carrying scholars on their way to Peking to present themselves for the examinations, and the throngs of travellers and goods on the waterway. Its decline as a main artery came in the nineteenth century with the elimination of piracy on the seacoast and increased safety of sea traffic to the north; a decline hastened by the building of the railways. But the canal at Suzhou is still busy and important for the local traffic that crowds beneath its picturesque stone bridges.

In the 1850s the Taiping armies captured the lower Yangtze cities. They were led by a young man calling himself the Heavenly King, who had received instruction from a Protestant missionary in Guangzhou and had come to believe that he was the younger brother of Jesus called by God to overthrow the Manchu Emperors and rule China. After his army took

Suzhou, he lived in the building that now houses the Historical Museum. The Taipings were finally driven out in a terrible battle in which three-quarters of the city was destroyed and more than half the inhabitants killed or made homeless. The horror of civil war at that time is vividly illustrated by the story of twelve of the descendants of the nineteenth century Suzhou bibliophile Huang Pei-lieh, who drowned themselves in the lake in front of the family cemetery rather than fall into the hands of the Taiping army.

Suzhou gradually recovered, and today what is left of the old town retains much of its former charm. Many of the houses and open-fronted shops facing the tree-lined streets back onto one of the small canals that thread through the city. It is pleasant to walk beside the canals under the arched stone bridges, and past the old white-walled houses with grey tiled roofs.

Suzhou was once called the City of Pagodas; one of the most famous, the North Temple Pagoda (Beisi Ta), can be seen from the train as it draws into the station. Founded in the third century and recently restored, it towers 350 ft above the city.

The Twin Pagodas (Shuang Ta) in the east city were built in the tenth century by successful graduates in honour of their teacher. Suzhou was always proud of its scholars. The official Examination Halls had three thousand cells for candidates, and many Suzhou men won the highest honours and became members of the Hanlin Academy in Peking. Foreign residents dubbed the towers the Pen Pagodas, and the nearby Bell Tower, now ruined, the Ink Pagoda because it was shaped like a stick of Chinese ink. The Bell Tower was built in the seventeenth century as a gentle reminder to the God of Literature that local scholars were no longer doing so well.

When the Pagoda of the Temple of Benevolent Light (Ruiguang Si Ta), now in the southwest city was founded in the third century, it was in the city centre. Built in honour of the mother of the King of Wu, its condition was believed to govern the health of the ruling family. In the eighteenth century the Qian Long Emperor commanded hundreds of lanterns to be hung on it to light his mother's soul out of purgatory. A four foot high Buddhist column of silver and pearls, dedicated in 1013 by the wife of a Song official, was recently discovered during repairs to the pagoda.

The famous gardens of Suzhou go back to the tenth century. Unlike western gardens they contain no vistas and great fountains, few sweeping lawns and fewer formal beds of flowers. Some are extensive and some tiny, but all use concealment and suggestion to give the impression of a whole landscape in a small space. Water, rocks and pavilions are essential to the scene. The quiet enjoyment of walking round a Chinese garden is similar to that of slowly unrolling a handscroll painting of a natural landscape and being drawn step by step into the vision of its creator.

In the street outside a Suzhou garden the blank wall and inconspicuous gate offer no clue to the secret world within. From the gate an enclosed passage, decorated with patterns of stones, may lead to an ornamental window or a moongate framing a sudden view of pavilions and water; another opening may reveal a hill and trees, or rocks and plants against a plain white wall. In small pavilions there may be calligraphy extolling the view, penned by visiting scholars or by the tiny-footed ladies who passed so much time here and had little chance of wandering in a real landscape. Winding bridges cross lakes with goldfish, mandarin ducks and waterlilies. Small paths mount hillocks of piled-up rocks to stone seats on the summit, overlooking the waterside pavilions where friends gathered to talk and paint, to eat and play literary and drinking games, to watch the goldfish and the carp in the pools, and in the summer moonlight to compose poems on the shifting shadows of bamboo against a silver wall, or to get drunk and gamble away their inheritance, perhaps the garden itself.

Each decoration in the garden has a meaning; the bamboo, pine and prunus, called the Three Friends, are often planted or depicted together. The peony, lotus, chrysanthemum and prunus represent the four seasons. The pine tree and cranes mean longevity; the bat happiness; pomegranates fertility; and the mandarin ducks represent married bliss as they mate for life and pine away and die when separated. The decorative grey bricks set in the walls and carved with animated scenes of stories, plays and everyday life have been a distinctive feature of Suzhou gardens since the Ming dynasty.

Once there were more than a hundred gardens belonging to wealthy retired officials or merchants. Today only a few are preserved and open to visitors. Four of the most famous are described.

Wangshi Yuan
This beautiful small garden, dating back to the twelfth century, is down a quiet lane only a few minutes' walk to the west of the Suzhou Hotel. Restored in the eighteenth century by a retired official who named it the Garden of the Master of the Nets, it is known for its intricate and delicate lattices. A surprising number of buildings are placed harmoniously round the lake and stone hillock, and this garden provides a good illustration of the subtle art of creating an illusion of distance in a restricted space. A copy of the Ming style 'Hall for Staying the Spring' (Dianchun Yi), has been built in the Metropolitan Museum in New York.

Zhuo Zheng Yuan
Perhaps the most famous and one of the largest is the Humble Administrator's Garden in the northeast city, also known as the Garden of Plain Man's Politics. It is over four hundred years old, and was built by an imperial official who retired from a busy life in Peking to spend his old age in Suzhou. Sadly, after he died his son gambled the garden away. His residence beside the garden now houses the Suzhou Historical Museum, which contains local discoveries and exhibits connected with life in Suzhou.

Three fifths of the garden is occupied by lakes and it is noted for its exquisite pavilions and the harmony created between sumptuous and simple designs. Of the three distinctive parts, the new east garden is informal with lawns and streams; the central and main garden has large lakes, islands, pavilions and rocky hillocks; the west garden has smaller lakes, galleries and pavilions, and an inner section for azaleas, miniature gardens and dwarf trees.

Shizi Lin

Also in the northeast city, opposite the Humble Administrator's Garden, is the Lion Rocks Garden, built in the fourteenth century by four famous architects for the superior of the adjoining temple. He wished to create a memorial for his master, who had lived at 'Lion Cliff'. A maze of artificial hills, grottos and caves encircle the lakes. There are islands, a stone boat and strange lion-headed stones reflected in the water. Rocks such as these were chosen for their unusual shapes and then submerged in the nearby Taihu Lake for as long as twenty years to allow the waves to perforate and sculpt them. Connoisseurs would pay enormous sums to obtain one.

Ten wellknown painters are said to have helped lay out the garden, and one, Ni Can, left a famous ink painting of it. However, not everyone liked this garden. The eighteenth century author of a charming tale of married bliss, *A Floating Life*, Shen Fu, said that despite its ancient trees and elegant rocks, it looked to him more like heaps of clinker than hills and forests and concluded, 'for a uncultivated person like myself, I just fail to see where its beauty lies!'

Liu Yuan

The Liu, or Tarrying Garden is west of the city on the Liu Yuan Road. The name of an early owner of this sixteenth century Ming garden was Liu. True to the Chinese love of puns, when the garden was sold the sound 'Liu' was retained, but the meaning of the character chosen to write the name was changed to 'tarrying' or 'remaining', possibly because this was one of the few gardens not destroyed during the Taiping wars in the mid nineteenth century. It was restored and opened in 1954. The halls in the eastern section contain fine Ming furniture. Outside the Hall of Mandarin Ducks is a tall rock called the Cloudcapped Peak. Such rocks, reminiscent of modern sculpture, are a vital element in Chinese gardens and should ideally be 'unblemished, perforated, porous, textured, graceful, and rare'.

Further west along Liu Yuan Road is the seventeenth century West Garden Temple (Xi Yuan Si) which was rebuilt in the last century. Its Hall of 500 Lohans with larger than life gold figures and Buddhist shrines is important because it is a copy of the now destroyed Hall of 500 Lohans in the Lingyin Temple in Hangzhou.

Tiger Hill, about two miles northwest of the city, is the site of the tomb of King He Lu of Wu, the founder of Suzhou. When the King died in about 500 B.C., the outer compartments of his three-fold coffin were filled with treasure and his collection of the magnificent swords for which Suzhou was famous. Legend has it that just as the coffin was sealed in the tomb, a tiger sprang out of the hill to keep guard, hence its name.

From the foot of the hill a wide path leads across a stone bridge to a thirteenth century gateway; and up to a great stone that was cleft in two when the King tried his sword on it. The little pavilion honours a faithful widow who ended her own life when she was sold to a brothel after her husband's death.

At the top of the path is the Thousand Men Stone, said to be still stained with the blood of a thousand of the King's retainers who were slaughtered at his burial so that they could serve him after death.

Beyond a large rock carved with the words Tiger Hill Pool of Swords lies a deep cleft pool. Its waters cover the entrance to the King's tomb and successfully prevented later rulers from stealing the three thousand swords buried with him. The path crosses a bridge with two holes where the monks drew water, and winds up to the leaning pagoda that crowns the hill. This tenth century pagoda, one of the earliest to be decorated with paintings, was already leaning and in need of repair by the seventeenth century. The 'lean' of over 9 ft can be clearly seen from the east side; the pagoda rises to a height of 150 ft. During recent repairs a workman discovered cavities containing caskets and Buddhist offerings that established the exact date of the building as 961 A.D. The finds can be seen in the Suzhou Museum.

The Yenyan temple nearby was rebuilt in the last century.

Three miles west of Suzhou the Cold Mountain Temple (Hanshan Si), founded in the sixth century, was famous for its sonorous bell that inspired a haunting Tang poem still preserved on a stone tablet in the temple. The attractive buildings were recently restored.

Wuxi

Wuxi is an old silk city about thirty miles west of Suzhou on the edge of the Taihu lake, which is now a thriving commercial and textile centre with a population of 650,000. One of China's most ancient towns, its name was changed about two thousand years ago from 'Yuxi' (with Tin) to 'Wuxi' (Without Tin), when the local tin vein was exhausted. Since 1949 there has been extensive modern development, but the busy city is still crisscrossed with canals and cobbled streets. The Grand Canal, jammed with boats manoeuvred by voluble oarsmen, flows through the town centre past old whitewalled buildings with wide grey roofs.

Silk was first produced in the area about 1500 years ago. The Wuxi weavers still make some of the finest white silk in China, and sericulture remains one of the area's main industries.

In the northwest city the Huishan potteries make painted clay figurines similar to the ones they sold in the markest in the Ming dynasty. Then the figures were usually characters from literature or drama but today many modern subjects have been added.

Xihui Park contains the sixteenth century Longguang Pagoda and the Jichang Garden. This Ming garden was so admired by the Qian Long Emperor in the eighteenth century that he had it copied in the Summer Palace outside Peking where it is called the Garden of Harmonious Interests (Xiequ Yuan).

Most visitors stay on the shores of Taihu, famous for magnificent scenery

15 The famous Hall of the Sacred Mother at the Jin Ci Temple near Taiyuan, shaded by an ancient cypress said to be three thousand years old.

16 The Great Wild Goose Pagoda was built to store Buddhist scriptures brought from India in the Tang dynasty.

17 Before the Qian Ling, tomb of the Emperor Gao Zong and Empress Wu Zetian, stand the now mostly headless statues of border princes who gave allegiance to the Tang Emperors.

18 The entrance to the Forest of Tablets, the famous national collection of stone engravings at Xi'an.

19 Women from a commune near Suzhou stitching cloth shoe soles as they are rowed to work.

20 A workroom in the Suzhou Embroidery Research Institute.

21 The Leaning Pagoda on top of Tiger Hill at Suzhou is more than nine feet out of true.

22 Twilight at Five-Pavilion Bridge on the Narrow West Lake at Yangzhou.

23 A Jingdezhen artist painting a fragile 'eggshell porcelain' bowl.

24 Hanpokou Pavilion in the Lushan mountains.

25 The landscapes of classical Chinese painting come to life in Guilin.

26 Water buffalo ploughing in the flooded ricefields.

27 A lotus pool in the garden of Sansu Ci at Meishan, the birthplace of the poet Su Dongpo, on the road from Chengdu to Mount Emei.

28 Children sitting in a cart pulled by the ubiquitous 'walking tractor' which is making life easier for farm workers.

and for natural gardens and ornamental garden stones. It has more than ninety islands and fleets of picturesque fishing junks. Tours on the lake stopping at lakeside gardens, wooded islands and beauty spots provide a welcome break from city sightseeing.

It may be possible to go to one of the lakeside communes where they grow rice, tangerines and tea, and catch the fish and shrimps for which the lake is famous. Some communes produce cultured pearls.

Yangzhou

Yangzhou is one of the historic Yangtze Valley towns near the junction of the Grand Canal and the river, about fifty miles northeast of Nanjing. The Sui Emperor Yang Di linked it by canal to his capital at Luoyang in the seventh century and celebrated by arriving in a procession of spectacular dragon boats drawn by thousands of beautiful girls. It grew into one of the most prosperous, cultured and cosmopolitan cities in the empire. The range of its products casts doubts on Marco Polo's claim to have governed Yangzhou in the thirteenth century; he remarked only on its production of accoutrements for horses and men-at-arms, which does not suggest great knowledge of the city. The government salt monopoly, based on Yangzhou, made its salt merchants fabulously rich. Visits by the Qian Long Emperor in the eighteenth century gave them the opportunity for lavish display and gala performances by their superb private opera companies.

The White Dagoba (Bai Ta) beside the Narrow West Lake (Shouxi Hu), was built by a saltmerchant hoping to gain the Emperor's favour. He overheard the Emperor remark that only the lack of a white dagoba made the lake inferior to the North Lake in Peking. This attractive lake has developed from the old Tang city moat; its unusual Five Pavilions Bridge (Wuting Qiao), was added in 1757. South of the Lake Park the canal leads eastwards to the Imperial Landing where the Emperor's barge was moored beside his palace, a site now occupied by the Xiyuan Hotel.

Near the hotel a shrine on Plumblossom Hill (Meihua Ling) commemorates Shi Kefa (1601-45) who died defending Yangzhou against the onslaught of the Manchu conquerors. Down beside the moat, the picturesque Yangzhou Museum exhibits paintings by the seventeenth and eighteenth century 'Eight Eccentrics of Yangzhou' whose brilliant work was so unconventional that it was not admitted to the Manchu imperial collections.

During the Tang dynasty Yangzhou was already famous for its scholars, poets and gardens, but the vogue for beautiful gardens reached its peak in the eighteenth and nineteenth centuries. The city still maintains four fine examples in the seventeenth century Houyechun Garden, the nineteenth century Ge Yuan which belonged to a saltmerchant, the Xiaopangu, Little Winding Valley Garden of a governor-general, and in the nearby He Family Garden, one of the latest and more original of the Yangzhou gardens.

Not far away, the Peak of Literature Pagoda (Wenfeng Ta), dominates the Grand Canal. It was built in 1582 in the hope that its benign influence would help Yangzhou men to succeed in the official examinations and thus bring prestige to the city. The old Wenfeng Temple is now a park.

To the north on Wenhe Road, the sixteenth century Promoting Literature Pavilion (Wenchang Ge), with its triple circular roofs stood at the entrance to the Provincial College, established by edict of the first Ming Emperor in 1369. Wenchang, the God of Literature, was honoured by printers and bookbinders here. The nearby Stone Pagoda dates back to the Tang dynasty.

On the canal in the eastern suburb there is a Moslem cemetery with its own small mosque and the tomb of Behao Aldin (Puhading), a Moslem teacher who died in Yangzhou in 1275, a reminder of the time during the Tang and Song dynasties when thousands of Arab and Persian merchants lived in the city.

The renowed Buddhist monk Jian Zhen (688-763) was abbot of the Daming Monastery which lies in a low range of hills to the north. When two Japanese monks came to China to seek help from a master of sufficient authority to impose discipline on the lax Buddhist community in Japan, Jian Zhen decided to go back with them himself. After five voyages had ended in disaster he succeeded in reaching Japan in 753. Although blind he founded many monasteries including the Toshodai Temple in Nara where a dry lacquer statue of him, made from life, survives to this day. A copy of the main hall built by Jian Zhen at the Toshodai Temple was completed here in 1974 to commemorate the 1200th anniversary of his death, and a reproduction of the Nara statue of him, made by the Peking Central Academy of Arts, has been placed in it.

The different views from the three stories of the Level Distance Tower (Pingyuan Lou) not far away are said to demonstrate the theory of perspective devised by the Song painter Guo Xi; and legend says that the flowers of the ancient tree in the courtyard are the fabulous Red Jade Flowers whose fame brought the Sui Emperor Yang Di to Yangzhou in the seventh century.

Yangzhou today is the centre of a great rice producing area, with light industries and traditional crafts. One of China's major flood control and irrigation schemes, the Jiangdu Water Control Project, is east of the city.

Nanjing (Nanking)

Nanjing (Southern Capital), a provincial city with pleasant treelined streets, lies on the south bank of the Yangtze River. Its old Stone City wall rising above the river against a background of curving mountains has conjured up in the Chinese imagination an image of a 'crouching tiger' beside a 'coiling dragon'. Much of Nanjing was destroyed during the uprisings of the Taipings against the Manchus in the middle of the last century but there are still many things to be seen, even though they are only a modest reminder of the colourfulness of the city's history.

By the fifth century B.C. iron weapons were being made at Forge City Hill. The town grew steadily in importance until in the third century A.D. it became capital of Wu, one of the Three Kingdoms, whose founder built the Stone City fortress to command the Yangtze. As the capital of the Six (or Southern) Dynasties, it was a centre of learning, art and Buddhism; one of the best known sculptures of this period is a huge stone winged lion at the sixth century Liang tombs northeast of the city. It later became capital of the Southern Tang, one of the minor dynasties which followed the collapse of the Tang dynasty itself.

Nanjing next came into prominence when a Buddhist ex-monk overthrew the Mongol Yuan dynasty and in 1368 chose the city as capital of the new Chinese dynasty, the Ming. Enough of the city wall and gates which he built remain to show how he exploited the defensive potential of Lion Hill (Shizi Shan) in the north, the lakes to the east, and the old third century Stone City Fortress along the Qinhuai River on the west. The use of these natural defences explains the irregular shape of the city. For the building of the wall the Ming Emperor ordered one hundred and fifty-two prefectures to provide standard bricks each stamped with the name of the prefecture, the brickmaker and the overseer so that responsibility for any inferior materials would be clear. Inside the walls he built an Imperial City and Palace. Neither have survived: the site and a few remains are opposite the Provincial Museum on East Zhongshan Road. Only the Drum Tower (Gu Lou) remains of the Ming city. Its companion, the Bell Pavilion, opposite, was rebuilt in 1889 but it retained its bell, one of an original pair cast in 1388.

The third Ming Emperor transferred the capital to Peking in 1421 but Nanjing remained a city of consequence. Its textile industry continued to flourish and it became the home of an Imperial Manufactory, a bureau headed by a Textile Commissioner, charged with organising craftsmen to fulfil the enormous orders placed by the court in Peking. The Commissioner was personally responsible for the court pattern books but the skills and secrets of manufacture were handed down from father to son. There was a saying that 'when a stranger enters the workshop the looms stop and the craftsmen fall silent.' Modern Nanjing is still justly famous for silks and brocades.

In 1853 Nanjing was taken by the Taipings and remained their capital until 1864. Their leader, Hong Xiuquan (1814-64), having been influenced by Christian tracts into believing that he had been called by God to rule China, provided a focus for popular opposition to Manchu misrule. Temples were destroyed wherever the Taipings passed, a devastating loss to the beautiful Yangtze Valley, but they also introduced reforms, abolishing footbinding, opium and intemperance. Hong used as his palace the residence of the Manchu governor in the centre of the town. Much of Nanjing was burned during the recapture of the city by the imperial forces, but some larger buildings were reconstructed in the late nineteenth century. The Heavenly King's Palace has in recent decades been used for official residences and offices.

In 1927 Nanjing became the capital of the new republic of China. It was chosen in preference to Peking in order to offset some of the influence of the northern warlords and political factions.

In planning their capital the republican government sought to combine the old and the new, and the hand of Chinese architects who had studied abroad can be seen in a number of government offices in the city; not all were successful but at their worst they put up what one eminent Chinese architect called 'a Western building with a Chinese hat' and at their best achieved a harmonious blend of modern and traditional design.

Occupied by the Japanese in 1937, the city was reoccupied in 1945 by the Nationalists who abandoned it to the Communist forces in April 1949. Once again the capital was moved to Peking. Nanjing is now the capital of Jiangsu, a major industrial centre and China's largest inland port with a population of two and a half million. The double decker road and rail bridge across the Yangtze, opened in 1968, is the pride of Chinese bridge engineers. It dominates a river busy with merchant shipping, and passenger vessels and cruise boats plying between Shanghai and the upper Yangtze. Inside the walls the town has been extensively planted with trees to mitigate the oppressive summer heat that once earned it the title of 'one of the three furnaces' of China.

Some pleasant gardens and lakes remain to give a glimpse of the beauty of the old city. The Xuanwu Lake just outside the northeast wall, overlooked by the square Sanzang Pagoda, has been a pleasure garden for centuries and in summer is a mass of lotus blossoms. The Grieve-not Lake (Mochou Hu) outside the west wall is named for a girl who pined away after her young husband was posted to a distant frontier in the sixth century. In the Winning at Chess Hall (Shengqi Lou) General Xu Da won Mochou Lake from the first Ming Emperor. He also owned both the White Egret Park (Bailuzhou) in the southeast city and another of Nanjing's beauty spots, the traditional Zhan Garden, which though small still manages to combine all the features of the classic gardens in Suzhou. The Sweeping Leaves Tower (Saoyelou) in the west city was the home of the seventeenth century painter Gong Xian.

The Jiangsu Provincial Museum on East Zhongshan Road has a well-known and representative collection of paintings and ceramics with emphasis on regional finds, including some fine tomb figurines. A jade funerary suit from an Eastern Han tomb (25-220 A.D.) is among the exhibits.

The Purple Mountain (Zijin Shan) to the east of the city has several sites of interest, including the Xiaoling, the tomb of the first Ming Emperor, Hong Wu (1327-98). The approach to the tomb is guarded by pairs of massive stone figures of animals, generals and ministers. The tomb was badly damaged during the Taiping Uprising and little remains of the original buildings apart from the ramps leading up to the 50 ft high terrace that stands before the tumulus. Remains of the tombs of Ming officials and generals are scattered over the surrounding area.

Standing out against the green forest of the slopes of the mountain are the white stone and blue roofs of the Sun Yat-sen Mausoleum. It is a long but rewarding climb up the three hundred and ninety-two steps up to the hall containing his statue, carved in Paris in 1930 by Landowski, and inscribed quotations from his works. Regarded by Chinese as the Father of the Revolution which overthrew the Manchus in 1911, Sun Yat-sen died in Peking in 1925 where his body lay in state until his burial here in 1929.

Given the enormous destruction of temples and other buildings at the time of the Taiping Uprising it is not surprising that Nanjing has few monasteries compared to other cities of its size and historic importance. One of the survivors was the Monastery of the Valley of the Spirits (Linggu Si). It was moved to its present position at the foot of the mountain when its original site was chosen for the Emperor's tomb. In the wooded grounds is the vaulted Beamless Hall (Wuliang Dian), an unusual all-brick building, which may explain why it survived, and behind it a pagoda built in the 1930s.

The Qixia Monastery, restored in 1908, is fifteen miles away in the hills east of the city. Founded in 489 A.D. it was one of the four great monasteries of China in Sui and Tang times (sixth to tenth century). The 65 ft pagoda, decorated with carved reliefs, was built in the tenth century and to the left of it a path leads up to the Thousand Buddha Cliff beside rock carvings dating from five centuries earlier.

The scientifically minded will enjoy a visit to the Nanjing Observatory at the top of Purple Mountain which has a collection of ancient astronomical instruments including seven sent from the old Peking Observatory in 1931.

The tombs of the first and second Emperors of the Southern Tang dynasty (937-75) on Bulls Head Hill (Niu Shou Shan) have remarkable relief carvings of door guardians and dragons at the vault entrance. They lie south of the city, a few miles beyond the Terrace of the Rain of Flowers (Yuhua Tai), now a park, where in the sixth century a Buddhist monk is said to have preached so eloquently that flowers rained down from heaven. The coloured 'Rainflower Pebbles' on sale on the hill may interest flower arrangers. The park has a memorial to Communists executed here by the Nationalist Government.

Not far away an avenue of stone figures marks the tomb of the King of Borneo who died while visiting the Ming court in 1408.

Lushan

The Lushan mountains lie about fifteen miles south of the Yangtze town of Jiujiang. Motor roads now give access to its beautiful scenery and peaks rising above 4500 ft. Flowers familiar in European and American gardens grow wild in the mountains which abound in waterfalls, ruins and inscriptions left by a legion of scholars, and in romantic legends often at variance with history.

Visitors stay in the pleasant mountain town of Guling which grew out of a missionary estate. It began in 1895 when a Mr Little obtained from the local magistrate a ninety-nine year lease on some land which he sold in lots to missionary societies and businessmen for summer houses. The 'Guling Estate' developed quickly and soon had its own administration, hospital and even police force. A census in 1917 showed a foreign summer population of nearly two thousand living in over three hundred houses. Lushan had always been popular with Chinese visitors and the Nationalist Government built a summer retreat here. Since the Communists took power in 1949 the area has been developed as a health resort using the old summer houses and much new purposebuilt accommodation.

The road up the western valley out of the town passes the Flower Path (Hua Jing), a scenic area made famous by the Tang poet Bo Juyi (772-846) who, surprised to find the peach blossom still in flower in the mountain temples when it had already faded on the plain below, wrote a poem expressing his delight at discovering this 'second spring'.

The name of the Cave of the Immortals (Xianren Dong) nearby originates in the legend of the visit of one of the eight Daoist immortals, Lu Dongbin, who was presented with a sword there by the Fire Dragon.

On a hill to the west a pavilion shelters the Imperial Stone Tablet (Yubei Ting) erected by the first Ming Emperor, Hong Wu, who began his career as a monk in a temple at the foot of Lushan. Here he joined the uprising which eventually overthrew the Mongol dynasty and made him Emperor. The tablet tells the strange story of his relationship with a monk-magician who plagued him with weird prophecies, but finally sent a brother monk to cure him of a mortal illness. The site of the Heavenly Pool Monastery (Tianchi Si) further up is marked by the ruins of a pagoda from which there is a panoramic view to the west.

Many of the views in the area are breathtaking. Some claim that on a clear day the Han River 150 miles away to the west can be seen from the Hanyang Peak, the highest in the range. The pavilion on the hill above Hanpokou commands a superb view eastward over the Poyang Lake, hence the name 'the Pass which holds the Lake in its Mouth'. Not far away is one of the highest of the many waterfalls in the mountains, the Three Cascades (Sandie Quan), over which the water pours in three successive falls on its way to the Poyang Lake beneath.

Away to the south of Hanpokou lies the lovely Valley of the Residing Worthy One with the remains of the monastery of the same name (Qixian Si), founded in 489 A.D. The Residing Worthy One was probably Li Bo of White Deer Grotto fame (see below). Rivers and streams from the surrounding peaks fall in cascades into the gorge beneath, where they are transformed into torrents and whirlpools before finally plunging into the Bottomless Pool of Jade (Yuyuan Tan). The scene is a reminder in miniature of the Three Gorges of the Yangtze. Descending from the pool the path crosses the Bridge of the Three Gorges (Sanxia Qiao). This historic stone bridge, built one thousand years ago during the Song dynasty, crosses thirty yards in a single span, 90 ft above the pool called the Golden Well, and is one of the sights of Lushan.

The fame of Lushan as a Buddhist centre began when the monk Huiyuan (334-417) built himself a retreat beside the Dragon Spring. Time, the elements and anti-religious movements have taken their toll of the many monasteries built in the mountains since his time. But some modest and recent temple buildings and tea houses still mark the older sites, and are visited for the beauty of their surroundings. One of the most famous was the Monastery of the Yellow Dragon (Huanglong Si) near Guling. It was known then, as it is now, for the Three Precious Trees, a ginko (salisburia andrianifolia) and two enormous cedars (cryptomeria Fortuneii), reputed to have been planted more than a thousand years ago.

Scholars too came to Lushan. In the tenth century a State College was established at the White Deer Grotto (Bailu Dong), named after a deer kept by a scholar named Li Bo (773-831), not to be confused with the Tang poet of the same name. The college developed into one of the four great Academies of the Song dynasty. Zhu Xi, the commentator, editor and exponent of the Confucian Classics whose interpretation became a standard of Confucian orthodoxy, lectured and spent his declining years here. He is buried in the vicinity.

Keen gardeners will not want to miss the walk along the mountain ridge from Hanpokou Pavilion down to the 700-acre Botanical Gardens. Many of the flowers, shrubs and trees which grow wild on the mountain were introduced into European and American gardens early in this century, among them syringa, hydrangeas, forsythia, wisteria and azaleas, whose pinks, mauves and yellows cover the slopes in April.

At the end of a day in the mountains there is nothing more refreshing than a bowl of Cloud Mist Tea grown on the hillside, and perhaps a plate of the delicious local dish called the 'Three Rocks' made from an edible fungus, local frogs and fish, popularly called 'rock ears', 'rock chicken' and 'rock fish'.

Nanchang and Jinggang Shan

Nanchang, the capital of Jiangxi province, was the home of a great Ming painter, Bada Shanren, who was born in 1626, and lived at the Qingyunpu Monastery where there is an exhibition of his works.

The city owes its place in modern history to the Communist Uprising which took place here on 1 August 1927 in which Zhou Enlai, later Prime Minister, played a leading role. After the failure of the uprising the insurgents moved south to join the peasant forces led by Mao Zedong at their base high in the Jinggang Mountains, in the village of Ciping. In the valley on the other side of the pass are two more historic villages; Ninggang, where Mao and the future leader of the People's Liberation Army met in the spring of 1928, and Maoping, where they and other Communist leaders assembled to map out their strategy. The short village street in Ciping, where the revolutionaries lived and stored their weapons, is preserved as a national monument, and a number of buildings in Nanchang connected with the uprising have been turned into museums. Apart from their historic interest, the school and clan house in Maoping, and particularly the lovely old Ming academy in Ninggang, where the meetings took place, are fine examples of Jiangxi provincial architecture.

In 1934 the Communist forces broke through the 'iron noose' which the

Nationalists under Chiang Kai-shek had tried to draw around them, and set off on their historic Long March to their new base in Yan'an in Shaanxi province in northwest China.

Jingdezhen (Chingtechen)

Jingdezhen, a city famous for porcelain, is on the Chang River sixty miles east of the Poyang Lake. It acquired its name, which means the Market of Jing De, at the beginning of the eleventh century during the reign of the Song Emperor Zhen Zong whose reign title was 'Jing De'. Demand for the products of the southern kilns increased substantially after the Song Emperors lost north China, together with the northern kilns, to invaders from beyond the Great Wall and established the Southern Song court at a new capital at Hangzhou. Large supplies were also needed to support the profitable export trade to Japan, Korea and Southeast Asia and beyond, which helped to compensate for lost northern taxes. The Mongols, who conquered China in the thirteenth century, continued to encourage production both for their own use and to push up the tax revenues from the kilns. It was at this time that the world famous 'blue and white' ware was first made.

The succeeding Ming dynasty established an Imperial Manufactory in the town and the number of imperial and private kilns grew rapidly, producing a wide variety of wares, and, in the fifteenth century, blue and white of superb quality. Some of the great master potters of Jingdezhen were famous for hoodwinking solemn antiquarians with apparently perfect copies of famous pieces from earlier dynasties.

Jingdezhen was devastated in the wars which established the Manchu dynasty in power, but the potteries were soon rebuilt, and producing the exquisite wares for which this period is justly famous.

In Europe during the eighteenth century there was an enormous demand for Jingdezhen blue and white, and later for enamel painted ware. Many pieces were made to order from models and painted patterns sent from Europe. These alien designs were faithfully copied, even to the point of reproducing smudges caused by the patterns getting wet. Consignments to Europe went through Guangzhou. To reach that city the porcelain had to be carefully bound into straw bundles, shipped down the Gan River on junks similar to those still seen today, carried overland across the mountains and then on again by river to Guangzhou, where it was at last loaded onto the East Indiamen and other great sailing ships bound for Europe and America.

Jingdezhen owed its development in large degree to the availability in the surrounding area of fine clays, kaolin, and other materials used in the production of porcelain. The name 'kaolin' comes from the Chinese 'Gaoling' (high mountain range), a village thirty miles east of the town, where the fine clay was dug out. The work was highly organised in the potteries with specialisations closely tailored to production processes, mixing clays, colours, glazes, potting and decorating, etc. At the end of the line came the firing, for which the responsibility was heavy and where a mistake could mean disaster. Successful firing was rewarded, but failure brought punishment. Skills were handed down from father to son, and many families continued in the tradition until the decline of the industry in the mid nineteenth century, when the Taipings overran the town destroying the imperial kilns and scattering the potters.

Subsequent attempts to re-establish the prosperity of Jingdezhen were bedevilled by uncertain markets and increasing competition from foreign machine-made imports. The potteries today are producing increasingly fine wares but have still to rediscover the inspiration of the past. The museum provides a glimpse into the history of this unique town.

Wuhan

Wuhan, the capital of Hubei province, is a large industrial city passed by travellers on the train from Peking to Guangzhou. Six hundred miles from the sea, it comprises the three cities of Wuchang, Hanyang and Hankou and stands at the confluence of the Han River and the Yangtze River which is navigable at all times of the year. One of China's largest iron and steel complexes is ten miles down river at Qingshan.

The old city of Wuchang on the south bank has a special place in Chinese history. A revolt of the garrison here on 10 October 1911 was the spark for a much wider uprising which overthrew the Manchu dynasty and brought to an end centuries of imperial rule. There are few antiquities of note in the city, but a number of monuments mark the revolutionary sites. Wuhan University lies on the shore of the beautiful East Lake (Dong Hu). The statesman-poet Qu Yuan, in whose memory the Dragon Boat Festival is held, used to walk near the Xingyin Pavilion in the lake park. He drowned himself in the third century B.C. in despair over the misery brought on his country of Chu by the King's disregard for his wise counsel. The Hubei Provincial Museum nearby has an exhibition of regional discoveries and revolutionary history.

The second city, Hanyang, south of the Han River, was the site of China's first modern industry in the 1890s. Not far from the station a group of Chinese buildings mark the terrace named after a celebrated lute player, Boya, of the Spring and Autumn period (770-475 B.C.), remembered for destroying his lute in his grief when the one friend who really understood his music died. The nearby three hundred year old Guiyuan Si Monastery still has a Gallery of Five Hundred Lohans and its library of ancient sutras, containing some seven thousand texts and manuscripts from India, Burma and Sri Lanka.

In the third city, Hankou, on the north bank of the Han River, the architecture of some of the buildings on the riverfront is a reminder of the foreign concessions that flourished here after the city was opened to foreign trade in 1861.

Changsha

Changsha is the capital of Hunan, one of the great rice growing areas of China. Its major industries are still rice milling and transport, and tall white-sailed rice junks and small matcovered barges sail along the Xiang River past Orange Island with its groves of mandarin oranges and old houses once occupied by foreign merchants. Foreigners were not always welcome here. Some of the first missionaries attempting to land were repulsed by hails of brickbats from the shore. But this unpromising beginning did not deter the Yale Foreign Missionary Society from choosing Changsha early in the century as the site of the Yale in China centre which established a respected medical and scientific institute and a nursing school in the city.

Visitors come to Changsha today because Mao Zedong lived and taught here, to see the Mawang Dui exhibition at the Hunan Provincial Museum, and some to visit the historic Changsha Embroidery Workshops, where they make superb copies of early paintings.

Mao studied (1912-18) and later taught at the Hunan Teachers' Training College, a European style building rebuilt after 1949, which now houses a museum about his life in Hunan. He founded a political society in 1918 that met at Enjoying the Evening Pavilion (Aiwan Ting) on the other side of the river near Hunan University. The Pavilion is on Yuelu Hill, now a park, but once the site of the Yuelu Academy, famous in the Song dynasty. Only a few old temple buildings remain today.

One of the most fascinating exhibitions in the world is in the Hunan Provincial Museum. It comprises the tomb and the body of a woman buried in Changsha two thousand years ago. Sixty feet below ground the massive wooden tomb, now exhibited in a separate building and not to be missed, lay encased first in a layer of charcoal, then in a thick layer of white clay. To the astonishment of the archaeologists these were unbroken and provided a seal that almost perfectly preserved the contents of the tomb. Inside was a black outer coffin surrounded by rectangular compartments containing over one thousand items. Woven bamboo cases full of silk, clothes, food and medicine were still tied and sealed with the seal of 'the Chamberlain of Marquis Dai.' There were embroidered, painted and printed robes, and rolls of silk, gauze and brocade. The one hundred and eighty four pieces of red and black lacquerware, some in perfect condition, included many objects never seen before and known only from descriptions in literature.

The wooden figures placed in the coffin symbolised living retainers, some painted, others dressed in exquisite woven silk robes. Musical instruments, games, fans, mirrors and even a false hairpiece and a staff were not forgotten. An inventory written on three hundred and twelve bamboo slips has been invaluable to paleographers, and imitation money helped date the tomb to 174-145 B.C.

The black coffin proved to be the outermost of four fitting perfectly into each other. The second, again black, was painted with striking swirling figures; the third was red with dragons, tigers and deer, and the innermost covered with silk with a pattern made of downy feathers, the first example of such an outer cover on a coffin. Over this cover lay the earliest painted silk funeral banner ever found, probably placed there after having been carried in the funeral procession. It is T shaped, six feet long and depicts the occupant of the tomb herself leaning on her staff and surrounded by mythical figures to help her through the underworld. When archaeologists removed the twenty embroidered and painted shrouds of silk and linen they were amazed to find a body with skin and muscles still elastic and internal organs intact. They identified her blood group and also discovered that she died soon after overindulging in musk melons. She proved to be the Marchioness of Dai buried close to her husband and son.

Her body and the contents of her tomb are now in the museum, together with weapons and other items from the two other less well-preserved tombs. Excellent reproductions of some of the tomb contents are sold in the museum shop.

Shaoshan

Many people also visit Mao's birthplace at Shaoshan, a journey of about fifty miles through picturesque villages and intensively cultivated farm-land. The home where he was born in 1893 is a typical mudbrick Hunan farmhouse with wide overhanging roof, set in pleasant countryside. The Mao Family Clanhouse which Mao Zedong frequented when he was in the village is an attractive building with grey roofs and white walls and anyone you talk to in the vicinity will probably also be surnamed Mao. It is common in Chinese villages for many families to have the same surname.

The exhibition in the modern museum illustrates Mao's life and early Communist party history. A visit there can be preceded by lunch at the small new hotel.

5. The South

South China is a semitropical region of forested hills, with many rivers draining into the main West River (Xijiang) system, and densely populated valleys so fertile that rice can be double cropped. The superb scenery in areas where fantastic outcrops of limestone rock ('karst') tower above the plains is renowned throughout China. In the mountains, nature reserves, such as the sub-tropical rainforest on Dinghu Mountain, now protect many rare species of trees, plants and animals, ranging from the rarer bamboos the huge xianmu tree (bairetiodrendon Hsienmu) and scaly anteaters, gem-faced civets and chestnut backed bulbul birds.

The inhabitants of this area speak dialects which are completely different from those of their northern compatriots.

Guangzhou (Canton)

The capital of Guangdong province is Guangzhou (Canton) a large and sprawling city of two and a half million people which combines a trade centre, port and industrial area. Originally a walled city, it was substantially modified in the 1920s when the walls were removed and new roads laid out. The Guangzhou Kowloon Railway was opened in 1911. The inhabitants of the city, very different in temperament from those of the north, have always demonstrated a fiery independence of spirit, and during the first three decades of this century it was the scene of regular revolutionary activity. After the arrival of the Communists in 1949 there began a second and more ambitious phase of reconstruction and industrial development. Until the 1970s the Guangzhou Export Commodities Fair, held in the spring and autumn of each year, was, apart from Peking, the main point of contact for foreign businessmen. The Fair is still held but commercial contacts with the west are now conducted direct by a larger number of Chinese cities.

Guangzhou is the entry point for many visitors. It is not as rich in historical monuments as many other cities of its size, but it offers some fine gardens, a few temples, visits to communes and craft workshops, shopping in the large Friendship Store and other department stores, and the Guangzhou Antique Shop in Wende Bei Lu, not far from the Peasant Institute, and superb food in restaurants serving dishes from the celebrated

Guangzhou cuisine. There is an extensive exhibition of the products of the area in the former Ancestral Temple of the Chen Family on Zhongshan Road.

Guangzhou can trace its origins back to two hundred years before the birth of Christ, when at the time of the Qin empire, General Zhao Tuo came to conquer the 'southern barbarians', the numerous non-Chinese races who inhabited the area. The walls that he put up were rebuilt many times, but all that remains of them today is the 5-storey Tower that Dominates the Sea (Zhenhai Lou) first built in 1381 which marks the highest and most northerly point of the old walls. Its strategic position as a fort commanding the whole city was evident to the British and French forces who used it as a strongpoint during their occupation of Guangzhou from 1857-61. It now houses the Guangzhou Museum which displays a collection of local ceramics and has an exhibition illustrating the history of the region.

Indian monks preached Buddhism in Guangzhou where it gradually grew in influence until the city could boast four great monasteries. The oldest and most famous is the Guangxiao Si. The Indian monk, Dharmayas as taught here in the fourth century, followed in 520A.D. by his fellow countryman Bodhidharma, founder and first Patriarch of the Chan (Zen) School of Buddhism in China. A Chinese monk, Hui Neng, is honoured in the Hall of the Sixth Patriarch. In the Tang dynasty (618-907) a rival named Shen Xiu of the northern Chan School claimed the succession from the Fifth Patriarch but Hui Neng's southern School carried the day. The hair shaved from his head at his ordination is reputedly buried beneath the monastery pagoda, one of the few Tang pagodas still existing in south China. The iron pagodas dating from 963 and 967 are also much prized as two of the oldest in the area.

The Haichuang Temple south of the river in a park named after it was much enlarged by the Manchu Emperors in the eighteenth century. It has an interesting connexion with England. Both Lord Macartney in 1794 and Lord Amherst in 1816 were lodged at the temple on their journeys home via the Grand Canal and the river route to Guangzhou after leading the first two British Embassies to China.

Although an older foundation, the buildings of the Hualin Temple date from 1655 and its Hall of 500 Lohans only from 1846. No. 108 in the list of the Lohan is often presented as representing Marco Polo and unlike others he does wear a wide hat: but his inclusion among the Lohan is no more than a local fancy. The 'Flowery Pagoda' (Hua Ta) of the Temple of the Six Banyan Trees (Liurong Si) has also been restored and rebuilt many times since it was first erected in 537. The temple takes its name from the trees in its courtyards which were admired by the Song poet Su Dongpo when he visited the temple in 1099.

The minaret of Guangzhou's oldest mosque, called by the Cantonese the Bare Pagoda (Guang Ta) because of its plain exterior, can trace its ancestry back to 627 when large numbers of Arab and Persian traders lived in the city; but the present building is modern. Equally impressive are the twin

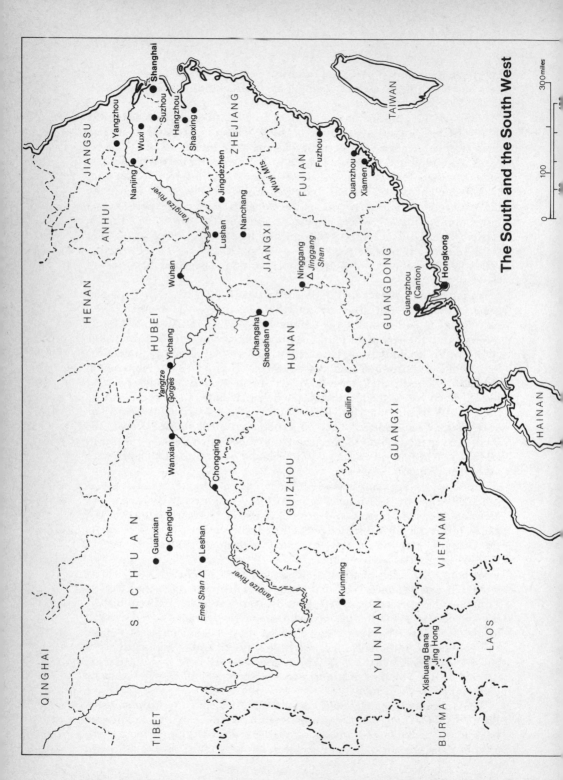

The South and the South West

Gothic towers of the former French Catholic Cathedral, consecrated in 1863, which stand out against Guangzhou's skyline as the symbol of a once thriving Catholic community.

It is as 'the cradle of the revolution' that Guangzhou is best known to the younger generation of Chinese. Sun Yat-sen failed in his first attempt to organise an uprising in the city against the Manchus in 1895 partly because his supporters from Hong Kong failed to arrive in time. In April 1911 a further revolt was staged in the city. It too was a failure and the seventy-two heroes who died in it are commemorated in the Huanghuagang Park and Mausoleum where they are buried. The Wuchang Uprising of October of the same year brought about the downfall of the Manchus and China fell into disunity. By 1921 Sun Yat-sen was back in Guangzhou as Provisional President but his power was confined to the south. The blue roofed Memorial Hall built after his death in 1925 stands where he took his oath of office. In the following year Chiang Kai-shek led the northern expeditionary forces out of the city in a campaign that would eventually unify China. But in 1927 having won the Yangtze cities, he turned on his erstwhile Communist allies. The thousands who died in the fighting in Guangzhou are honoured in the Memorial Park to the Martyrs of the Guangzhou Uprising.

Before the split Nationalist and Communists had co-operated. Mao Zedong himself taught at the Peasant Institute where revolutionaries were trained for work in the rural areas, which was housed in one of the city's three Confucian temples. Now preserved as a museum it has a double interest as a revolutionary monument and as one of the few remaining examples of a Confucian temple where the simplicity of the architecture and decoration is in marked contrast to the elaborate decoration of its Buddhist and Daoist counterparts.

The Foreign Trade Centre

Thousands of Arabs and Persians were trading in Guangzhou in the seventh century, in ivory, precious stones, incense, rhinocerous horn and other medicaments. There was little trace of them left when the Europeans arrived in the sixteenth century to establish their 'factories' and start three hundred years of bickering over trading rights with Chinese officialdom. The factories, part warehouse, part office, and part living quarters grew as opulent as any London club. There were elegant dining rooms on the upper floor capable of seating a hundred beneath crystal chandeliers, libraries, billiard rooms and gentlemen's bedrooms. The clublike atmosphere was enhanced by the refusal of the Chinese to allow European women to reside there. So seriously did they take this prohibition that when a few wives visited the factories all trade was stopped until they left.

The factories were destroyed during the Opium War in 1842 and again in 1857. The British and French then abandoned them in favour of a water logged site which they converted into a foreign enclave, Shamian Island. It proved a profitable proposition for the British Government, who sold off lots to merchants from Hong Kong for more than the cost of the site. 'The parsees bid right royally against our first class merchants for front lots', observed the British Consul with satisfaction. The modern visitor can spend a pleasant evening taking a Chinese meal in the Economy Restaurant on the island and strolling through the old streets and along the river front of the former British and French concessions. The opening of many other ports to foreign trade in the second half of the nineteenth century somewhat reduced the importance of Guangzhou as a foreign trade centre but it came into its own once again when the Chinese Export Commodities Fair was set up there in 1957.

For the garden lover the extensive Guangdong Botanical Gardens and the smaller Chinese Orchid Garden at Yuxiu Hill can offer more than two thousand species of semi-tropical plants and the favourite Chinese orchids (cymbidieae).

For the adventurous gourmet Guangzhou is a paradise. The names of the Snake Restaurant on Jianglan Road, and the Game Restaurant on Beijing Road speak for themselves. The food at the Beiyuan (North Garden) on Dongfeng Road (known for sweet-sour fish with pine seeds, and stuffed crab), and the Nanyuan (South Garden) south of the river on Qianjin Road, may be less exotic, but its standard is matched by the charm of the 'teahouse' architecture. Both as a teahouse and a restaurant the Banxi Restaurant at Liwan Park is superb — the price matches the quality (try crabmeat and sharks fins; tea leaf chicken; and excellent fried rice). The Guangzhou specialities, the delicious small savoury or sweet stuffed dumpling and rolls (dim sun) are served in the mornings. The park is the successor to the pleasure gardens and villas which once drew to Liwan the high society of old Guangzhou.

Outside the city there is typical southern scenery in the White Cloud Mountain Park (Baiyun Shan) nine miles to the north but the old monasteries once there have largely disappeared. For those with time to go further afield, it is fifty miles to one of China's favourite spas, the Chonghua Hot Springs and seventy miles to Seven Star Crags (Qixing Yan) where the combination of hills, lakes and caves is a small scale version of the fantastic scenery of Guilin.

Much nearer is the old town of Foshan, once one of the Four Great Marts of China and a port which could rival Guangzhou. Its historic potteries, now producing tableware and figurines, still preserve their original Dragon Kiln which featured a series of connected firing chambers each one step higher than the other between the firebox at one end and the chimney at the other, to allow a variety of wares to be fired at different temperatures. From the Shiwan potteries nearby, which also produce figurines and tableware, have come a large proportion of the highly decorated ceramic tiles, with scenes from Chinese folk tales, animals and fish which decorate the roofs of Daoist temples in China and Hong Kong.

Foshan's Ancestral Temple (Zumiao), a Song foundation, has a remarkable array of these tiles on its typically southern steeply pitched roofs. The central feature of the Zumiao is the Temple of the Spirit's Response (Lingyin Si) whose three halls are dedicated to the Emperor of the North

(Bei Di), a Daoist god of whom there is a large bronze statue, cast in 1452, in the Hall of the Purple Clouds (Zixiao Gong) the main hall of the temple (Bei Di is the Pak Tai of the Hong Kong Daoist temples). There is a story that in the Ming dynasty when Foshan was surrounded during a peasant rebellion the defenders prayed for deliverance to Bei Di and when the rebellion was defeated, attributed the defeat to 'the Spirit's Response', hence the name given to the temple and the ceremonial archway in front of it.

The temple stage with its fine gilded wooden screen carved with scenes from traditional stories was erected in 1658. The Taipings, who came near to overthrowing the Manchu dynasty in the middle of the last century, are said to have raised funds through performances on this stage.

The Renshou Temple is now an exhibition centre displaying paper cuts, lanterns and other local handicrafts.

Guilin

The town of Guilin is a Chinese painting come to life. Soaring pinnacles of limestone jutting into the sky tower over the Li River and the surrounding countryside. This fantastic scenery has been celebrated by Chinese poets and artists for thousands of years. One described the river as 'a green gauze sash' and the pinnacles as 'dark jade hairpins'.

The city was once known as the 'City of the Banyan', probably on account of the trees which grew on the wall next to the modest Tang dynasty gate which still stands on the banks of the Banyan Lake. The lake was once part of the city moat. The tree grew to such a size that its roots reached from the top of the wall to the ground beneath and people emerging from the gate appeared to come out from the Banyan tree itself.

The Ming rulers abandoned the old Tang Wall when the nephew of the first Ming Emperor, Jing Jiang, expanded Guilin. In 1372 he commenced work on the palace in the centre of the city. Of its complex of great halls, ancestral temple, sacrificial altar and other buildings only the wall and gates and a fine carved marble stairway which led to the main palace still remain.

Within the grounds, the Peak of Solitary Beauty (Duxiu Feng) towers over the town. The pool at the foot is all that remains of the palace garden. The last of the Mongol Emperors was for a time exiled to a temple on the peak before his accession to the throne. It was alleged that his mother, a concubine, had already been pregnant by the last descendant of the Song Emperors when she was taken into his supposed father's harem, and that in consequence he was not the true heir.

The Duxiu Feng is typical of the pinnacles in and around the city which give fine views of its lakes and the Li River. Each has its descriptive name, such as the Peak of Layered Clouds (Diecai Shan), the Eddying Waters Hill (Fubo Shan) and Elephant Trunk Hill (Xiangbi Shan) to name but a few, so called because of natural features or some supposed likeness. Most are covered with inscriptions carved on their rock faces or temple relics. Each has engendered a variety of folk tales to go with its name.

To add to its remarkable scenery Guilin can offer those interested in art a number of fine engravings and carvings. The walls of the Huagaishan Temple carry engravings made in the seventeenth century of drawings of sixteen Buddhist lohan, originally made by the monk Guan Xiu (832-912) in his craggy caricature style. Other rare examples of his work are in the Tokyo Museum. A self-portrait of Mi Fei (1051-1107) who served as an official in Guilin is carved on the walls of the Returned Pearl Cave (Huanzhu Dong) at the foot of Fu Bo Hill. His style, known from the works of imitators, had great influence on Chinese painting but no work attributable to him has yet been fully authenticated. Some Buddhist statues dating from the Tang dynasty are in the same riverside cave. Two each of a set of eight engravings of paintings of orchids and bamboo by the seventeenth century Guilin painter, Li Bingshou, are at Diecai Hill, Fubo Hill, Yu Hill and Sixian Hill.

Military operations over the centuries and Japanese bombing during the last war have left few historic buildings in Guilin. The Flower Bridge (Huaqiao) to the east of the city is of Song construction. The stupa in the south of the town is all that remains of a former seventh century temple, the Kaiyuan Si.

But tourists come to Guilin, not for its buildings but for its scenery and for the six hour trip down the Li River to the little town of Yangshuo. The combination of tree covered pinnacles reflected in the water, miniature gorges, racing currents, traditional boats and cormorant fishing on the river produces scenes that are unique and breathtaking in their loveliness. The one hour bus ride back to Guilin has its own delights in the stop at the huge and ancient banyan tree near the traditional ferry to an old Tang dynasty village and the ride through flooded rice fields reflecting the surrounding pinnacles.

Those with time to spare can also visit the extensive Reed Flute Cave (Ludi Dong) and the Seven Star Crag Cave (Qixingyan Dong).

Fujian (Fukien Province)

Large numbers of overseas Chinese who live in Southeast Asia and elsewhere in the world trace their ancestry to the coastal areas of Fujian province and still maintain family connections there. The province, famous for its tea and lacquer, is mountainous, difficult of access and throughout history has looked towards the sea. Its people have their own dialects, largely unintelligible to the rest of China. Over the centuries many of them have sought their fortunes overseas and succeeding generations are now returning in increasing numbers to visit their home towns. Since the opening of the province to tourism in 1979 foreign visitors are beginning to follow in their wake.

The provincial capital is Fuzhou (Foochow) a thriving port on the Min River, whose two most famous temples are the Xichan and Hualin Monasteries. The Song dynasty Luoxing Pagoda down river at Mawei has been a navigation mark for Fuzhou sailors for nearly a thousand years. China's earliest naval college was established in the city in 1867.

About seven miles from Fuzhou the Gu Mountain rises 3000 ft over the north bank of the river. The centre point of this scenic area is the Monastery of the Ever-Flowing Spring (Yongquan Si) founded in 908 but repaired and expanded many times. Its library still preserves a large collection of sutras donated by the Manchu Kang Xi and Qian Long Emperors.

Quanzhou

Further down the coast is the ancient port of Quanzhou, Marco Polo's 'Zaiton' which he believed to be one of the two biggest ports in the world. It had a large community of Arab merchants, and the tombs of two Mohammedan teachers who taught there in the seventh century are preserved at Lingshan east of the city. The Quanzhou Mosque, founded in 1010, is one of the most famous in China. A rare reminder that Manichaeism found its way to China still exists in a stone tablet at a modest monastery on Wanshan Mountain. Daoism is represented by a monumental statue of Laotze carved in the Song dynasty from the natural rock in the hills to the north of the city. Another link with Quanzhou's past as a major trading port was discovered in 1974 when the hull of a wooden junk built in the latter part of the Southern Song dynasty (1127-1279) was found with the remains of tortoiseshell, frankincense, mercury and rare woods still in its hold. A special exhibition hall has been built to preserve it.

The magnificent Kaiyuan Buddhist Monastery nearby was first founded in 686 when it was known as the 'Lotus Temple'. When in 738 the Tang Emperor decreed the establishment of Kaiyuan temples in all prefectures ('kaiyuan' indicated a reign period: 738 was the 26th year of 'kaiyuan'), some compromised by changing the names of existing temples, as did Quanzhou. The monastery has a fine Great Hall, known as the Hall of a Hundred Pillars, but it is more famous for the twin pagodas on each side of the hall which have become a symbol of the city. First built in wood, they were later reconstructed in brick and then in turn clad in granite between 1228 and 1250.

Xiamen (Amoy)

The port of Xiamen, further south again, is better known to foreigners as Amoy. Until the oubreak of the war with Japan there was an International Settlement on the small island of Gulangyu, west of the harbour, where most of the foreigners lived. A memorial hall on the island is dedicated to Zheng Chenggong, often known as Koxinga, whose naval forces defied the Manchus at the end of the Ming dynasty. Driven off the mainland, he expelled the Dutch from Taiwan and established his own rule there. The sharply upturned roofs and ornate architecture of Xiamen's South Putuo Temple is in striking contrast with the more restrained lines of northern Buddhist temples.

The South

The town of Jimei, about fifteen miles away was the home of Chen Jiageng, better known as Tan Kah-kee, the Chinese philanthropist, who having made his fortune in Singapore, endowed many educational establishments in and around his home town including a navigation school, and was one of the founders of Amoy University. Many of the buildings are a remarkable mixture of Chinese and western architectural styles.

Wuyi Shan

Among the scenic attractions of the province are the landscapes of Wuyi Mountain near the town of Chong'an, close to the border with Jiangxi, where the beautiful Nine Curves Stream winds through spectacular ravines and wooded hills. By the eleventh century the area was famous for its tea, the best of which, Dragon Tea, was reserved for the Emperor. During the Mongol Yuan dynasty a large tea garden was planted here and named the Imperial Tea Garden.

For many years people were intrigued by 'boat coffins' which were lodged high on cliffs overlooking the rivers and in inaccessible caves. Local superstition had it that they were 'fishing boats of the immortals'; Daoist influence in the area was strong. In 1978 one was recovered complete and found to contain human remains. There is still much discussion about their date. Carbon 14 tests suggest that they are more than three thousand years old, but a number of experts date them several centuries later because the standard of workmanship suggests the use of iron tools. The practice of lodging coffins on cliffs and in remote caves was apparently widespread among peoples in a number of south China provinces. Similar coffins have been recovered in Box Bellows Gorge (Fengxiang Xia) in the Yangtze Gorges.

6. The Southwest

Sichuan

The western part of the province of Sichuan bordering Tibet is mountainous and sparsely populated, much of it lying nearly 10,000 ft above sea level with peaks rising to 25,000 ft. The Sichuan Basin in the east and centre of the province is surrounded by mountain ranges and watered by navigable rivers and is one of the most fertile and densely populated parts of China. The name 'Sichuan', the Four Rivers, originated in the eleventh century division of the province into four areas, called the Four Circuits of Rivers and Gorges (Chuanxia Silu). The names of the old kingdoms which once existed in the province, Ba for the east and Shu for the whole area, are still sometimes used.

Although so fertile and well watered that it was called the Earthly Paradise, Sichuan was extremely difficult of access. The route from the east lay through the powerful rapids of the Yangtze Gorges, and from the old capitals in the Yellow River area along precarious wooden walkways over dangerous mountain passes. This isolation engendered a fierce sense of independence and Sichuan became at times a separate or virtually separate kingdom.

The province is the home of the Giant Panda. A recent survey has shown that a thousand still live in eight specially protected nature reserves in Sichuan, and in two other reserves in the neighbouring provinces of Gansu and Shaanxi. Scientists from the World Wildlife Fund are assisting with the design of the research and protection centre at the Wolong Nature Reserve in Wenchuan county northwest of Chengdu.

Chengdu

Coveted for its riches by all Chinese dynasties at times of turmoil, Sichuan became a refuge for aristocrats and scholars who enhanced the reputation of its capital Chengdu as a centre of art and learning. It was an ancient city already renowned for weaving, lacquer and crafts in 220 A.D. when the Han dynasty fell and the Chinese empire split into the Three Kingdoms of Shu in the west, Wu south of the Yangtze and Wei in the north. Liu Bei, the heir to the Han dynasty, became ruler of the Kingdom of Shu, with Chengdu as his capital. This period is immortalised in the *Story of the Three Kingdoms,* a swashbuckling tale of battles and heroes constantly retold by storytellers, in plays and opera.

For more than a thousand years there has been a memorial temple dedicated to Liu Bei's Prime Minister Zhu Geliang in Chengdu. The two original temples, one dedicated to Liu Bei himself and one to Zhu Geliang, were combined in 1672. Some of the buildings in what is known as the Warlords Temple date from that time. In the side buildings in the second courtyard the painted seventeenth century statues of generals and officials who served Liu Bei have tablets inscribed with their exploits in front of them.

The central building is the Memorial Hall to Liu Bei who is shown wearing a golden robe. He is flanked by his sworn brothers, the generals Zhang Fei, with his grandsons, and Guan Yu with his sons. Guan Yu, who was later deified as God of War, is shown wearing an Emperor's long beaded mortarboard because he was posthumously granted the rank of Emperor. These three heroes, as familiar in China as the Three Musketeers in the west, took an oath to fight, live and die together in the attempt to win the empire for Liu Bei. But after years of campaigning, the Kingdom of Wei triumphed in 263 A.D.

Beyond the next courtyard is the Memorial Hall to Zhu Geliang, the fourth member of the band of heroes and their brilliant military strategist. Holding his characteristic feather fan he is shown with his son and grandson. In front of the hall is a striking iron incense burner with twin standing figures as handles. The path to the west leads through gardens to the tomb of Liu Bei, who was buried here in 223 A.D.; the present tomb was set up in the eighteenth century. The modern building to the south built in traditional style houses a collection of exhibits from the Three Kingdoms period together with a small art and souvenir shop.

In the mid-eighth century the Tang Emperor Xuan Zong took refuge in Chengdu after being driven from his capital at Xi'an by a rebellious general, once the protegee of his imperious concubine, the beautiful and extravagant Yang Guifei. As they began their perilous journey through the mountains to Sichuan the imperial guard threatened mutiny if Yang Guifei, to whom they attributed the empire's misfortunes, were not punished by death. Forced to consent to her being strangled, the Emperor never recovered from his grief and finally abdicated in favour of his son.

A few years later the poet Du Fu, who wrote movingly and bitterly about the horror of these wars, arrived in the city. He built a modest retreat just outside the walls known as Du Fu's Thatched Hall (Du Fu Cao Tang) and on its site a group of attractive buildings now house a museum of his life and writings.

In the Riverview Pavilion Park (Wangjianglou) on the south bank of the Brocade River (Jinjiang) there is a well named for another writer of the period, the Tang poetess Xie Tao who made a special paper with the well water. Xie Tao paper is still sold today for painting and calligraphy. New brocades were washed in the Brocade River and Chengdu was known as the

Brocade City at the time, and in the following Song period, because of the superb quality of its weaving. Paper was also produced in qualities fine enough to be offered as tribute to the Song court and the city was a centre of printing. In 972 the first Song Emperor chose the city to undertake the first complete printed edition of the Buddhist scriptures, the Tripitaka, a task that took ten years and involved the cutting of 130,000 wood blocks. At the time more books were being printed in Chengdu than anywhere else in China. The steady growth of its commercial importance is illustrated by the fact that ten of the great merchant families were issuing their own notes, constituting what would today be a note-issuing bank.

When the Mongols arrived they devastated Chengdu after overcoming a heroic defence, but the city quickly recovered its prosperity. When the Ming came to power the son of the first Emperor was made Viceroy. At the strictly controlled official Horse and Tea Mart established here, tea was bartered with the border peoples for their horses, so vital to the defence of the realm. But with the decline of the dynasty the area was once more plunged into the misery of war.

Again Chengdu recovered and became a beautiful walled and moated provincial capital which combined an imperial city, a Manchu city housing the Manchu garrison and a residential Chinese city. Fifty mandarins of high rank lived there and the triennial provincial examinations attracted fifteen thousand candidates. Chengdu's reputation as a centre of education has continued. It was the home of the West China Union University, a missionary enterprise founded in 1910 in which the Canadian Methodist Mission had a strong contingent, and today Sichuan University occupies a site next to the Wangjianglou Park.

The Sichuan Provincial Museum in the People's Park has a collection of tiles from Han tombs decorated with vivid pictures of daily life, as well as rubbings, tomb figurines, bronzes and exhibits from regional excavations. These include a jade belt and buckle believed to have belonged to Wang Jian, who at the end of the ninth century ruled his independent state from Chengdu. His tomb was discovered in 1942 in the western suburbs of the city. Part of the museum is devoted to an exhibition on the Long March.

The Wenshu Yuan, formerly a Buddhist monastery, is now the Museum of Religion. Its most famous building, the Sutra Library (Cangjinglou) still retains some volumes of its once large collection, including rare Indian and Japanese sutras.

Modern Chengdu is of growing importance as the capital of Sichuan province, an industrial centre and the junction for the railways which link it with Chongqing in the east, Kunming in the south and Baoji to the north. Its smaller workshops still produce the ornaments, silver filagree jewellery and decorated knives so popular with the border peoples, particularly the Tibetans. There is a shop in the market reserved for them to which foreign visitors may also be admitted.

Chengdu restaurants specialise in hot food; it is the home of hot beancurd with beef and chillies (mapo doufu). Other good dishes are pork with onions (huiguo rou), and hot diced chicken (hula jiding).

Xindu

In the town of Xindu, northwest of Chengdu, the Cassia Lake Park (Gui Hu) was once the home of the Ming scholar Yang Shen and his poetess wife. To symbolise their happiness together they designed a pavilion with two wings of the kind seen in the park today. The newly built library has an exhibition devoted to them.

Xindu is more famous for its large and once influential Buddhist monastery, the Baoguang Si. There has been a temple on the site for nearly two thousand years. It was much expanded when the young Tang Emperor Xi Zong established a temporary palace here in 881 after his capital at Changan had been occupied by rebels; two carved pillars remain from that time. The thirteen storey square pagoda in the second courtyard is in the Tang style; some of the present buildings are Ming but most are Qing and later. In layout the Baoguang Si follows the typical pattern of the larger Buddhist monasteries. The wealth of the monastery is reflected in some good antique furniture in the abbot's quarters and in his attractive gardens. It has been the custom since Song times for visiting artists to present a painting to the monastery, and its collection includes works by modern painters such as Xu Beihong.

The large Sutra Hall built in 1851 is of particular interest. The library upstairs, whose walls are decorated with Qing paintings, still has a complete set of the more than six thousand volumes of the Buddhist canon in Chinese. In the Hall of Meditation below, the Abbot's chair stands before a large painting of a lion. The screens on either side can be removed to reveal the platform where new monks were ordained. The Hall of Lohan with the Qing statues is intact, and there is also a Hall of Patriarchs which housed memorial tablets in honour of former abbots and founders of 'monk families'. As each novice entered the monastery he was assigned to a 'master' as his new spiritual father; in time he became a master himself, thus continuing the 'family'.

Qingcheng Shan

About thirty miles west of Chengdu is the old Daoist monastery at Qingcheng Shan, the Grotto of the Heavenly Teacher (Tianshi Dong). Its main hall, the Hall of the Three Pure Ones, stands on a wooded hill wrapped in an atmosphere of dark tranquillity. The upper storey is lightened by a magnificent series of decorated Ming panels. Daoist monasteries have dominated the mountain since 842 A.D. when a dispute with the Buddhists about the right to build temples on it was settled in favour of the Daoists by the Tang Emperor Xuan Zong.

Guanxian

The prosperity of Chengdu in the earliest times depended on fertile land and good irrigation. Near the town of Guanxian on the Min River about 25 miles northwest of Chengdu a scholar-engineer, Li Bing, devised a scheme in 256 B.C. for controlling the floodwater and diverting it into an irrigation system. Although the modern system has been enormously expanded, Li Bing's dyke, the Dujiangyan, remains the key to it to this day. He built up a long island in the middle of the river dividing it in two and making a new inner channel. To provide an outlet for this inner channel he cut a gorge through a rock face which diverted the waters into irrigation canals beyond the gorge. The rest of the river water followed its natural course down the outer channel. When melting mountain snows swell the river, part of the flood water surging down is still diverted through Li Bing's manmade gorge; the overflow, unable to get through the gorge swirls back over the central island and into the main stream. The Chinese call this island, or dyke, the Flying Pebbles Dyke, because it traps much of the silt from the excess water.

Each winter the river was dammed with large wooden tripods set right across the stream, with huge baskets of stones packed between and inside them, and the two channels were cleaned out. Just before the spring flood waters were due to arrive, the local Intendant came from Chengdu for ceremonies of homage to the Gods of the River at nearby temples. To breach the dam long ropes of bamboo fibre were secured to the tops of the tripods and as soon as a few were hauled clear the water surged through the gap and quickly demolished the rest. The Intendant was then hurried into his official chair to be carried swiftly back to Chengdu to welcome the waters there. Failure to arrive in time could have cost him his office.

The former Daoist Subduing the Dragon Temple (Fulong Guan) has an exhibition on the irrigation system and provides a superb vantage point for viewing Li Bing's great work. The stone statue of Li Bing in the entrance hall, carved in 168 A.D. for a riverside temple, had been swept away by flood waters and was only rediscovered during work on the new sluice in 1974. One of China's oldest statues in the round, it fortunately fell face down in the mud and so is reasonably well preserved. In 1868 the spirit of Li Bing was elevated to the position of honour in the Subduing the Dragon Temple in contrast to the sad state of affairs in the Erlang Temple, now the Temple of the Two Kings by the river. There Li Bing's son, Erlang was honoured and Li Bing was placed in a rear hall, in part because Chinese stories were not always at one on the respective contributions made by father and son in subduing the dragon whose activities were believed to cause the flooding; and in part because the son became confused with his namesake who is a famous character in the well known Chinese story 'Monkey'. The namesake Erlang was a nephew of the chief deity of Daoism and so he naturally took precedence over the mere mortal Li Bing. The main halls of the temple were burned down in the 1920s and both father and son are now commemorated in the reconstructed halls. The design of their new statues made in 1974 was approved by the historian Guo Moruo, the leading authority on the period.

The Guanxian irrigation system based on the Min and nearby Tuo and Fu Rivers now serves the whole of the Chengdu region (over 530,000 hectares) and has been extended to previously inaccessible areas by the creation of reservoirs and tunnelling through the mountains.

An important route to Tibet crossed one of the oldest rope suspension bridges at Guanxian. Over 900 ft long, it was supported by three masonry piers, one on the dyke in the centre and one at each end housing the pulley systems and capstans for tightening the bamboo ropes. Animals too terrified to go onto the swaying bridge were slung on poles to be taken over. Crossing the steadier steel cable bridge that has replaced it can still be an unnerving experience.

Leshan

The ancient river town of Leshan, once known as Kiating, has a history going back 1300 years. Three turbulent rivers meet here, the Qingyi Jiang, the Dadu He and the Min Jiang. Its grey weathered city walls rise from rocky banks above stone steps busy with people hurrying to the ferry, still in charge of skilled oarsmen. Opposite Leshan and dominating the three rivers is one of the great Buddhist monuments of China, a 220 ft high carving of a seated Maitreya Buddha begun in 713 A.D. and cut out of the sandstone cliff of Lingyun Hill in the pious hope that he would calm the waters and prevent shipwrecks. On either side stand 30 ft figures of guardian gods visible only from the river. Visitors can climb the steep narrow steps from his monumental toes to his carefully sculpted head. Drainage channels incorporated in the Buddha have successfully protected the carving from serious erosion. It took ninety years to complete.

In the park at the top of the hill the Lingyun Monastery, founded during the Tang dynasty and reconstructed in 1667, still has its seventeenth century statues, including Samantabhadra (Puxian) the patron deity of nearby Mount Emei. The Song poet, Su Dongpo (1036-1101) is commemorated in a hall in the garden built in the Ming dynasty. He washed his inkstone in the pond outside the hall and local legend says his ink dyed the delicious 'black fish' caught in the river nearby.

Above the buildings towers the Lingbao Pagoda reconstructed in 1534; its foundation is not recorded but the construction of the interior staircase suggests a date contemporary with the eighth century temple.

The Wuyou Monastery is close by on the 'Separated Island on the Qingyi River' (Qingyi Biedao) which was originally a peninsular called Black Ox Rock. It was 'Separated' some two thousand years ago when the engineer-official Li Bing cut a channel through the rock to allow the spring floodwater surging down the Dadu River to be diverted into the Qingyi River. Li Bing is famous for his flood control system at Guanxian northwest of Chengdu. The Wuyou Monastery, founded in 742 A.D. by the monk Hui Jing, was restored in the nineteenth century. From the river steep steps lead up to the entrance guarded by a standing Amitabha Buddha. The now empty Hall of 500 Lohans is used for local art exhibitions. The bell is still in the creeper-clad belltower in the first courtyard and a 'wooden fish' hangs ready to be struck to summon the monks to the refectory. In the Great Hall the three Tang style gilded camphorwood figures of the Sakyamuni Buddha flanked by the Bodhisattvas Manjusri and Samantabhadra (Wenshu and Puxian) were carved in Hangzhou during the Ming dynasty. They were carried nearly 1500 miles by junks hauled by trackers through the rapids in the Yangtze Gorges and up the Min River to this hall. In the narrow confined courtyard in front of the Tathagata Hall (Rulai Dian) the pillars are decorated with delicate carvings of figures, animals and plants, and complete scenes of both the Lingyun and Wuyou Hills. The abbot's rooms are still furnished with provincial antique furniture. In a side hall a small exhibition of local finds includes a tenth century pottery monk's funerary casket and sets of tomb figures.

Not far away at Mahao Ya is a Han cave tomb with wall carvings which include one of China's earliest known carvings of Buddha.

Emeishan

Emei Shan is one of the Four Renowned Mountains of Chinese Buddhism each of which has a patron deity. The patron of Emei is Samantabhadra (Puxian) who is represented riding on an elephant. He is the protector of those who follow the Buddhist Law. At the top of the mountain, some 25 miles from Leshan, the Thousand Buddha Peak (Wanfo Ding) towers 10,000 ft above the plain. On a clear day the snowcapped mountains of Tibet are visible in the west and late in the afternoon the fortunate pilgrim may see the Glory of Buddha, a shimmering light floating on the clouds below the peak like a halo on which his shadow casts a Buddha-like silhouette. Many have hurled themselves over the mile-high precipice in a state of religious ecstasy, believing that they would be enfolded in the arms of Buddha.

Before climbing the mountain, visitors register at Protect the State Monastery (Baoguo Si) whose buildings date from 1615 A.D., where they can consult a map and see a painting of the whole mountain. The bronze pagoda in the inner courtyard was cast in the late sixteenth century. From the monastery the road goes part of the way up the mountain but it is still a seven mile climb to the top up rocky paths and innumerable steps where Tibetan pilgrims mingle with elderly ladies who may have travelled hundreds of miles to make this ascent. Fast moving porters carry children, and loads of supplies for the temples above, on wooden carriers strapped to their backs. Early in this century there were many monasteries and pagodas on the mountain, now only a few remain. It is possible to stay in monastery guestrooms: accommodation is basic with no running water or electricity but the food is usually delicious and the setting idyllic.

Two of the more accessible temples are the Monastery of Eternity (Wannian Si) and the Pavilion of Clear Sounds (Qingyin Ge). The Wannian Monastery at 3800 ft is about an hour's walk from the road. A fourth century foundation, its present buildings are late sixteenth century and include simple guestrooms on the upper floor. A magnificent bronze statue of Samantabhadra riding in a lotus seat on his 6-tusked white elephant and draped with long offering scarves stands in a large domed brick structure. He is said to have first alighted on Mount Emei to give his elephant some water. The statue, 23 ft high and weighing 62 tons, was cast in Chengdu in 980, and brought up the mountain in sections to be assembled in the monastery. Niches with iron Buddhas and shelves of small statues line the walls. The rare 'Handkerchief' or 'Dove Trees' (Davidia Involucrata) flower here in April.

A pleasant mountain walk leads past the little White Snake Cave Temple (Bailong Dong) down to the Pavilion of Clear Sounds overlooking a stream cascading into two pools spanned by twin Flying Bridges.

A more remote monastery, the Hongchun Ping, is about two hours walk beyond the pavilion. On the far side of a narrow gorge a steep path goes up beside the stream and across a covered mountain bridge not far below the monastery. Half hidden in the huge trees and seeming to hang on the side of the mountain, the Terrace of the Hongchun Tree (Hongchun Ping) takes its name from an ancient Chinese mahogany (cedrela odorata) outside its gate. It is popularly known as the Terrace of Drenched Trees because, even at an altitude of 3600 ft the air is so humid that, as the local saying goes, 'even on a fine day clothes are soon drenched when walking on the mountain'. Some of the simple guestrooms lead out to a balcony with a breathtaking view over the forest. The mists swirling through the trees surrounding the dark roofs and deep red pillars of the monastery buildings evoke an ethereal atmosphere quite unlike that of the temples in the plain.

The monastery is a fourth century foundation, but like most on the mountain it has been reconstructed and probably the oldest of its buildings date from 1790. Its original name was the Monastery of 1000 Buddhas: and in the upper story of the Great Hall the Myriad Buddha Tower has shelves for many small statues and a bronze 'Lotus Lantern of a 1000 Buddhas'. The layout does not follow the standard form. Maitreya is honoured in the gate house, Guan Yin in the first hall and Samantabhadra in the rear behind the Great Hall.

The temperature difference of 30°F between the summit and foot of Emei Shan accounts for the variety of its fauna, monkeys, bamboo squirrels and Bearded Frogs, and of its flora which includes the broad leaved evergreen shrubs and ferns of the warm temperate zone below 6000 ft and rhododendrons, silver firs, and deciduous trees in the cool temperate zone from 6000 ft to the summit. Farmers collecting the profusion of medicinal herbs on the steep slopes wear straw sandals spiked with hardened bamboo, and thick leggings to protect themselves against snakes.

Chongqing (Chungking)

Often shrouded in mist between autumn and spring, Chongqing stands on a rocky promontory overlooking the confluence of the Jialing and Yangtze Rivers in east Sichuan. Steep flights of steps lead down to the crowded riverside quays where the journey through the Yangtze Gorges begins. Chongqing suffered heavy bombing damage during the war against Japan and its historic buildings, temples, and the city walls that once protected them have now been replaced by a modern industrial city with more than two million inhabitants. Historically a commercial centre the city was opened to foreign trade in 1891, but the first English missionaries had made the hazardous journey up the Yangtze in 1868. To escape the stifling summer heat and the crowds in a town known as one of the Three Furnaces of China the newcomers built bungalows in the hills on the south bank: there was one in the second range for the British consul and another nearby for naval officers of the gunboats that then regularly visited the city.

During the war against Japan Chongqing became from 1938 to 45 the temporary capital of the National Government and rapidly developed as an industrial centre. At that time the tiny airstrip on the low island in mid-river was a vital link with the world outside. A delegation of representatives of the Chinese Communist Party stayed during the war at 13 Red Cliff Village (Hongyan Cun) and at 50 Zengji Yan, now maintained as museums of China's revolutionary history.

There are hot springs in the area; fifteen miles south at Nanwenquan and thirty miles away at Bei Wenquan, near Jinyun Shan, Red Silk Mountain.

The Chongqing Museum has a collection of local discoveries including bricks from Han tombs decorated with scenes from daily life, ceramics, and a coffin of the third century B.C. from Box Bellows Gorge.

The Yangtze Gorges

Until the turn of the century the voyage through the Yangtze Gorges was a hazardous one. At high water in spring the current flowed through the narrower stretches at speeds up to 18 knots; at low water the jagged rocks in the rapids churned the waters into maelstroms. To travel upstream each junk hired a crew of trackers who made their way painfully along narrow towpaths cut into the cliffs as they hauled on bamboo ropes against the current. Even in the 1890s the first steam vessels still needed help from the trackers. Since 1949 many of the dangerous rocks and shoals have been blasted out of the riverbed, navigational marks and light systems have been installed, and though still exciting, the journey now presents few of the perils of former days.

The comfortable specially-built cruise boats of some two to three thousand tons spend the first day winding along the river to Wanxian, below which the Yangtze begins its precipitous fall through the Three Gorges. About eighty miles from Chongqing, opposite the town of Fuling, is the White Crane Ridge, a mile long stone bank which divides the river at low water. Carvings of fish and inscriptions dating from 763 A.D. appear at a level used by the modern hydrological station as the zero point for its guage. Uncovered only about once every ten years, they have provided hydrologists with accurate details of water levels in the Yangtze for more than a thousand years.

Beyond the old town of Fengdu is the Stockade of the Stone Jewel (Shibaozhai), a picturesque town set below the Jade Seal Mountain (Yuyin

Shan), a square pinnacle of rock with a temple perched on its summit. The way up is through the 12 storey pagoda built close to the cliff in 1819 to provide access to the temple at the top.

A night stop is usually made at the busy town of Wanxian, where the plaited bamboo ropes used for hauling junks up the rapids were once made. On the way to Fengjie and the entrance to the Gorges the boat passes the village of Yunyang. The temple, shaded by trees with golden roofed pavilions clinging to the rocky hillside on the opposite bank is dedicated to Zhang Fei, one of the heroes of the Three Kingdoms of the third century A.D. who are honoured in the Warlords Temple in Chongdu. Stories of the Three Kingdoms and other martial tales are told about many places in the Gorges illustrating their strategic importance as one of the few lines of communication between two of the Kingdoms, Shu in Sichuan and Wu south of the Yangtze. The third Kingdom was Wei in the north.

Just below the ancient walled town of Fengjie at the entrance to the Qutang Gorge, steps lead up to Baidicheng, the City of the White Emperor. The old city got its name 2000 years ago when the local ruler saw a great swirl of white mist in the shape of a white dragon. Believing this to be a good omen, he adopted the name of 'White Emperor' (Baidi) and is now commemorated in the Baidi Temple. In 223 the Emperor of Shu, Liu Bei, died at Baidicheng after a battle to avenge the death of his sworn brother Guan Yu. His body was taken home for burial to his birthplace, Chengdu, where the tomb can be seen today. The main hall of the Baidi Temple, restored in the sixteenth century, contains statues of the four heroes, Emperor Liu Bei, the generals Guan Yu and Zhang Fei and the Prime Minister Zhu Geliang. Zhu Geliang once studied the stars in the Stargazing Pavilion in front of the main hall. The spectacular views over the river and ancient battlefields have been the subject of countless poems through the centuries.

Local people tell a story about the marks in the cliff on the opposite bank which they call Meng Liang's Ladder. They say the corpse of a defeated Song general, Yang Linggong, was exposed by his enemies on a ledge high above the river. His faithful friend Meng Liang, scaling the sheer rock at night in an attempt to recover the body, hammered in iron pegs to support wooden rungs but was detected before he could achieve his objective. The prosaic fact seems to be that the 'Ladder' is the remains of an ancient man-made exit from the gorge.

At this point the river has already entered the Gorges by the great Kui Men, the Kui Dragon Gate, where it is flanked by two precipitous cliffs. For the next five miles it surges through the narrow Qutang Gorge, in some ways the most impressive of the Three Gorges. The narrow channel facilitated the slinging of iron chains across the river to obstruct naval operations which gave it the second name of Iron Lock Gorge. Within it is a section called Box Bellows Gorge (or Windbox Gorge) from the long wooden box-like objects lodged in crevices high on the cliff face, and known locally as the Box Bellows of Lu Ban (the patron deity of carpenters). Old Chinese bellows were in the form of a long box with a plunger which worked on the same principle as a pump. When in 1971 one was brought down, they proved to be coffins made from whole tree trunks by the Ba people whose custom was to lodge their coffins in crevasses and caves. The contents, which included coins and engraved bronze swords, proved that they dated from the third century B.C. Some of the objects recovered can be seen in the Baidicheng Museum and a coffin is in the museum in Chongqing. Similar coffins lodged high on cliffs and in caves have been found at Wuyi Shan in Fujian province. The river emerges from Qutang Gorge at Daixi, Eyeblack Canyon.

At Wushan, famous for herbs and fruit, the river enters the Sorcerer's Gorge (Wuxia), twenty-six miles of turbulent water rushing between precipitous cliffs. Legend says the twelve mountain tops, and the lofty Goddess Peak (Shennu Feng) at this spot were once the daughters of the Goddess of the West. After they had helped the Great Yu to create the Gorges they decided to remain on earth as beautiful peaks to guide boatmen shooting the dangerous rapids. This gorge too is associated with Zhu Geliang. Beside the river not far from the Goddess Peak there is an engraved stone. During the war between Shu and Wu, the general came upriver to attack the Shu forces. Here he found a stone engraved with a poem by Zhu Geliang proposing an alliance. The Wu general was so impressed with Zhu's argument that he withdrew, and the stone became known as the Stone that Made Everything Clear.

The third of the gorges, the Xiling Gorge is 45 miles long and within it were once some of the most dangerous rapids and whirlpools in the whole river. The Military Manual and Precious Sword Gorge (Bingshu BaojianXia) lies in this stretch of the river. It is said that when Zhu Geliang fell ill he had his manual of military strategies lodged so high on the cliff face that only a daring hero worthy to be his heir would be able to retrieve it. The rocks do resemble a pile of books and a sword. Further downstream and high above the river, the Huangling Temple was built in 1618 but it was reputed to have been founded by Zhu Geliang. Although high on the cliff, it was not far enough above the river to escape flooding in 1860 and 1870.

The river leaves the gorges at Nanjing Guan. There is a startling contrast between the depth and power of the current where it is compressed between sheer cliffs only 300 yards apart and the placid flow as the banks allow it to widen to 2000 yards outside.

Just above the busy river port of Yichang, the first stage has been completed of a giant river control and hydro-electric project which will, when in full operation, be among the largest in the world. At the beginning of the century Yichang was to have been the terminus of a railway upriver to Wanxian and Chongqing which was badly needed to improve access to the resources of Sichuan. Sixteen miles of track were laid between 1910 and 1911 funded by local Chinese capital. But the attempt of those in power in Peking to take it over and finance it with the help of foreign capital provoked such violent local opposition that it helped to precipitate the revolution of 1911 which overthrew the Manchus. The project foundered and not until after the Communists came to power was Sichuan linked by rail with the rest of China.

Yunnan

To the south of Sichuan lies the province of Yunnan, South of the Clouds, hemmed in by Tibet on the northwest and by mountainous borders with Burma, Laos and Vietnam to the west and south. Its distinctive and independent peoples were the scourge of Chinese rulers seeking to extend their empire. In 109 B.C. the Kingdom of Dian, a local kingdom with an individual and highly developed culture, submitted to Chinese suzerainty, but the Chinese hold on the province continued to be a tenuous one. In the eighth century, there was strong resistance to Chinese rule from the King-dom of Nanzhao which had its capital at Dali, the source of a decorative marble widely used in Chinese buildings. With the armies seeking to subdue the province came a strong Moslem contingent. In the course of time the Moslem settlers in their turn revolted, taking advantage of the fact that the imperial armies were desperately fighting the Taipings far away in the Yangtze Valley. Their rebellion, which lasted from 1855 to 1872, left the two main cities of Kunming and Dali in ruins, and the province in a poor state from which it only gradually recovered.

Yunnan is still home to more than twenty minority nationalities, all of whom cherish their distinctive language, dress and customs. Students from these peoples are trained in administration in the Yunnan Institute of Nationalities in Kunming. One of the groups, the Dai, lives in the Xishuang Bana Autonomous Region on the banks of the Mekong River in the south-west corner of the province, where the scenery, palm thatched houses, white stupas and the traditional dress are reminiscent of parts of Southeast Asia. At the New Year they celebrate the Water Splashing Festival shown in the mural at the Peking International Airport.

The expansion of industry in Yunnan has been helped by the building of the railway linking Kunming to Chengdu, a remarkable feat of engineering: bridges tunnels and culverts make up nearly a third of its length.

In contrast to its violent history, the climate of the Yunnan plateau is mild and it is the home of many of the flowers, trees and shrubs in European and American gardens, including such favourites as camellias, rhododen-drons, primulas and roses. The migration of plants began in the seven-teenth century and in the late eighteenth and the nineteenth centuries professional collectors – Fortune, Maries, David, Delavey, Wilson and Henry to name but a few – often risked their lives in the sometimes uncomfortable, often dangerous but always fascinating search for plants among what Ernest Wilson, the famous English naturalist, described as 'the richest temperate flora in the world'.

Kunming

Kunming, the capital of Yunnan, is known as the City of Eternal Spring and its spectacular displays of flowers including the renowned Yunnan camellias are at their best in February and March.

29 Pinnacles of rock in the Stone Forest in the picturesque Sani National Minority Area near Kunming.

30 A guardian at the gate of the
Huating Temple in the Western
Hills of Kunming

31 Lion with friend outside the
Huating Temple.

32 The National Minorities Shop at Kunming attracts tourists as well as local people.

33 Waiting for the train on the Kunming–Chengdu railway: members of National Minorities in their colourful costumes are a common sight in Yunnan province.

34 Inside the beautiful Yuantong Temple in Kunming.

35 A gravel junk on the Dian Lake at Kunming.

36 A Mongol nomad family in their '*yurt*', a traditional round felt tent.

37 The Potala Palace at Lhasa, capital of Tibet.

38 Tibetan women herding their sheep in southwest Gansu.

39 Working on the golden roofs of the Jokhang Monastery at Lhasa.

40 The path to the Twin Flying Bridges on Mount Emei in Sichuan province.

The city stands on the old route to Burma: here missions carrying tribute from the Kings of Burma to the Chinese Emperor would be received before starting on the 1500 mile, eight month journey to Peking. To ensure the safe passage of the sandalwood, rugs, unguents, jade, gold and silver leaf and most important, elephants for the imperial stables, roads and bridges would be repaired, escorts arranged and their arrival and safecrossing into the next province reported to the throne by each provincial governor along the route.

During the 1937-45 war with Japan Kunming was the busy terminus of the Burma Road, and of the airbridge over the 'Hump' (the Himalayas), the routes used for supplying the Chinese army from India. It was also a refuge for many Chinese and for Chinese universities from the occupied provinces.

In spite of the development of industry and the rise in the population to one million, the city has not lost its charm. Many old houses with sweeping roofs and latticed windows still line attractive lanes near the hotel in the north of the city beside the Green Lake Park (Cui Hu). Not far away Yuantong Hill, clothed in a mass of cherry blossom in spring, overlooks the gold roofs of the Yuantong Temple. A Tang foundation, and the only remaining Buddhist temple within the city, it has a perfect setting. Its buildings look out on a charming pavilion in the centre of a small lake. The clear water reflects the graceful arches of the marble bridges which cross the lake and the golden roofs of the temple buildings round about. The eclectic nature of traditional Chinese religious beliefs is illustrated in the Main Hall where scaly dragons coil around pillars on each side of the Sakyamuni Buddha. The dragons are credited with the power of bringing rain in times of drought.

The approach to the old Confucian temple is through narrow streets lined by traditional houses of the old town. It was damaged in the Cultural Revolution but is now being restored.

East of the city the vast Kunming Lake (Dian Chi), the largest lake in Yunnan, covers an area of over 200 square miles. The Tower with the Magnificent View (Da Guan Lou) stands in a park on the lakeside. First built in 1696 soon after the park was laid out and restored by the governor of Yunnan in 1866 it is well known for its pair of inscriptions, one extolling the beauties of the lake and the other reviewing epic events in the history of the city. They were written in the eighteenth century by Sun Ran, a scholar loyal to the memory of the Ming dynasty who refused to accept office under the Manchus.

A breathtaking view over the lake and its fleets of tall sailing junks can be obtained from the Dragon Gate in the Western Hills, not far from the city. The steep path up to it begins at the Sanqing Pavilion, originally a group of thirteenth century buildings perched on the side of the cliff which were a summer resort for a prince and later a Daoist temple. The paths and caves on the way up were carved out of the rock between 1781 and 1853 by masons who worked supsended on ropes along the cliff. One of the many local stories is that of a young artist disappointed in love who began carving at the Dragon Gate. One day he spoiled his work in a moment of carelessness and in despair hurled himself from the cliff. The gate leads onto a tiny terrace and shrine to the God of Literature high over the lake.

The road from the Dragon Gate passes the Taihua Temple originally founded in the Yuan dynasty (1271-1368) but much restored. It boasts a huge ancient camellia and fine magnolias among its many flowers and trees. Further on is the Huating Monastery; an imperial summer resort in the Kingdom of Nanzhao it became a temple in 1320. Huge Gate Gods mark its entrance.

The Golden Temple (Jin Dian) north of Kunming has a beautiful setting on Mingfeng Hill. Its main hall was cast in bronze in 1670 by Wu Sangui, the Ming general who co-operated with the Manchus in their conquest of China but later turned against them. It is one of the best places to see the famous Yunnan camellias, including the 'Butterfly Wing', on trees said to have been planted in the Ming dynasty. The temple bell was cast in 1423.

Further to the north is the Black Dragon Pool with its Black Water Temple (Heishui Si). Of the 'Han Temple' which historians say existed near the pool, and which is listed among its 'Four Beauties', nothing remains; the present temple dates only from the Manchu dynasty. The other 'Beauties' are a plum tree, a cypress, and the tomb of a Ming scholar. Stone steps lead on through the forest to the gate of the Daoist Dragon Fountain Temple (Longquanguan) a fine example of Ming architecture.

The Yunnan Botanical Research Institute, one of the largest in China and known for its camellias, has its gardens in the park.

The Bamboo Temple (Qiongzhu Si) set on a wooded hill eight miles northwest of the city is its most ancient temple. The present thirteenth century buildings were restored in the 1880s and it was at this time that the famous painted clay sculptures of 500 Lohan and Four Guardian Kings were added. They were made by a Sichuanese sculptor, Li Guangxiu, a lay-brother deeply versed in Buddhist theology who followed the tradition of including contemporary portraits of monks and laymen in religious art that goes back to the Buddhist cave art of Dunhuang, Yungang and Maijishan. He also painted the river landscape on the wall of the west hall. Of the Four Heavenly Kings, the King of the West playing his guitar and singing is unusually lifelike. A majestic five hundred year old Peacock Cedar (Cunninghamia) shades the courtyard outside. Another example of the eclectic nature of the Chinese attitude to religion is in the inclusion of a statue of the Daoist Jade Emperor behind the Buddha in the Great Hall.

The Anning Hot Springs are some thirty miles from the City. On a hill not far away the Caoxi Temple has a Song dynasty Buddha and an intriguing circular hole in the upper part of its walls, so placed that at the mid-autumn festival at intervals of sixty years (a traditional time cycle in China) the moon shines directly onto a mirror on the forehead of the Buddha.

A visit to the Stone Forest in the Yi Nationality Autonomous District entails a three hour journey through picturesque villages and the varied Yunnan countryside. The forest is a fantastic karst formation of towering limestone pillars with deep pools lying between sheer walls of rock decorated with inscriptions extolling the beauty and strangeness of the scenery. Some visitors stay overnight in the pleasant guesthouse and visit the Sani people (a branch of the Yi nationality) who hold their Torch Festival on the 26th of the 6th Lunar month at nearby Beida Village. The Sani girls wear pretty wide flat headbands caught above each ear with a triangle of cloth which they call 'butterflies' and carry shoulder bags embroidered with their traditional crossstitch designs.

The Yunnan Provincial Museum in Kunming exhibits some of the outstanding bronzes of the second to early first century B.C., recovered in 1955-60 in the south of the city from tombs of the Dian Kingdom whose distinctive culture was only fully appreciated after the tombs were excavated. The gold seal of office now in the museum was granted to the Dian Kings when they accepted the suzerainty of the Emperors of China in 109 B.C. Among the bronzes are powerful representations of animals including bulls, tigers, deer, snakes and peacocks. Bronze drums filled with the cowrie shells used as currency as late as the Qing dynasty have tops covered with birds, animals, scenes of daily battle and human sacrifice. The variety of drums found has led experts to suspect that Yunnan was the original home of the bronze drums found all over Southeast Asia.

7. The West and Northwest

Inner Mongolia

The Inner Mongolian Autonomous Region stretches along part of the northern border of China, a great belt of mountains and grasslands with vast deserts to the west. The grasslands are the breeding grounds for sheep, cattle, horses and camels. The Mongol herdsmen have lost none of their fabled skills of horsemanship, wrestling and archery, and gather together every summer to take part in races and competitions at the Nadam Festival. The original Mongol population is now outnumbered by immigrant Chinese from south of the Wall, and although many who once followed a nomadic way of life have settled on farms to engage in mixed arable and stock farming, the round felt 'yurts', tents which are the traditional homes of the Mongol people, are still seen on the steppes.

The climate is extreme, ranging from − 15°F in the northern section and 10°F in the southern, to over 65°F in the short Mongolian summer when the steppe is transformed into a colourful carpet of wild flowers. There are bears and deer in the hills, antelope, foxes, racoons and lynx on the grasslands. This also the home of the Steppe and Golden Eagles, Upland Buzzard, the Cinereous Vulture and the Mongolian Lark, prized by the Chinese as a favourite singing bird.

In winter both men and women wear heavy furs and felt boots, but at summer festivals they show off their bright silk robes tied with contrasting sashes, turquoise and coral jewellery and embroidered boots with great panache. They entertain their guests with mutton, cheese and tea brewed from Brick Tea and drunk with mares' milk with a flavouring of salt and millet.

The hero of the Mongols is still Genghis Khan, whose invincible hordes rode west to the very gates of Vienna, only turning back when Genghis died in 1227. His remains were so revered that during the war with Japan they were removed first to Gansu province and then to Qinghai to prevent their falling into the hands of the invaders. They are now at Ejin Horo Qi, his original burial place near the present Shaanxi border, with those of his three wives and relics including the sword and saddle said to have been used by the Great Khan himself. The mausoleum in which they are housed was built in 1954.

The region's main industrial city is Baotou on the upper reaches of the Yellow River, one of China's major iron and steel towns. There are two small lamaseries in the city, but for the visitor the site of greatest historical interest is the Wudang Zhaomiao in the Yinshan Mountains, fifty miles to the northeast. First built during the reign of the Manchu Kangxi Emperor, and once a great centre of learning, with colleges of astrology, divination, theology and medicine, and a population of over a thousand lamas, it was substantially reconstructed in 1749. This massive collection of temple buildings in the flatroofed Tibetan style covers an area of nearly fifty acres. The main halls are richly decorated with murals and statues, and in the mausoleum gilded reliquaries in the form of stupas contain the ashes of seven generations of Living Buddhas once resident in the Lamasery; (the last one died in 1955). In the Ganzhur Buddha Mansion, where they lived, there is now a collection of statuary, decorations, wall hangings and ceremonial objects.

The capital and university town of the region is at Hohhot (Huhehot), a town of four hundred thousand people, many of them engaged in producing wool textiles, carpets and in food processing.

In the Manchu Qing dynasty there were eleven large lamaseries in the city. At the Five Pagoda Temple (Wuta Si) established in 1727, only the building which gave it its name, a high tiled square terrace crowned by five square pagodas, still stands. The Great Sutra Hall of the Yanshou Si, a Ming dynasty foundation, is an interesting example of a Sino-Tibetan style lamasery, combining a Chinese roof structure and open verandah with the heavier vertical lines of Tibetan architecture. The nearby Double-Eared Dagoba gets its name from the two curving scrolls on its spire; another landmark is the White Dagoba, of which seven octagonal brick stories remain of a much taller structure dating from the Liao dynasty (947-1125).

Six miles away, on the south bank of the Great Black River (Dahei Ho) is the tomb of Wang Zhaojun, a lady-in-waiting in the palace of the Han Emperor Yuan Di. She was given in marriage in 33 B.C. to a ruler of the Huns (Xiong Nu) as a pledge of peace. Since sixty years of tranquillity followed the marriage she became a symbol of friendship between the Chinese south of the Great Wall and the peoples of the northwest. A small memorial hall has been built near her tomb mound to display documents and artefacts connected with her story.

Silinhot is a small town of about sixty thousand people with a leather and felt factory that produces traditional boots and saddles. The Prince's Lamasery (Beizi Miao), built in the Chinese style, stands in front of Aobao Hill. 'Aobao' are the cairns of stones seen all over the steppes that were erected originally to placate the spirits; they were adopted by Lamaism as places at which prayers could be offered and where long poles bearing prayer flags could be put up.

Xinjiang (Sinkiang)

The Xinjiang Uighur Autonomous Area is China's largest and most westerly province, about five hours flight from Peking. In the centre of the province the snowcapped Tian Shan, the Mountains of Heaven, divide the dry Junggar Basin in the north from the Tarim Basin and the blistering shifting sands of the Taklimakan Desert to the south. Of the population of eleven million, almost half are Uighur farmers, forty per cent are Han Chinese, and the remainder are Mongols, Kazaks, Uzbeks, Kirgiz and other minority races. Most of the non-Chinese peoples are Moslems. The northern slopes of the Tian Shan, watered by the melting snows, have been the home for centuries of Kazak and other herdsmen who still lead a seminomadic life, tending their horses and sheep and living in felt tents (yurts) in the summer months, before returning to their wooden houses for the winter. A popular visit from Urumqi is to the alpine Dongfeng Commune forty miles to the southwest where the local people put on a dashing display of riding, shooting and Kazak dancing. The oasis towns are famous for their fruit; Hami for its melons, Turfan for its grapes, Korla for pears, and Kuqa and Kashgar for apricots, figs, peaches and pomegranates.

Over a century before the Christian era the Han Emperor Wu Di (140-86 B.C.), having beaten off the Central Asian Huns, who were a constant source of trouble on his western borders, sent an envoy Zhang Qian to the far west to make contact with the Huns' old enemies. Zhang returned after thirteen years and many adventures with invaluable intelligence and tales of the fleet bloodsweating horses of Ferghana. The Emperor was determined to possess these wonders, whose bloodlike sweat ran red from a parasite on their hide. Countless Chinese soldiers perished in campaigns across the deserts and mountains of Xinjiang before their comrades returned in triumph with the horses after conquering Ferghana, thousands of miles away beyond the high snowbound Pamirs.

During the first century A.D. Chinese silk carried westward over the trade routes through Xinjiang became the height of fashion in Rome, and in the Chinese imperial capital the spices and latest novelties brought in by the returning caravans were eagerly awaited. At the same time Buddhism was spreading slowly from India through the oasis towns. Gradually the shifting desert sands crept over the southern oases, and the caravans on the Silk Road followed the northern rim of the Tarim Basin through Turfan and on to Kashgar. To secure their hold on the trade routes the Chinese established forts, settlements and staging posts, the remains of which can still be seen. Islam came to Xinjiang in the ninth century in the wake of increasing Arab incursions from the west. Four hundred years later the Mongols under Genghis Khan took all of Central Asia in their grip. Highly mobile, they could exist on raw meat carried under their saddles, mares' milk, and blood from the opened veins of their horses. Marco Polo travelled through their Empire along the reopened Silk Road in the 1270s noting that although some country was 'much devastated by the Tartars', there were also 'cotton, vineyards . . . and orchards in plenty' at the oases. The City of Lop where he rested is now buried in the desert sands. The discovery of the easier searoute to China from Europe in the sixteenth century brought about a decline in the overland trade through Central Asia.

In the late nineteenth century a Moslem leader, Yakub Beg, gained control of the province, and although he was defeated, Xinjiang paid scant allegiance to the Central Government until the arrival of the People's Liberation Army early in 1950. Large numbers of these troops stayed on to irrigate new areas for the cultivation of cotton and grain, and develop local industry.

Urumqi

Urumqi, the provincial capital, with a population of eight hundred thousand, has little to offer the tourist. The dry climate is bitterly cold in winter and hot in summer. Its most attractive feature is the local people in their distinctive national dress. The history of Xinjiang's connection with China is traced in an exhibition in the museum, where there are also recent finds from the ancient city of Turfan. A popular excursion to the beautiful Lake of Heaven, high in the Tian Shan mountains, includes a boat ride on the lake.

Turfan

The small town of Turfan is in the Turfan Depression, the lowest place in China, 500 ft below sea level. The four-hour journey from Urumqi by road crosses the Tian Shan mountains through some spectacular passes. The area relies on irrigation through a system of covered canals, called the Karez, which draw on a large underground lake fed by the mountain snows. The predominance of Uighurs in its population, the oasis style architecture and the vine arbours give it a distinctive Central Asian atmosphere.

Gaochang

The remains of the ancient city of Gaochang lie twenty five miles to the southeast of Turfan. The Han Emperor ordered the establishment of a garrison here in 68 B.C. It was an important walled city built in the same style as the Chinese capital at Changan with an inner and outer city, but it was abandoned in the fifteenth century. Today the clay wall, three miles in circumference, and the ruins of the old city are still an impressive sight full of the atmosphere of the past. In the remains of a monastery in the southwest it is possible to trace the gate, the Buddha Hall and the base of a pagoda. Recent excavations of tombs northwest of Gaochang have produced a variety of silk textiles, foreign coins from Persia and Rome, and documents such as the passes which had to be checked and stamped as travellers passed along the Silk Road in Tang times. Many of the finds are in the museum at Urumqi, but there are some also in the Turfan Museum.

Jiaohe

Another ancient city, Jiaohe, lies six miles west of Turfan where the remains of its walls, streets and a temple can still be traced. It was founded in the second century B.C.

Dunhuang

Dunhuang is an oasis town at the western end of the Gansu corridor through which travellers have passed between China and Central Asia for centuries. Its position made it a natural trading centre where the cultures of east and west met, and an ideal base for military expeditions preparing for arduous campaigns in the desert. Just beyond the town the old Silk Road divided, one spur leading north through the Jade Gate to Turfan and along the northern edge of the Taklimakan Desert, the other going west through the Yang Gate and south of the desert. Buddhism spread from India through the oasis towns along the Silk Road, and by the end of the third century a community of monks in Dunhuang were constructing cave-temples in the Indian style. The prosperous town became a haven of learning and culture where monks and scholars sought refuge from the wars then ravaging China.

In the fifth century the Northern Wei, a tribal dynasty, having emerged victorious in north China, and taken Dunhuang, transported thousands of its monks and citizens to work in their new capital at Datong in Shanxi province, and to build the Yungang cave temples. The Northern Wei created many such cave complexes, not only at Yungang, and at Longmen near Luoyang, but at sites spread right across north China. In some, where the rock was hard enough, as at Yungang and Longmen, the figures were carved from the stone. In others, such as the Dunhuang and Yulin caves, the sandstone was too soft for successful carving, and the painted sculptures were modelled of clay built up with layers of cloth and coated with lacquer and paint. In the following centuries hundreds of temples were completed, many filled with sculptures, wall and ceiling paintings, painted silk banners and hangings, and treasured collections of manuscripts.

In 1035 a Tibetan people, the Tanguts, overran the town. It may well have been at this time that a group of monks determined to save their temple's manuscripts and paintings from destruction by walling them up in a small chapel and carefully repainting the walls. They did their work well for it remained undisturbed for nearly nine hundred years.

Even though after peace was restored new caves were constructed and old ones repaired, the town and the temples never regained their former glory, and Dunhuang became once again a remote outpost.

In 1899 a Daoist priest named Wang Yuanlu settled in the valley and began restoring the caves. Clearing sand from a neglected temple one day he noticed a crack running through one of the wallpaintings. On examining the painting closely he found that it masked the entrance to a hidden chapel, packed high with more than twenty thousand scrolls and bundles. They were well preserved by the dry climate and proved to date from the fifth to tenth century. When he reported this amazing discovery to the Manchu authorities they decided the treasure would be too costly to move, ordered the monk to wall it up again, and took no further interest. Rumours about the manuscripts soon spread. In 1907 Sir Aurel Stein and later the French scholar Paul Pelliot came to Dunhuang and bought thousands of the manuscripts and paintings which they transported with great care back to London and Paris. A succession of collectors followed, until in 1910 the Chinese Government ordered the remainder of the collection to be sent to the National Library in Peking. In 1943 the National Art Institute of Dunhuang was set up to study and care for this priceless museum of Buddhist art. There are three groups of cave-temples at Dunhuang; the Yulin caves, the West Thousand Buddha caves and, the largest and most frequently visited, the Mogao caves. They lie twelve miles southeast of the town in a small desert valley between the Sanwie and Mingsha mountains.

The four hundred and fifty-odd caves are in tiers, accessible from safe and solid balconies. The first cave was built in 366 by a monk inspired by the beauty of the sun setting behind Sanwei Mountain, and although it is no longer identifiable, a record of its construction is preserved on a seventh century tablet. For the remaining caves nothing short of an encyclopaedia could do justice to the hundreds of sculptures and wall paintings that still survive. It is only possible here to identify some of the better known caves and note some of the changes in form, style and costume that occurred through the centuries.

The wallpaintings are not frescoes painted onto wet plaster. In Dunhuang the walls were prepared by smearing on clay mixed with chopped wheatstraw and hemp fibre which was smoothed and covered with a thick lime wash. The colours were applied after the surface had been dried and polished.

The influence of Indian Buddhism is noticeable in the early caves where Indian patterns were probably copied for some main figures. In many paintings the red shading of the Indian style, a technique not then used in China, has turned black with age and produced strange dark lines and blobs on the figures. Caves 275 and 254 show sombre stories of Buddha's sacrifice in this style.

One of the most famous early sculptures is the enigmatic seated Sakyamuni Buddha of the Northern Wei period in Cave 259.

Nearly a hundred caves were decorated in the Northern Zhou (557-581) and Sui (581-618) period. Faces became rounder, clothes and ornament more elaborate and worshippers appeared in voluminous Chinese robes rather than in the closer fitting Central Asian dress. Cave 296 has a painting of merchants travelling the Silk Road: a temple is being built; Chinese traders with horses meet merchants from the west with large noses and deepset eyes leading their camels. The sculptures in Cave 419 have early portrayals of Buddha's disciples, the youthful Ananda and elderly Kasyapa; they appeared for the first time at this period. An early Tang version of these figures may be seen in Cave 220, and a mid Tang version in Cave 45.

The two hundred Tang caves are filled with beautiful rounded and worldly figures. The life and entertainments of the court at Xi'an are reflected in paintings of two Pure Land Western Paradises in Caves 217 and 112. The Persian influence in art and music can be traced in instruments and the decoration of pearls and wild geese on the ceiling of Cave 361. In Cave 103 there is a vivid painting of the sage Vimalakirti who sits holding his fan as he debates with the Bodhisattva Manjusri. The nine-storey pavilion, Cave 96, houses a huge Tang Buddha, as does Cave 130 which has worshippers 25 ft high. In the tenth century Cave 98 the King of Yutian stands 6 ft tall and is accompanied by ladies in Tang dress.

A later painting in Cave 61 of the Song period is an illustrated map of a large area of north China. Those interested in costume might be interested to compare the dress of the female worshippers in this cave with that worn by the Princess of Yutian in the earlier Cave 98. The Tangut, or Xi Xia, costume can be seen in the eleventh century Cave 409 — it was fear of these people that led the monks to wall up the manuscripts in Cave 16. During the last half of the eighth century the Tibetan occupation of Dunhuang led to the introduction of the Lamaistic art and the many-armed and 'thousand'-eyed Avalokitesvara appeared in the iconography. Lamaism returned during the Mongol dynasty in the thirteenth century; when Marco Polo came to Dunhuang he noted the 'many abbeys and monasteries, all full of idols'.

By early in the tenth century the space on the cliff had run out. Most new caves had to be made by enlarging or repainting old ones. Occasional masterpieces appeared, but after the Mongol period no more caves were built.

Jiayuguan

A visitor to Dunhuang travelling on the Lanzhou-Urumqi railway will pass the still well preserved walled garrison town of Jiayuguan built in 1372 to guard the western end of the Great Wall during the Ming dynasty. Its triple-roofed towers stand high on crenellated walls against a background of desert and snowcapped mountains. Thirteen centuries earlier in Han times the Wall stretched far to the west beyond Dunhuang, but only a rampart of rammed earth remains to mark the legendary Jade Gate at the threshold of Central Asia.

Tibet (Xizang)

Tibet was for centuries the world's most inaccessible and isolated country, jealously guarded against outside influences by a theocracy determined to preserve its unique character. Almost half the country is more than 15,000 ft above sea level. There are salt lakes and borax fields in the barren northern wastes; further south nomad herdsmen with savage watchdogs to scare off wolves and leopards tend herds of yak and sheep. The most fertile area is the land watered by the Tsangpo River (the Brahmaputra). Here the greater part of the population of three million are employed in agriculture, tending animals and growing barley and hardy vegetables, or in the local industries of the three main cities of Lhasa, Gyantse and Shigatse. The mountains of the east are covered by subtropical forest, and channel three great rivers, the Yangtze, the Mekong and the Salween in a narrow fifty mile corridor for a distance of nearly two hundred miles.

In the seventh century the Tibetans were strong enough to trouble the Chinese Tang empire, and to appease them their young King Srongtsan Gampo was granted the hand of the Chinese Princess Wen Cheng in marriage. The King also had a Nepalese wife, and between them the two princesses played a large part in introducing the civilisation of China and Nepal, and the Buddhist religion.

The form of Buddhism which entered Tibet had already absorbed Tantric influences from India and took in elements of the old animist Bon religion of the Tibetans. Its iconography is in consequence in part traditional but it reflects also Tantric and Bon influences. Lamaist deities are portrayed in terrifying as well as benign aspects, the better to struggle with the forces of evil; gods are sometimes represented coupling with their female consorts, symbolising the union of compassion and wisdom; and Lamaism developed a deep attachment to ritual repetition of prayers written on paper slips and rotated in prayer wheels. Towards the end of the fourteenth century a new sect, the Gelugpa or Yellow Sect, became dominant, advocating reform, discipline and a return to spirituality. In 1578 the Third Grand Lama of the Sect converted the followers of Altan Khan, the most powerful of the Mongols, who conferred on him the title of Dalai, Ocean of Wisdom. He promptly raised his two predecessors retrospectively to the same title. The Dalai Lamas were regarded as incarnations of the Tantric god Avalokitesvara. At the time of the fifth Dalai Lama (1617-82) the Grand Lama of the Tashilumpo Monastery at Shigatse was recognised as the Panchan, Great Scholar, a reincarnation of Amitabha, the God of Light. The Dalai was held to have temporal pre-eminence and the Panchan the spiritual leadership, but there was constant rivalry between the two. As each Lama died a child was sought by the monks as a new reincarnation to carry on the line.

When the People's Liberation Army occupied Tibet in 1951 they found life continuing much as it had for hundreds of years. Thousands of monks were living in the huge townlike monasteries. There was serfdom on the great estates. Polyandry, which had its roots in nomad life, still occurred. Groups of pilgrims walked enormous distances to visit famous shrines or to circumambulate the great sacred mountains. Divining, consultation with oracles and the casting of lots were still popular among the common people. The attempts of the Chinese Communists to bring about change precipitated a rebellion in 1959 which led to the flight of the Dalai Lama to India and the dissolution of the monasteries. The process of modernising agriculture, health and education has continued but progress has been difficult. The present population is 1.8 million.

Lhasa

Some visitors to Lhasa, the capital of Tibet, find they are affected by its high altitude, 10,000 ft above sea level. But this does not spoil the interest of this unique city with its many traditional houses, markets and monasteries, whose architecture is completely different from that of China. Tibetan palaces and monasteries look more like fortresses than settings for a cultured and religious life. Built on the sides of hills, their massive walls slope inwards giving an impression of great height. The largest of them all, the Potala, which towers over the city, was begun in 1645 in the reign of the fifth Dalai Lama. He died in 1682, during its construction, but the Regent succeeded in keeping his death a secret for nine years while the work was completed in the Dalai's name. Like the Vatican, the Potala is as much a city as a palace. Within it were the Dalai's private apartments, the great shrines of his predecessors, his private monastery and treasury, a monastic college, a library with its own printing works and, in its base, the much feared dungeons. The private apartments were at the top of the White Palace. Their ornate decoration combined both Chinese and Tibetan styles, the walls of his living chamber being lined with richly carved and gilded cupboards, and the audience hall hung with 'thangkas', the religious scroll paintings executed on linen or silk with Buddhist figures in the centre surrounded by deities and attendants. Thangka painting was an art handed down from father to son.

Among the most impressive sights are the great jewelled shrines containing the remains of the Dalai Lamas from the fifth onwards. The two largest are those of the Great Fifth himself and of the thirteenth who died in 1933. The stupa of the latter rises through three stories of the building to the golden roof above, where once the Dalai Lama walked and enjoyed the magnificent view over the city.

The Tibetans believed that before the New Year could be celebrated the evil influences of the old year had first to be exorcised. This was the purpose of the Devil Dances performed on the 29th of the last month of the year on the Eastern Terrace. The Dalai himself and all the officials of the capital came to watch war dances performed by men in ancient Tibetan armour, 'skeleton dancers' who postured around a mock corpse, and 'demons' wearing horrific papier-mache masks. The dances were accompanied by the clashing of cymbals and deafening boom of the ceremonial Tibetan horns, so long that they had to be supported on richly carved stands.

The thirteenth Dalai Lama did not enjoy living in the oppressive atmosphere of the Potala and spent much of his time at his summer residence, the Norbulinka, about a mile to the west of the city. This residence, now a park, was built at the end of the nineteenth century with magnificent living quarters, throne rooms, prayer rooms and pavilions around an artificial lake; even the walls of the stables were decorated with frescoes and the pillars richly painted. It was from here that the fourteenth Dalai Lama fled to India in 1959.

The oldest and most holy monastery in Lhasa, the Jokhang (Dazhao Si), is said to have been founded in the seventh century by the Princess Wen

Cheng herself to house the sacred image of the Sakyamuni Buddha which she brought from China. Situated in the centre of the old city, it is built in a mixture of Tibetan, Nepalese and Chinese styles with a heavy flat roof crowned with gold ornament, its woodwork protected by dark yakhair canopies. In the entrance gate the faithful donned their nailstudded wooden hand-protectors and began the repeated prostrations that have worn deep grooves in the flagstones. Once inside they made their way round the innermost of the Three Sacred Ways turning the prayer wheels, some 8 ft high, in the pious hope of sending thousands of prayers to heaven. The second Sacred Way was round the outside of the building, and the third, followed on holy days, round the city itself. In addition to the life-size Buddha gleaming with gold and precious stones in the Great Hall, the temple houses statues of the Princess Wen Cheng, King Srongtsan Gampo and his Nepalese consort, and of the Palden Lhamo, a goddess protector of the Dalai Lama, who in her terrifying form was once paraded through the streets of the city. In the middle of the first month the Dalai Lama himself used to circumambulate the second Sacred Way to inspect the huge frozen yak butter sculptures, some 40 ft high, made for the popular Butter Festival.

The representative of the Manchu court in Tibet, the Amban, occupied a Chinese building to the southwest of the Jokhang.

Although the Dalai Lama was the temporal as well as a spiritual leader, power was shared with the noble families and great monasteries such as the Tashilumpo, the seat of the Panchen Lama at Shigatse, the oldest monastery in Tibet, the Samye, and the Kumbum in Qinghai. In Lhasa itself the Three Pillars of the State, the monasteries of Drepung, Sera and Ganden (which was destroyed in the Cultural Revolution), dominated the life of the city.

The white buildings of the Drepung, the Riceheap, stand on a hill six miles northwest of the city. Founded early in the fifteenth century it became the second most powerful in Tibet. About half its ten thousand monks were engaged in religious duties, and half in running the huge temple complex. It houses a great library, hundreds of images and some celebrated murals, blackened by years of smoke from yak butter lamps but now being restored.

Nestling in the foothills four miles north of Lhasa are the red and white buildings and golden roofs of the Sera, the Wildrose Fence. The second largest but the most powerful monastery, it was founded like the Drepung in the fifteenth century by disciples of Tsongkapa, the founder of the Yellow Sect, of whom it contains some fine statues. The separate meeting rooms for its Three Colleges are richly furnished with carpets and hangings on pillars, walls and ceilings. In the tolerant eighteenth century the Jesuit, Desidera, and a Capucin Father were permitted to live here and study Tibetan. For more than a century thereafter very few westerners were allowed to visit Tibet and it is only in recent years that it has been open to tourists.

8. Practical Information

Advice

Most people go to China on an organised tour, either for a general holiday or with a group pursuing a specialised interest such as art and archaeology, architecture, Chinese gardens, botany or ornithology. It is important to make a careful choice and to have a clear idea of the areas to be visited. Not all tours go to Peking, and not all towns included in the tours are of equal interest. A glance at the appropriate sections of this book will give an idea of what is to be seen at each place. It is sometimes possible in special cases to organise independent visits, but these are rare and can be expensive unless they are made at the invitation of the Chinese authorities.

Visas are required and can be arranged through the tour organiser, the Chinese Embassy or the China International Travel Service in Hong Kong. The services of the China Travel Service are essential in China itself since they arrange hotels, transport and interpreter-guides. It is not the custom to tip for services in China.

Visitors are rarely given a choice of hotels. Accommodation will have been arranged between the tour organisers and the China Travel Service — or simply allocated by the latter according to availability. With a few exceptions in the larger cities, hotels in China are oldfashioned with simple amenities, but as a rule tours use hotels with private bathrooms. In remote areas the accommodation will be basic, and the good fortune of being able to stay in mountain monasteries will be balanced for some by the complete absence of all mod. cons.

Hotels generally provide both Chinese and western food but not unnaturally the Chinese food is of a higher standard; the waiter will always bring a knife and fork if manipulating chopsticks proves too difficult. Chinese beer and sweet soft drinks are served at meals. Western wines and spirits are available only at a few of the largest hotels. Mineral water, of which the best is called 'Lao Shan', is usually available, as is Chinese tea. It is wise, as in many places, to use boiled water for drinking and cleaning your teeth. There is invariably a thermos of hot boiled water and a tea caddy in each hotel room; coffee drinkers have to provide their own instant coffee. Chinese coffee is served at breakfast.

Tourist hotels usually have post offices, and it is possible to telephone abroad from the main cities. Foreign currency and travellers cheques can be changed at hotels, banks and some tourist shops, and receipts must be kept; any remaining Chinese currency must be changed back before leaving China. There are two forms of currency — standard notes and special notes issued for foreign exchange. Some tourist shops accept only the latter. The unit of the Yuan (colloquially called a 'kuai'), which is divided into a hundred 'fen'. Notes for units of ten fen, marked 'jiao', are colloquially called 'mao'.

Shopping for presents and souvenirs can be done in the hotel shops, at Friendship Stores reserved for overseas visitors in the larger cities, local shops and the main museums. Chinese silks and silk scarves, embroidered jackets and table linen make good, easily transportable presents, as do Chinese tea, sets of stamps, scissors, jewellery, basketwork, dolls in Chinese dress.

Many art shops and art departments stock a wide variety of paintings, jade and ivory carvings, carved and painted lacquer, porcelain and reproductions of tomb figures, such as Tang horses and figurines, stone rubbings, papercuts, prints and cards with reproductions of classical paintings. Those who enjoy embroidery will find superb examples in the larger cities and the homes of the famous embroidery schools, Guangzhou, Suzhou, Hangzhou, Changsha and Chengdu.

It is prudent to seek up-to-date advice from your guide on whether there are specialised antique shops for overseas visitors other than at the Friendship Store and the Hotel, since arrangements for the sale of antiques are constantly changing. Prices are high, and the red authenticating wax seal must be kept intact to be shown to the customs on departure.

Sightseeing is usually done on a tour bus. But for those who wish to supplement the official programme the China Travel Service or the hotel shop will provide a town map, arrange for a taxi, and, most important, tell you what the cost will be. If you go out alone take a piece of paper with the name of the hotel written on it, just in case you get lost. You will find local people very helpful.

In the hotels ladies' and gentlemen's lavatories are marked in English and toilet paper is usually provided. But at tourist sites they may be 'open plan', with no paper provided. The Chinese word for lavatory is pronounced 'T' sir saw': but if faced with identifying the men's toilets from the ladies, remember that the character for 'Men' has a sign like a four-paned window at the top.

In China everyone dresses informally. Good non slip walking shoes are essential and lightweight rainwear is useful. In warm weather most men wear slacks and open-necked short sleeved shirts, with a light jacket or sweater for evenings. For women trousers are acceptable everywhere, but a dress is useful for the occasional evening out. Cotton — or a high cotton content mix — is more comfortable than synthetics in hot weather.

A packable lightweight bag is invaluable for camera, spare films, raincoat, guidebook, notebook, a torch, insect repellent and other odds and ends for all day outings, and for one night stays if you are going off the beaten track. Although some hotels in large cities keep camera film be sure to take a good supply; don't forget to check the battery in your camera and to take a spare with you.

Take a supply of your usual medicines, cosmetics and toiletries. It is wise to take advice from the travel agent and your doctor on innoculations and other essentials such as an effective remedy for stomach trouble. In case of illness the China Travel Service guide will arrange for medical treatment; an insurance policy to cover medical expenses taken out before departure is an essential precaution.

It is polite in China to be punctual or even a little early for appointments.

In Chinese names the surname comes first, so Mr Liu Bei is addressed as Mr Liu: and Miss Hua Mulan as Miss Hua.

It may help to have an easy approximate guide to the pronunciation of consonants in 'pin yin' that differ markedly from English;

'q' is 'ch';	e.g. the Qian Long (Chien Lung) Emperor of the Qing (Ching) dynasty.
'x' is 'hs';	e.g. the Kang Xi (Kang Hsi) Emperor and the city of Xi'an.
'c' is 'ts';	e.g. the Empress Dowager Ci Xi (pronounced 'Tser-Hsee')
'zh' is 'j';	e.g. the city of Hangzhou (pronounced Harng-Joe).

Some useful phrases:

	Pin yin	*Pronunciation*
Hello	Ni hao	nee how
Goodbye	Zai jian	dzigh jenn
Thank you	Xie xie	hsye hsye ('ye' as in yet)
No thank you	Bu yao	boo yow (as in cow)
Sorry	Dui bu qi	dwey boo chee
Sorry to bother you	Mafan ni	mar-fan nee
How much	Duo shao	door shao
British Embassy	Yingguo Dashi Guan	ying-gwor dar-shir guan
U.S. Embassy	Meiguo Dashi Guan	may-gwor dar-shir gwan
Please wait a moment	Deng yi deng	dung-ee dung
Please bring . . .	Qing lai . . .	ching lie
Hot boiled water	Kai shui	kigh shway
Cold boiled water	Liang kai shui	leearng kigh shway
Beer	Pi jiu	pea jyo
Tea	Cha	char
Milk	Niu nai	new nigh
Sugar	Tang	tarng
Coffee	Ka-fei	kar-fay
Bread	Mian bao	mee-en bough
Rice	Mifan	mee-fan

I don't feel very well — wo bu shu fu (war boo shoo foo)
Please call the doctor — qing daifu lai (ching die-foo lie)
Please call the interpreter — qing fanyi lai (ching fan-ee lie)
It is broken — huai le (hwigh ler)
Please bring the bill — qing suan zhang (ching swann jarng)

Chinese Food

China, the home of one of the great cuisines of the world, has four regional schools of cooking. Not to be missed in Peking are Peking Duck and Mongolian Hotpot, steamed breads and sesame buns. Sichuan and Hunan cooking is known for its lavish use of hot chillies. In Guangzhou and the south the flavour is fresh and ingredients can be exotic — snake, pangolin and rice birds. Shanghai and the lower Yangtze Valley are known for soft crabs, fish and dishes cooked in the local yellow wine. There are restaurants cooking in all four styles in many of the big cities.

The most famous restaurants specialise in 'banquets'. These are set meals featuring the specialities of the restaurant, usually of ten to fifteen dishes beginning with a selection of cold food followed by a succession of meat, fish and vegetable dishes, each of which will be placed on the table in turn and shared by all. The soup may well come near or at the end. The meal will probably be concluded by one or two sweet dishes and fruit. Given the length of the menu, the best way to enjoy it is to take a little of each dish. A yellow rice wine, a white spirit (maotai), beer and soft drinks are served. Toasts are announced with the words 'Gan bei' (dry glass), but it is not necessary to take more than a token sip. Banquets begin early, often at six or seven in the evening, and the custom in China is to take your leave soon after the end of the meal. Banqueting tables are almost invariably round; traditionally the seat of honour in China is on the host's left but today the western custom of seating the guest of honour on the right is also followed.

Everyday Chinese food in hotels will be often of a good standard but much less elaborate. The more enterprising may like to venture out into Chinese restaurants, and a rough guide to ordering is to ask for one dish for each member of the party (again they will all be shared) plus a soup, perhaps an extra vegetable dish, or a sweet dish with which to bring the meal to a close. One of the hazards is that the restaurant staff may not speak English and if you doubt your acting ability, ask the guide to telephone from the hotel and order in advance. The menu can then be determined by the price you wish to pay. The more exotic and expensive dishes are often those more difficult for the western palate to appreciate; not many westerners share the Chinese love of hai-shen (beches-de-mer or sea slugs).

If you have to choose, try the following simple menu for six; if you are four, leave out two main dishes.

A plate of hors d'oeuvres (leng pan).

Main dishes:

1. Crisp chicken (xiang-su ji)

2. Sweet-sour fish (tang-su yu).

3. Pork with chillies and vegetables (la-zi rou-ding)
or fried chicken liver (zha ji-gan),

or duck liver (zha ya-gan), with bamboo shoots (dong sun).

4. Dry-fried prawns in the shell (gan-shao da-xia).

5. Mixed vegetables (luohan cai),
   or green vegetables (qing cai)
   or young Chinese cabbage in cream sauce (nai-you bai-cai)

6. Beef slices (niu-rou si).

Ham and winter-melon soup (huo-tui dong-gua tang),
   or delicious cabbage soup (bai-cai tang),
   or hot-sour soup (suan-la tang).
la tang).

Plain rice (bai mi-fan).

For sweet dishes:

Apple in hot caramel (ba-si ping-guo),
   or cold almond soup (xing-ren dou-fu).

You may not want or get all these dishes everywhere you go, but this is an example of the variety of dishes that makes a good meal. Replace them as you like with regional specialities, of which a few are mentioned in the main text. If you want birds' nest soup ask for 'yan-wo tang'; sharks' fins are 'yu chi'. Both will be expensive.

See page 160 for guide to pronunciation.

CLIMATE AND CLOTHING (Temperature in Fahrenheit)

Place	Winter	Spring	Summer	Autumn	Comments and Clothes
Peking and the North	Dec-Mar 15-40	Apr-May 50-80	June-Sep 75-95	Oct-Nov 70-40	Is extremely cold in winter but dry and often sunny. Very little snow. Very warm clothing essential for outdoors; efficient heating in modern hotels. Summers are very hot and humid. Windy and often dusty in the spring.
		Rainy season June, July and August			
Shenyang and the Northeast	Nov-Mar 0-40	Apr-mid Jun 40-75	mid Jun-mid Sep 60-80	Sep-Oct 70-35	In winter bitterly cold. Very warm lined clothing including hats, boots and gloves essential for outdoors. In Harbin and the north winter temperatures are even more extreme.
		Some rain April to September with most in June, July and August			
Xi'an and the Northwest	Dec-mid Mar 30-50	Mar-May 50-70	Jun-Sep 60 - 90	Oct-Nov 70-40	Although the temperature is not extreme, in winter it can be very cold, and heating is not always efficient. Medium weight winter clothing. For summer, very light
		Some rain throughout the year with most in July to September			

Place	Winter	Spring	Summer	Autumn	Comments and Clothes
Shanghai and Central China	Dec-Feb 30-55	March-May 40-70	May-Oct 60-95	Oct-Dec 70-35	Medium weight clothing except in the hot and humid summer. Rain-wear essential. Summers hotter and very humid inland.

It rains throughout the year with May to August as the wettest months.

| Chengdu and the Southwest | Jan-Feb 40-60 | Mar-Apr 50-75 | May-Oct 60-90 | Nov-Dec 60-40 | Medium weight winter clothing and light summer clothes. |

December and January are the only two months with little rain. The province of Sichuan is noted for its cloudy skies, 'when the sun shines the dogs bark'; but there are many sunny days in this beautiful province.

| Kunming | | | | | Medium to light weight clothes. |

The City of Eternal Spring, with a temperature range from a minimum of 40 in winter to about 70 in summer. Most rain from May to October. January and February dry. February is one of the best months for flowers.

| Guangzhou (Canton) and the South | Jan-Feb 50-70 | March 65-75 | Apr-Oct 70-90 | Nov-Dec 80-60 | Light weight clothing all the year round with a 'sweater just in case'. |

Very humid and wet all the year round but with tropical downpours during the summer months, and least rain in December-January.

Suggested Reading

China: Tradition and Transformation, Fairbank and Reischauer (George Allen & Unwin, 1979)

Imperial China, Raymond Dawson (Pelican, 1976)

China Readings 2: Republican China, ed. Schurmann & Schell (Pelican, 1968)

China Readings 3: Communist China, ed. Schurmann & Schell (Pelican)

Red Star over China, Edgar Snow (Pelican, 1978)

The Chinese, David Bonavia (Allen Lane, 1981)

China — a geographical survey, T. Tregear (1980)

The Chinese Potter, Margaret Medley (Phaidon, 1976)

Chinese Art, Mary Tregear (Thames & Hudson, 1980)

The Arts of China, Michael Sullivan (Thames & Hudson, 1973, revised 1977)

The Art and Architecture of China, Sickman & Soper, Pelican History of Art (Penguin, 1971)

Three Ways of Thought in Ancient China, Arthur Waley (George Allen & Unwin, 1939)

Buddhism in China, Kenneth Chen (Princeton, 1973)

A History of Christian Missions in China, K. Latourette (S.P.C.K., 1929)

Emperor of China; Self Portrait of Kangxi, Jonathan Spence (Knopf, 1974)

The Dragon Empress, Marina Warner (Cardinal, 1974)

Chinese Provincial Cooking, Kenneth Lo (Elm Tree, 1979)

A Cultural History of Tibet, Snellgrove and Richardson (Weidenfeld & Nicolson, 1968)

My Journey to Lhasa, Alexandra David-Neel (Penguin, 1940)

Traditional Fiction

Pilgrimage to the West, Wu Chengen, trans. by Arthur Waley as *Monkey* (Unwin Paperbacks, 1979)
Romance of the Three Kingdoms; trans. by C. Brewitt-Taylor (Kelly and Walsh, Hong Kong; 1929)
Story of the Stone, trans. by David Hawkes (Penguin Classics) (The same novel is often translated as *Dream of the Red Chamber*)
The Scholars, Wu Ching-tzu, trans. by Yang Hsien-yi and Gladys Yang (This has a good appendix on the examination system) (Foreign Languages Press, Peking, 1973)

Modern fiction published by the Peking Foreign Languages Press

Short Stories, Lu Xun (1972)
Midnight, Mao Dun (1979)
Family, Ba Jin (1958)

Table of Dynasties

SHANG		c. sixteenth to eleventh century B.C.
ZHOU		c. 1027-256 B.C.
	Western Zhou	c. 1027-771
	Spring and Autmn period	770-476
	Warring States	476-221
QIN		221-206 B.C.
HAN		206 B.C.-220 A.D.
	Western Han	206 B.C. -9 A.D.
	Xin	9-23
	Eastern Han	25-220
THREE KINGDOMS (Wei, Shu and Wu)		220-265
NORTHERN AND SOUTHERN DYNASTIES		265-589
	Northern Wei	386-534
	Liang	502-557
SUI		581-618
TANG		618-907
FIVE DYNASTIES		907-960
SONG		960-1279
	Northern Song	960-1126
	Southern Song	1127-1279
	In North China:	
	the Liao	947-1125
	the Jin	1126-1234
YUAN (Mongol)		1271-1368
MING		1368-1644
QING (Manchu)		1644-1912
REPUBLIC OF CHINA		1912-1949
PEOPLE'S REPUBLIC OF CHINA		1949-

Index

Index

Index

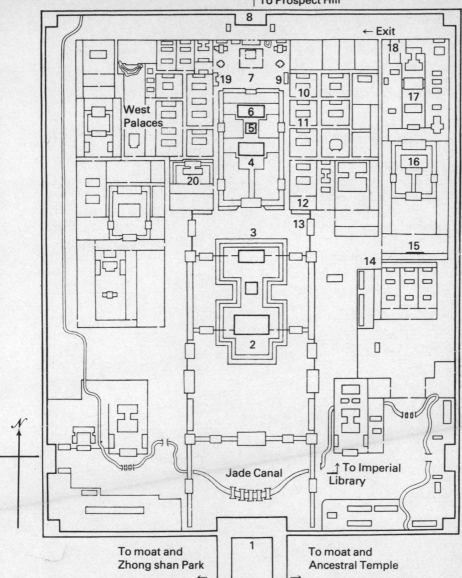

↑ To Prospect Hill

← Exit

West Palaces

Jade Canal

↑ To Imperial Library

N

To moat and Zhong shan Park ←

→ To moat and Ancestral Temple

The main places of interest in the Forbidden City, Peking (detailed maps in English can be bought at ticket offices and kiosks)

1 Meridian Gate (Wu Men)
   Ticket office

2 Hall of Supreme Harmony,
   main ceremonial hall

3 Carved ramp behind the Hall of
   Preserving Harmony

4 Palace of Heavenly Purity,
   where the Emperor lived

Index